THE WATCHMAN

THE MINISTRY OF THE SEER IN THE LOCAL CHURCH

DR. JOE IBOJIE

CROSS HOUSE BOOKS
Christian Book Publishers
245 Midstocket Road
Aberdeen
AB15 5PH, UK

"The entrance of Your Word brings light."

ISBN: 978-1-910048-18-4

For Worldwide Distribution.

2 3 4 5 6 7 / 20 19 18

To order products by Dr. Joe Ibojie & other Cross House Books,

contact info@crosshousebooks.co.uk.

Other correspondence: publisher@crosshousebooks.co.uk.

Visit www.crosshousebooks.co.uk.

Acknowledgments

I want to thank God for His great grace in my life. I can only say I am who I am because of God's mercies—they are new every morning!

I am grateful to God for the wonderful family He has given to me and for all the people He has placed on my path in life. I want to thank my wife, Cynthia, and to say that the dream lives on and the hope we share will not fail. I want to thank my children also: Eje, Ebi, Efe, and Effua; you are all precious to me, and thanks for all that we have been through together. The joy of our lives is the cheerful expectation of what lies ahead as the memories of our past make up the fabric of who we are. You have helped shape my story, the story of how my life has been touched and transformed by God's amazing grace. I will say, "Ebenezer, thus far the Lord has been faithful." If I were to do it all over again, I would not change a thing. You are simply the best!

ENDORSEMENTS

I am delighted to endorse Dr. Joe Ibojie's new book, *The Watchman*, and to commend it to the church in Scotland to read and be stirred to new understanding in this vital, yet often ignored or misunderstood, gift to the church.

Dr. Ibojie writes with his usual clarity and effectiveness to make a very complex and much maligned part of the church's ministry both understandable and necessary.

What I love about Dr. Ibojie is that his work is not that of a theorist but a practitioner! He leads a local church; he works in partnership with others in his city and the nation to which God has called him and around the world to release the Church into the fullness of all that God has for it.

God is doing a new and exciting thing in Scotland, and we need to see the recovery of all God's gifts to the church—for that I am grateful to Dr. Ibojie for this timely reminder of the vital role of the watchman.

Rev. Jim Ritchie
National Director, The Scotland Trust

Joe Ibojie has provided an invaluable manual for every pastor and prophet to understand those "weird" individuals within the church who seem to have more visions than Isaiah and more experiences than Ezekiel. *The Watchman* is full of wisdom and insight into the makeup and gifting of these individuals. This book expertly explains how the watchman fits within the local church, which is absolutely vital for a mature expression of anything prophetic. It is when things get separated from the local church that they start to get weird!

Joe's book lifts the veil of suspicion and mistrust and helps pastors lead certain members of their congregation, who up until now have been somewhat of an enigma, to their full potential.

For the watchmen themselves, this book gives validation. It tells them that they are not weird, that they don't need to be reclusive, and that they need, and are needed, by the Body of Christ.

Phil Sanderson
Senior leader, Third Day Church Aberdeen

Dr. Joe Ibojie runs with fervent pursuit the call of God in his life. His sound training and biblical foundation are evident in his work. Joe writes for matured minds, yet he ends up making difficult subjects easy to understand. If you are interested in influencing your world, this book is a must-read.

Bishop Fred Addo
Founder, International Praise Cathedral
Kaduna, Nigeria

Dr. Joe Ibojie is a seasoned, inspirational, and pragmatic author. His writings are uniquely appealing, succinct, and relevant to the times we live in. Little wonder, then, that his books are best-selling in Europe, the United States of America, Canada, and in the rapidly growing readership of Nigeria. That Dr. Ibojie is an anointed prophet of God, teacher, and preacher is evident in the pages of this book.

The Watchman: The Ministry of the Seer in the Local Church is a highly needed book for all believers going through difficult challenges when identifying genuine prophets and preachers of the Word.

Reading and meditating over the content of this book will give every believer fresh insight, new orientation, and divine strength for successful ministry in God.

Rev. Dr. Gabriel Adebayo
Senior Pastor, Yaba Baptist Church
Lagos, Nigeria

Once again, Dr. Joe Ibojie brings to us succinct revelations in an inspiring book. Bringing simplicity without compromising the eternal truth of God has become the hallmark of Joe's writing. Surely the anointing of the prophetic scribe rests on him, and we are all the better for it. This book cuts across all levels and can serve as a guide to the laity as well as to church leadership. I have no doubt that it will perfectly fit into the curricula of Bible institutes the world over. Keep the fire burning.

Bishop Calvin Antonza II
Supernatural Love Ministries, Inc.
Kaduna, Nigeria

CONTENTS

THE SECOND BOOK
ILLUSTRATED BIBLE-BASED DICTIONARY OF DREAM SYMBOLS

FOREWORD

As I read this book I am reminded of Isaiah 51:1, "Look to the rock from which you were hewn and the quarry from which you were dug," and I think pure gold! In the many years that I have known Dr. Joe Ibojie, it has been a joy to see the Refiner at work in him and the pure gold as this scholar of the Word of God pours forth the wisdom of his gift, experience, and character into the pages of this book.

At last we have a book for the prophet with the local church in mind. Whether you are a prophet or just a faithful everyday Christian, we all need to identify with the local church and its leadership to keep our feet on the ground. I believe the prophet should be accountable to the local church. Like in the days of Ezra, the prophet is to encourage the people as they build at the grassroots level! Ezra 5:1-2: "The prophets were with them encouraging the people."

As Joe puts it in this book, "The local church is the representation of this corporate Christ at our immediate environment, and this is the means by which we participate in the existence of Christ's corporate Body worldwide. So whatever you do to the local church, you are doing it for the Body of Christ worldwide." The Bible says, "Now you are the Body of Christ, and members individually" (1 Cor. 12:27). This must be our sober reflection!

I once met an anointed prophet who said he does not belong to a local church. Perhaps he has been driven into this state of "rejected prophet syndrome" because of his past experiences. Now is the time to check this drain of valuable resources; this book has come at an auspicious time in history. This is a tool that will help draw people into the Body, rather than allowing them to become loose cannons that can become a danger to us all.

The Watchman is also an excellent manual for training how the prophetic and intercession should work. Dr. Joe has done a great job bringing to us in simple terms what the prophetic should be in that "Prophets are not so much for platforms but for prayer, fasting, and pleading in intercession."

This book helps prophets grow both in character and in the prophetic anointing and is a wonderful tool for teaching many aspects of prophetic ministry.

As a generation, we have an awesome responsibility in these last days toward our children, to train them up in the way they should go. This book helps equip a prophetic generation to speak forth the prophetic word of God from within the local church to our communities, our nation, and the nations of the world. This is an outstanding book by a faithful servant of God, whom I have interacted with from the local church level to ministering at international conferences. His love for God's people is the motivation for writing *The Watchman*—a great work by a great man of God and friend.

Pastor Joseph Ewen
Founder and Leader
Riverside Christian Church Network Banff
Scotland, United Kingdom

PREFACE

There are different levels of watchfulness in the watchman ministry: for example, a watchman can be called to a local church, to a city or nation, to the Body of Christ, or even to a family unit. This book, however, while dealing with the fundamentals of the ministry of the watchman, focuses on the ministry of the watchman in the local church. In this era of rapid expansion of global communication, these lesser-known watchmen to the local churches often tend to be neglected. This book is dedicated to them and to the countless number of great women of God who make up a vast percentage of the watchman ministry. These "female watchmen" have worked under the name *watchmen*—a misnomer and perhaps a contradiction of terms—and have endured with excellence and honors. This one is for you!

Even at the local church level, there are very few true watchman ministries these days because many local church watchmen have restricted themselves through the narrowing of the perspectives in their calling to operating only in the "warn them" ministry. The twenty-first-century watchman ministries need to have a widened perspective. It is time that the conservative, narrow, and restricted perspectives of the watchman's ministry breaks out into the reality of its great potentials, values, and visions. The watchman's anointing remains a highly valuable tool in the Body of Christ that needs to be carefully harnessed.

There is what I call in-house responsibilities of the watchman. Apart from watching for approaching dangers, the watchman should be able to discern the spirits that may come against him and the local church. This book brings teaching on how to discern evil spirits that might come against the watchman's anointing and against the local congregation.

The discerning of spirits is one of the gifts of the Holy Spirit, and one of its purposes is to "see" into the invisible realm and discern the spirit or spirits behind any outward manifestation. This role also falls within the responsibilities of the watchman to the local church.

For the ministry of the watchman in the local church, avoiding prophetic pitfall is essential. This is equally important for the local church leadership. This book also provides a recipe on how to avoid prophetic and pastoral pitfalls as they work together to attain unity in the power of Christ's fullness.

Among the many questions that readily come to mind regarding the role of a watchman are:

- Who are these watchmen and how can we recognize them?

- How best can they be trained, appreciated, and integrated into the Body of Christ?

- How can their potentials be channelled to become valuable resources to the local leadership instead of the nuisance they can often become?

In this book I offer answers to these questions and suggest the way forward.

Note: Although referenced throughout as "he" and "watchmen" and "watchman," this verbiage refers to the universal "man" that includes women as equally important and vital as those fulfilling roles as God's servants to warn and advise His people.

INTRODUCTION

The ministry of the watchman in the local church is possibly one of the most common and yet most misunderstood ministries in the Body of Christ. Over time, the majority of these gifted people have been driven into reclusive lives because of relational issues that within the local church. Over the years, valuable time, resources, and knowledge have been wasted because of wrongly packaged warnings from true but immature watchmen. There is now a growing need for proper training, acceptance, and integration of these watchmen. Yet most local leaderships do not necessarily know how to handle someone who claims to receive the near-endless visionary revelations about the local church—especially when the watchman can fail to see the speck in his own eye.

The extent and the ability of the watchman to see into the spirit realm (known as spiritual acuity) are slanted toward the area of his call. So the watchman may receive endless revelations about a local church in excess of the average person and at the same time have comparatively less visionary revelations on personal issues. This is because the volume and proportion of revelations the watchman receives is slanted toward the area of his call. This situation requires tactful handling to help the watchman as well as to help facilitate their acceptance by the local leadership.

The ministry of the watchmen could be regarded as an offshoot of the seer's anointing. Indeed, most watchmen are seers. The following are some of the cardinal roles of the spiritual watchman:

- Watching and looking into the distance, especially in order to see approaching danger.
- Warning those who are endangered.

- ◆ Encouraging those who are righteous to continue in their righteousness.

- ◆ Warning the wicked to turn from their wickedness.

- ◆ Preparing the people to give the appropriate protocol to the coming of the King or His divine messengers.

Being a spiritual watchman is to be endowed by God to see things from afar. Therefore, this ministry is a conspicuous target and attracts the fury of the enemy.

On the other hand, seers are those gifted with visions and dreams and other forms of picture revelations on a consistent basis, and they operate mainly from the receptive dimension of the prophetic ministry. A majority of high-volume dreamers are seers. High-volume dreamers are those who dream around two or more dreams most nights on a consistent basis. Also, long and vivid visions are common with the seer's anointing. Most of the revelations that a seer receives are in picture form, and he may see and describe more than he hears and repeats. However, there are some seers who hear and repeat as much as they see and describe. From my experience, a major distinguishing feature in the ministry of a seer is that it is especially characterized by the occurrence of "strange spiritual experiences" and angelic interactions.

Strange spiritual events are occurrences that are curious, extraordinary, unique, unnatural, bizarre, or mysterious. They are common in the ministry of seers and distinguish the seer from the other dreamers. These strange events come in various forms and in varying degrees of strangeness or awesomeness. For this reason I have devoted a chapter in this book to discussing strange events.

THE BODY OF CHRIST—THE CHURCH

What is required of the Church of Christ is a concerted approach to training, acceptance, and integration of the seers and watchmen in the local congregation. In this book you will find guidance in these directions.

As Christians we called to be parts of one Body—the Body of Christ—called the Church. The local church is the representation of this corporate Christ at our immediate environment, and this is the means by which we participate in the existence of Christ's corporate Body worldwide. So whatever you do to the local church, you are doing it for the Body of Christ worldwide. "Now you are the Body of Christ, and members individually" (1 Cor. 12:27).

First, I would like to define what I mean by the Church. The word *church* "comes to us from the German 'Kirche' and the Scottish 'Kirk,' but the word has even older roots in the Aramaic word 'kenishta' and the Greek word 'kuriakon,' both of which means 'belonging to the Lord.' The church is thus the tribe of Jesus—called out of all tribes and nations. In the Old Testament the term used for such a group was 'qahol' (a people called together by Yahweh), which was translated into Greek as 'ekklesia' (those called out) and was used in the New Testament to refer to the church. The caller is God, the means of unity is faith in His Son, Jesus Christ, and the governing constitution is the Bible as read and obeyed under the guidance of the Holy Spirit. The members are referred to as believers in Christ."[1] This the picture of the local church portrayed in this book.

INTERCESSION

The role of intercession and the value of other intercessors in the ministry of a seer cannot be overemphasized. Working closely with intercessors is a vital asset in the ministry of the watchman in the local church. Every Christian should be an intercessor, and it is important that Christians pray for one another. However, some people have a greater measure of the gift of intercession than others. Intercession is a critical part of the watchman's ministry. Nevertheless, not all watchmen are intercessors in that technical sense, though every watchman should of necessity be able to intercede. The intercessory burden carried by the watchmen varies. For instance, I believe that the prophet Daniel carried a higher prophetic burden for intercession than did prophet Jeremiah. Yet both had outstanding watchman ministries.

This is what prophet Daniel said:

In the first year of his reign, I, Daniel, understood from the Scriptures [see Jer. 25:11-12] according to the word of the Lord given to Jeremiah the prophet, that the desolation of Jerusalem would last seventy years. So I turned to the Lord God and pleaded with him in prayer and petition, in fasting, and in sackcloth and ashes (Daniel 9:2-3).

On the other hand, the prophet Jeremiah was often quick to resort to weeping and self-pity instead of intercessory prayers:

O Lord, you deceived me, and I was deceived; you overpowered me and prevailed. I am ridiculed all day long; everyone mocks me. Whenever I speak, I cry out proclaiming violence and destruction. So the word of the Lord has brought me insult and reproach all day long. But if I say, "I will not mention him or speak any more in his name," his word is in my heart like a fire, a fire shut up in my bones. I am weary of holding it in; indeed, I cannot. I hear many whispering, "Terror on every side! Report him! Let's report him!" All my friends are waiting for me to slip, saying, "Perhaps he will be deceived; then we will prevail over him and take our revenge on him" (Jeremiah 20:7-10).

A clear and proper understanding of revelation is important for effective intercessory and watchman ministry. Without proper understanding of revelations, the best intercessory watchman's effort would be limited. I have noticed on several occasions that some devoted and well-meaning intercessors miss the main points of the revelations they have received and therefore have engaged in ineffective and sometimes unnecessary warfare. This must now change for both the watchman and intercessor. It is time to pray that intercessors and watchmen be clothed with the Daniel 1:17 anointing: "To these four young men God gave knowledge and understanding of all kinds of literature and learning. And Daniel could understand visions and dreams of all kinds."

This Daniel 1:17 anointing has a twofold manifestation: first, the granting of divine grace for skills to acquire knowledge; and second, the ability to interpret riddles, solve enigmas, and bring rare insight into difficult situations. This is what was said of Daniel in whom this anointing was amply manifested: "This man Daniel, whom the king called Belteshazzar, was found to have a keen mind and knowledge and understanding, and also the ability to interpret dreams, explain riddles and solve difficult problems. Call for Daniel, and he will tell you what the writing means" (Dan. 5:12). This aspect of the watchman's ministry is extensively dealt with in this book.

ENDNOTE

1. Samuel Ngewa, *Africa Bible Commentary* (Grand Rapids, MI: Zondervan, 2006), 1431.

Part I

The Seer Anointing

CHAPTER ONE

THE SEER

THE CALL, SPHERE OF INFLUENCE, AND OPERATION

Seers are those gifted with visions and dreams on a consistent basis. A majority of high-volume dreamers (those dreamers who consistently dream two or more dreams most nights) are seers. I believe high-volume dreamers are people the Bible describes as the "dreamer of dreams" (Deut. 13:1-5). Also, long and vivid visions are common with the seer's anointing. Most of the revelations that a seer receives are in picture form; therefore the seer may see and describe more than he hears and repeats. A key distinguishing feature is that the ministry of a seer is characterized by angelic interactions and strange spiritual encounters.

On the downside of the seer's anointing is the easy susceptibility to failure in relational issues, the lusts of the eyes, and failure to act on revelation. These are snares to the anointing and functions of the seer's ministry. Giving in to these temptations, particularly those involving the eyes, can make revelations in the seer's realm cloudy, smeared, jumbled, and filled with distorted images. Most seers need to work on relations with people; some have unfortunately ended up becoming reclusive because of relational issues. Working on the seer's character and living a life of continuous sanctification enable the seer to see more clearly.

A seer is one who sees visions and dreams consistently. On a wider perspective, the term expands to include one who perceives, looks, discerns, or stares into the supernatural to receive revelation mostly by pictures. A seer is therefore one divinely enabled to see or discern the will of God, one whose eyes have been divinely unveiled to see and to understand things that are not open to the ordinary man. The Hebrew word *ro'eh* is translated seer.

(Formerly in Israel, if a man went to inquire of God, he would say, "Come, let us go to the seer," because the prophet of today used to be called a seer.) (1 Samuel 9:9).

It is perhaps important that we realize that this verse is an explanatory note of an old custom or belief of the ancient Jews and that it was given for the benefit of the Jews in the era of the prophet Samuel. This verse does not mean that the term *prophet* has replaced the term *seer*. I believe what it means is that the term *seer* was more broadly applied in the ancient times by the Jewish people. In fact, by the time of King David, the term *seer* has narrowed down into its exact specifics and the office of the seer and that of the prophet were well-established and distinct from one another:

> *He stationed the Levites in the temple of the Lord with cymbals, harps and lyres in the way prescribed by David and **Gad the king's seer and Nathan the prophet**; this was commanded by the Lord through His prophets* (2 Chronicles 29:25).

> *King Hezekiah and his officials ordered the Levites to praise the Lord with the words of **David and of Asaph the seer**. So they sang praises with gladness and bowed their heads and worshiped* (2 Chronicles 29:30).

However, the nabi (meaning *spokesman*) prophet receives mainly by hearing things in the spirit realm. The Hebrew word *naba* means to prophecy, and a nabi prophet is one who speaks out or is a proclaimer of the will of God (one who speaks by divine inspiration).

Let me summarize the difference between the **seer** and the ***nabi prophet***:

SEER	NABI PROPHET
The seer is gifted with visual revelations on a consistent basis; Gad, Iddo, Hanani, and Asaph were seers.	The nabi prophet hears and speaks more than he sees and describes. The prophet Isaiah spoke of many future events as he heard them in the spirit realm, hence he was not too reliant on his personal vocabulary.

A seer is characterized by consistent and persistent visual revelation, experiencing strange spiritual events, and having common angelic involvement.

Seers see events in the supernatural realm before they happen in the natural.

Seers more often see and describe.

In describing what is seen, some seers grope for vocabulary. The seer's vocabulary capacity affects his ability to express what is received. Ezekiel and the apostle John relied on the capacity of their vocabulary to express what they saw. So on some occasions, seers gave different descriptions to somewhat similar pictorial revelations.

Seers are those gifted with visions and dreams on a consistent basis. Also long and vivid visions are common with the seer's anointing. A key distinguishing feature is that the ministry of a seer is characterized by angelic interactions and strange spiritual encounters.

On the downside of the seer's anointing is the easy susceptibility to failure in relational issues, the lusts of the eyes, and failure to act on revelation. These are snares to the anointing and functions of the seer's ministry. Giving in to these temptations, particularly those involving the eyes, can make revelations in the seer's realm cloudy, smeared, jumbled, and filled with distorted images.

By faith, a nabi prophet receives divine inspirations that spill out from within. Most nabi prophets get more inspiration once they have started to speak. So they might start slowly but soon advance into great speed and volume.

A nabi prophet can prophesy upon many people at a time.

They are good exhorters and often greatly used by God to bring inspiration or motivation to people in moments of despair.

They may give general or very specific messages.

The nabi prophets are in the communicative dimension of the prophetic ministry.

Some may be given to acting out prophetic messages.

On the down side, they tend to be extroverts and therefore should make efforts to avoid exaggerations that may give false hope or unattainable expectations.

Most seers need to work on relations with people; some have unfortunately ended up becoming reclusive because of relational issues. Working on the seer's character and a life of sanctification enable the seer to see more clearly.

Not all those who receive visual revelation are seers, as visual revelations may be evoked through intensive purification (fasting and prayers) and intercession.

The seer's anointing is very sensitive, as seers tend to pick up much visual revelation that leaves long, lingering effects.

A seasoned seer is adept in the understanding of the dark speeches or mysteries of God because of the frequent search to gain understanding of parables in picture revelations.

Seers are often deep thinkers, hence many people describe the seer anointing as the receptive dimension of the prophetic ministry.

Because of the reflective nature of the seer's anointing, the well-integrated seer soon becomes a great resource for other prophets. Seers can often become good teachers and administrators as exemplified by the lives of Samuel, Joseph, and Daniel.

However, some seers need to put forth much effort to have effective relationships with other people. Some may even become reclusive.

This is a rather simplistic categorization and is only meant to help rather than to restrict. Some people may find it hard to know which category they fall into. The main help I find in this categorization is that it reassures those in training that gifting may differ, and therefore this helps remove frustration. Some people may find it easy to *grow* in how to receive divine inspiration by faith without visual signals; whereas for others this may not come easily, if they are essentially seers. It is also important to remember that there are many who receive, or walk, in both categories or offices. Perhaps the prophet Gad moved in both realms:

> *Before David got up the next morning, the word of the Lord had come to Gad the prophet, David's seer: "Go and tell David, 'this is what the Lord says: I am giving you three options. Choose one of them for me to carry out against you'"* (2 Samuel 24:11-12).

I believe also that the prophet Zechariah operated effectively in both offices. In the beginning of the Book of Zechariah, the prophet received eight symbolic visions with significant angelic interaction as messages for the Jewish returnees in chapters 1 to 5, whereas in chapters 6 to 12, the prophet operated mainly as a nabi prophet.

Jim Goll writes on this topic:

> All true seers are prophets, but not all prophets are seers. A prophet may have the particular grace to hear and proclaim the word of the Lord and yet not necessarily function as profusely in the revelatory visionary capacity as a seer does. The seer, on the other hand, may move quite remarkably in this visionary dream capacity yet not be as deep in inspirational audible graces of hearing and speaking. Nevertheless, both move and operate in the prophetic realm, but in different capacities or dimensions.[1]

THE SEER AS STRATEGIST

The mature and seasoned seer is often a spiritual strategist because his revelations come with pictorial details about the plans of the enemy. A seasoned seer is also adept in understanding the ways and mysteries of God. The diligent and consistent quest for the meaning of the parable insights, which are coded or hidden in dreams, visions, and other pictorial revelations, brings understanding of the ways of God to the seer. Daniel, as a gifted seer, was a man known to be adept in understanding the dark speeches of God.

> *There is a man in your kingdom that has the spirit of the holy gods in him. In the time of your father he was found to have insight and intelligence and wisdom like that of the gods. King Nebuchadnezzar your father—your father the king, I say—appointed him chief of the magicians, enchanters, astrologers and diviners. This man Daniel, whom the king called Belteshazzar, was found to have a keen mind and* **knowledge and understanding, and also the ability to interpret dreams, explain riddles and solve difficult problems.** *Call for Daniel, and he will tell you what the writing means* (Daniel 5:11-12).

Angels are common in the ministry of the seer, which may include a great deal of angelic interaction. We see this in the ministry of Joseph, the earthly father of Jesus Christ, the apostle John, and the prophet Zechariah:

> *Then the angel who talked with me returned and wakened me, as a man is wakened from his sleep. He asked me, "What do you see?" I answered, "I see a solid gold lampstand with a bowl at the top and seven lights on it, with seven channels to the lights. Also there are two olive trees by it, one on the right of the bowl and the other on its left." I asked the angel who talked with me, "What are these, my lord?" He answered, "Do you not know what these are?" "No, my lord," I replied. So he said to me, "this is the word of the Lord to Zerubbabel: 'Not by might nor by power, but by My Spirit,' says the Lord Almighty"* (Zechariah 4:1-6) .

However, it is pertinent to be able to discern the appearance of angels in our revelations. In general this is how to recognize the appearance of angels in dreams, visions, and other pictorial revelations.

Most unknown people in dreams are symbolic of spirit beings and can be either good or bad. An unknown person who is helpful, protective, and instructive in dreams is often symbolic of angels; whereas an unknown person who is obstructive, deceptive, and has antiscriptural principles is symbolic of demons. A faceless person who is helpful, honest, protective, and instructive in dreams could be symbolizing the Holy Spirit.

The seasoned seer is more likely to give planned and rehearsed prophesies purely because his revelations often come in advance of the proclamation. As a consequence of this inadvertent or advanced notice, seers are less prone to errors of presumption, which could be common with spontaneous prophetic utterance particularly for the uninitiated—although presumptions remain a problem with the outworking of any revelatory anointing. Generally, it is a misconception that the majority of prophecies are spontaneous. A good proportion of prophecies are planned and rehearsed, as exemplified by many instances in the Bible. However, these phenomena of planned and rehearsed prophecies are more common in a seer's ministry than in the ministry of nabi prophets.

Often, such planned prophesies come with remarkable degrees of accuracy, wisdom, and practical relevance. The Bible records a very detailed prophecy given by Samuel, a notable seer in the Scriptures, with these remarkable features:

> *Then Samuel took a flask of oil and poured it on Saul's head and kissed him, saying, "Has not the Lord anointed you leader over His inheritance? When you leave me today, you will meet two men near Rachel's tomb, at Zelzah on the border of Benjamin. They will say to you, 'The donkeys you set out to look for have been found. And now your father has stopped thinking about them and is worried about you. He is asking, What shall I do about my son?' Then you will go on from there until you reach the great tree of Tabor. Three men going up to God at Bethel will meet you there. One will be carrying three young goats, another three loaves of bread, and another skin of wine. They will greet you and offer you two*

loaves of bread, which you will accept from them. After that you will go to Gibeah of God, where there is a Philistine outpost. As you approach the town, you will meet a procession of prophets coming down from the high place with lyres, tambourines, flutes and harps being played before them, and they will be prophesying. The Spirit of the Lord will come upon you in power, and you will prophesy with them; and you will be changed into a different person. Once these signs are fulfilled, do whatever your hand finds to do, for God is with you. Go down ahead of me to Gilgal. I will surely come down to you to sacrifice burnt offerings and fellowship offerings, but you must wait seven days until I come to you and tell you what you are to do." As Saul turned to leave Samuel, God changed Saul's heart, and all these signs were fulfilled that day. When they arrived at Gibeah, a procession of prophets met him; the Spirit of God came upon him in power, and he joined in their prophesying (1 Samuel 10:1-10).

This prophecy has exceptional details and outstanding specificities. It is also remarkable in the way that the sequence of events was accurately predicted.

It is not uncommon that the seasoned seer readily becomes a great support to other prophetic people around him, as most seers could easily become gifted prophetic teachers. (The prophet Samuel established the first school of the prophets in the Old Testament.) Trances, divine visitations, translations, and throne-room experiences are common with seers, as can also be seen in the ministry of Ezekiel.

The seer is also more likely to have frequent interactive dreams and visions than most other prophets. An interactive dream is one in which there is an exchange between the dreamer and God during the spiritual encounter. For appropriate interaction with God in dreams and visions, the ability to retain a certain level of adequate natural consciousness is required; for instance, knowing who you are and what you would normally stand for in your natural life during the dream encounter. King Abimelech had this required degree of retained consciousness in this encounter:

*Now Abraham moved on from there into the region of the
Negev and lived between Kadesh and Shur. For a while he
stayed in Gerar, and there Abraham said of his wife Sarah,
"She is my sister." Then Abimelech king of Gerar sent for
Sarah and took her. But God came to Abimelech in a dream
one night and said to him, "You are as good as dead because of
the woman you have taken; she is a married woman." Now
Abimelech had not gone near her, so he said, "Lord, will you
destroy an innocent nation? Did he not say to me, 'She is my
sister,' and didn't she also say, 'He is my brother?' I have done
this with a clear conscience and clean hands." Then God said
to him in the dream, "Yes, I know you did this with a clear conscience, and so I have kept you from sinning against me. That
is why I did not let you touch her. Now return the man's wife,
for he is a prophet, and he will pray for you and you will live.
But if you do not return her, you may be sure that you and all
yours will die"* (Genesis 20:1-7).

So did the apostle Peter in this visionary encounter:

*About noon the following day as they were on their journey
and approaching the city, Peter went up on the roof to pray.
He became hungry and wanted something to eat, and while
the meal was being prepared, he fell into a trance. He saw
heaven opened and something like a large sheet being let
down to earth by its four corners. It contained all kinds of
four-footed animals, as well as reptiles of the earth and birds
of the air. Then a voice told him, "Get up, Peter. Kill and eat.
Surely not, Lord!" Peter replied. "I have never eaten anything
impure or unclean the voice spoke to him a second time, 'Do
not call anything impure that God has made clean.' This happened three times, and immediately the sheet was taken back
to heaven. While Peter was wondering about the meaning of
the vision, the men sent by Cornelius found out where
Simon's house was and stopped at the gate. They called out,
asking if Simon who was known as Peter was staying there.
While Peter was still thinking about the vision, the Spirit said*

to him, "Simon, three men are looking for you. So get up and go downstairs. Do not hesitate to go with them, for I have sent them" (Acts 10:9-20).

ENDNOTE

1. James Goll, *The Seer* (Shippensburg, PA: Destiny Image Publishers, 2004), 23.

CHAPTER TWO

SPECIAL MINISTRY FEATURES

The seer's anointing is sustained and strengthened by the Word of
God, as it is evident in the following passages. The prophet Samuel
was a notable seer in the Scriptures. At a time when Samuel did not
yet know the Word of God, his word did not come to the people but
came to them after the Word of God had been revealed to him:

> Now Samuel did not yet know the Lord: **The word of the Lord
> had not yet been revealed to him** (1 Samuel 3:7).

> The Lord was with Samuel as he grew up, and he let none of his
> words fall to the ground. And all Israel from Dan to Beersheba
> recognized that Samuel was attested as a prophet of the Lord.
> The Lord continued to appear at Shiloh, and there he revealed
> himself to Samuel through his word (1 Samuel 3:19-21).

> **And Samuel's word came to all Israel.** Now the Israelites went
> out to fight against the Philistines. The Israelites camped at
> Ebenezer, and the Philistines at Aphek (1 Samuel 4:1).

The prophet Ezekiel was made to eat the scroll so he could have
solid foundation of the word inside of him:

> And he said to me, "Son of man, eat what is before you, eat
> this scroll; then go and speak to the house of Israel." So I
> opened my mouth, and he gave me the scroll to eat. Then he
> said to me, "Son of man, eat this scroll I am giving you and
> fill your stomach with it." So I ate it, and it tasted as sweet as
> honey in my mouth (Ezekiel 3:1-3).

Likewise, the prophet Jeremiah recalled that he, too, ate the word
of God because of the call of God in his life:

When your words came, I ate them; they were my joy and my heart's delight, for I bear your name, O Lord God Almighty (Jeremiah 15:16).

Later the prophet described that word of the Lord in him like fire;

Whenever I speak, I cry out proclaiming violence and destruction. So the word of the Lord has brought me insult and reproach all day long. But if I say, "I will not mention Him or speak any more in His name," His word is in my heart like a fire, a fire shut up in my bones. I am weary of holding it in; indeed, I cannot (Jeremiah 20:8-9).

The apostle John, the beloved of the Lord, also had to eat the word of God:

So I went to the angel and asked him to give me the little scroll. He said to me, "Take it and eat it. It will turn your stomach sour, but in your mouth it will be as sweet as honey." I took the little scroll from the angel's hand and ate it. It tasted as sweet as honey in my mouth, but when I had eaten it, my stomach turned sour. Then I was told, "You must prophesy again about many peoples, nations, languages and kings" (Revelation 10:9-11).

Strange or bizarre events are common to the manifestation of the seer's anointing. Some of the dramatization of the prophecies given to Ezekiel were weird, and Ezekiel's life was obviously complicated by these unusual requirements. Not only did God require him to deliver a very unpopular message, but He also instructed Ezekiel to dramatize the messages in bizarre ways, such as shaving his head, cooking with cow manure, and lying outside beside a model of Jerusalem and on one side for 390 days.

"Now, son of man, take a clay tablet, put it in front of you and draw the city of Jerusalem on it. Then lay siege to it: Erect siege works against it, build a ramp up to it, set up camps against it and put battering rams around it. Then take an iron pan, place it as an iron wall between you and the city and turn your face toward it. It will be under siege, and you shall besiege it. This

will be a sign to the house of Israel. Then lie on your left side and put the sin of the house of Israel upon yourself. You are to bear their sin for the number of days you lie on your side. I have assigned you the same number of days as the years of their sin. So for 390 days you will bear the sin of the house of Israel. After you have finished this, lie down again, this time on your right side, and bear the sin of the house of Judah. I have assigned you 40 days, a day for each year. Turn your face toward the siege of Jerusalem and with bared arm prophesy against her. I will tie you up with ropes so that you cannot turn from one side to the other until you have finished the days of your siege. Take wheat and barley, beans and lentils, millet and spelt; put them in a storage jar and use them to make bread for yourself. You are to eat it during the 390 days you lie on your side. Weigh out twenty shekels of food to eat each day and eat it at set times. Also measure out a sixth of a hin of water and drink it at set times. Eat the food as you would a barley cake; bake it in the sight of the people, using human excrement for fuel." The Lord said, "In this way the people of Israel will eat defiled food among the nations where I will drive them" (Ezekiel 4:1-13).

SEER MINISTRY SEASONS

There are seasons in the ministry of the seer. Often the seasons of low revelatory receptivity are the times to develop dependency on the supremacy of God.

The prophet Ezekiel experienced many seasons of highs and lows in his ministry. One of God's seasons was an incredible period of divinely instituted silence:

In the twelfth year of our exile, in the tenth month on the fifth day, a man who had escaped from Jerusalem came to me and said, "The city has fallen!" Now the evening before the man arrived, the hand of the Lord was upon me, and He opened my mouth before the man came to me in the morning. So my mouth was opened and I was no longer silent (Ezekiel 33:21-22).

The silence that Ezekiel experienced was present for about seven years until an exile arrived in Babylon with the news of the fall of Jerusalem. God ended Ezekiel's long silence just before the man got to him, by which time Ezekiel had learned valuable lessons. Notably after the arrival of the exile to Babylon, the tone of Ezekiel's message changed from that of doom to prophecies of hope for the rebuilding of the broken people of Judah. Often such seasons of low revelatory receptivity or divine silence could be a time to imbibe a paradigm shift from God (see Ezek. 33:23-34), as indeed, the prophet Ezekiel seemed to have demonstrated here.

As there are seasons of low revelatory receptivity, there are also seasons when revelations may be plentiful. What is important is that the seer must remain in the consciousness that it is God who gives revelations, that prerogatives will forever remain His, and those that dwell in the secret place of the most High shall abide under the shadow of the Almighty:

> *[Yet] first [you must] understand this, that no prophecy of Scripture is [a matter] of any personal or private or special interpretation (loosening, solving). For no prophecy ever originated because some man willed it [to do so—it never came by human impulse], but men spoke from God who were borne along (moved and impelled) by the Holy Spirit* (2 Peter 1:20-21 AMP).

In the days of the prophet Jeremiah, the people did not take cognizance of this fact and so sometimes in desperation, they compelled the prophets to tell their dreams whether they had received any or not. To save face, these prophets made up stories even though they did not receive dreams or visions. This is obviously dangerous because unless God gives the revelation, the prophet receives nothing. In a way, therefore, the prophetic person is like a postman and should not feel bad if the mail is scanty, because God can sometimes instigate this and the heavenly mail may be few.

> *Yes, this is what the Lord Almighty, the God of Israel, says: "Do not let the prophets and diviners among you deceive you. Do not listen to the dreams you encourage them to have"* (Jeremiah 29:8).

*I will bring the most wicked of the nations to take possession of their houses; I will put an end to the pride of the mighty, and their sanctuaries will be desecrated. When terror comes, they will seek peace, but there will be none. Calamity upon calamity will come, and rumor upon rumor. **They will try to get a vision from the prophet;** the teaching of the law by the priest will be lost, as will the counsel of the elders. The king will mourn, the prince will be clothed with despair, and the hands of the people of the land will tremble. I will deal with them according to their conduct, and by their own standards I will judge them. Then they will know that I am the Lord* (Ezekiel 7:24-27).

EACH SEER IS UNIQUE

The background and the setting for the seer and his message are unique and varied. Here are examples:

As a priest, Ezekiel had a special knowledge and interest to discern and warn against the misuses or abuses in the temple of the Lord. Ezekiel's background as a priest was obvious in his ministry. The vision of idolatry in the temple was given within the context of Ezekiel's meeting with the elders of Judah in his house. In the vision, Ezekiel saw the practices of idol and sun worship:

In the sixth year, in the sixth month on the fifth day, while I was sitting in my house and the elders of Judah were sitting before me, the hand of the Sovereign Lord came upon me there. I looked, and I saw a figure like that of a man. From what appeared to be his waist down he was like fire, and from there up his appearance was as bright as glowing metal. He stretched out what looked like a hand and took me by the hair of my head. The Spirit lifted me up between earth and heaven and in visions of God He took me to Jerusalem, to the entrance to the north gate of the inner court, where the idol that provokes to jealousy stood. And there before me was the glory of the God of Israel, as in the vision I had seen in the plain. Then He said to me, "Son of man, look toward the north." So

I looked, and in the entrance north of the gate of the altar I saw this idol of jealousy. And He said to me, "Son of man, do you see what they are doing—the utterly detestable things the house of Israel is doing here, things that will drive Me far from my sanctuary? But you will see things that are even more detestable." Then He brought me to the entrance to the court. I looked, and I saw a hole in the wall. He said to me, "Son of man, now dig into the wall." So I dug into the wall and saw a doorway there. And He said to me, "Go in and see the wicked and detestable things they are doing here." So I went in and looked, and I saw portrayed all over the walls all kinds of crawling things and detestable animals and all the idols of the house of Israel. In front of them stood seventy elders of the house of Israel, and Jaazaniah son of Shaphan was standing among them. Each had a censer in his hand, and a fragrant cloud of incense was rising (Ezekiel 8:1-11).

Amos spoke with strong country language. He was a farmer when he was called into ministry as a prophet and for the most part, he used a plain writing style, filled with strong country language that reflected his farmer background.

The words of Amos, one of the shepherds of Tekoa—what he saw concerning Israel two years before the earthquake, when Uzziah was king of Judah and Jeroboam son of Jehoash was king of Israel (Amos 1:1).

*Hear this word, **you cows** (meaning people) of Bashan on Mount Samaria, you women who oppress the poor and crush the needy and say to your husbands, "Bring us some drinks!"* (Amos 4:1)

Sentimentality has no place in the seer's ministry. It is pertinent to note that sentiment is an emotion and comes from the soul part of man. Once God had to warn the prophet Ezekiel when he was overwhelmed by what he saw in the natural. Perhaps Ezekiel had seen some remote reasons why the captives had lost faith in God. As a result, he sat unable to express or deliver his message for seven days until he received God's warning:

> *The Spirit then lifted me up and took me away, and I went in bitterness and in the anger of my spirit, with the strong hand of the Lord upon me. I came to the exiles that lived at Tel Abib near the Kebar River. And there, where they were living, I sat among them for seven days—overwhelmed. At the end of seven days the word of the Lord came to me: "Son of man, I have made you a watchman for the house of Israel; so hear the word I speak and give them warning from Me. When I say to a wicked man, 'You will surely die,' and you do not warn him or speak out to dissuade him from his evil ways in order to save his life, that wicked man will die for his sin, and I will hold you accountable for his blood. But if you do warn the wicked man and he does not turn from his wickedness or from his evil ways, he will die for his sin; but you will have saved yourself"* (Ezekiel 3:14-19).

The seer should move only in the compassion and mercies of God and not in emotions that natural circumstances dictate.

THE EYE GATE—LAMP OF THE BODY

There is an increasing relevance of the eye gate in the totality of our walk by the Spirit. The eye gate is the sensory gate by which we perceive or receive visual revelation or information. I believe that the eye gate functionally consists of the natural eyes, the spiritual eyes, how the two work, and how the human eyes influence the light within man. The eye gate is an important door through which things can get into man.

The Bible says that the eyes are the "lamp of the body." A good eye is symbolized as a useful lamp, and it gives true enlightenment to the whole body:

> *Your eye is the lamp of your body. When your eyes are good, your whole body also is full of light. But when they are bad, your body also is full of darkness. See to it, then, that the light within you is not darkness. Therefore, if your whole body is*

full of light, and no part of it dark, it will be completely lighted,
as when the light of a lamp shines on you (Luke 11:34-36).

Proper functioning of the eye gate is crucial for the effectiveness of seeing in the spirit realm. Evidence abounds in the secular world as to the significant role and the addictive nature of the eye gate in capturing the human attention. The human mind processes thoughts, ideas, and concepts in pictures. The part of the human mind known as the "pictorial depository" is where pictures are received and processed. The pictorial depository has a gripping effect on man's imagination and the pictures are often hard to erase. No wonder people struggle for days, weeks, or even months with persistent remembrances of a single pictorial flash accidentally seen on television or in a newspaper, even if the exposure was only a few seconds. Such is the power that images have on man's imagination. Impressions logged into our imagination are long-lasting. As a consequence, addictions such as pornography or phobias like the fear of heights, are the most difficult to overcome. We must be careful what we let in through our eye gate.

Many people have rightly called the prophetic ministry the eye of the Body of Christ. Indeed, this is why the prophet Isaiah described the darkness associated with the disobedience to God as prophetic blindness:

Be stunned and amazed, blind yourselves and be sightless; be drunk, but not from wine, stagger, but not from beer. The Lord has brought over you a deep sleep: He has sealed your eyes (the prophets); He has covered your heads (the seers). For you this whole vision is nothing but words sealed in a scroll. And if you give the scroll to someone who can read, and say to him, "Read this, please," he will answer, "I can't; it is sealed." Or if you give the scroll to someone who cannot read, and say, "Read this, please," he will answer, "I don't know how to read." The Lord says: "These people come near to me with their mouth and honor Me with their lips, but their hearts are far from Me. Their worship of Me is made up only of rules taught by men. Therefore once more I will astound these people with wonder upon wonder; the wisdom of the wise will perish, the intelligence of the intelligent will vanish" (Isaiah 29:9-14).

What use is a watchman if his eye gate is corrupted or blind? The main essence of the ministry of the watchman is to be able to see into the Spirit realm and report to the people. If a watchman is blind, he has virtually lost the core of the ministry:

*Come, all you **beasts** of the field, come and devour, all you beasts of the forest! Israel's watchmen are blind, they all lack knowledge* (Isaiah 56:9).

As the watchman, the prophet Isaiah looked into the future and saw where other ungodly nations, symbolized by beasts, were stirred up to attack Israel. Because of the laxity of the watchmen of Israel, being blind and lacking spiritual insights as to the plans of the enemy, the nation was left unprotected, vulnerable to attack.

Satan is after the human eye gate to pollute, hijack, or corrupt its functionality; "You will not surely die," the serpent said to the woman. "For God knows that when you eat of it your eyes will be opened, and you will be like God, knowing good and evil" (Gen. 3:4-5).

The eye gate was probably the first perceptive sense to be affected when man fell into sin in the Garden of Eden:

*When the woman saw that the fruit of the tree was good for food and pleasing to the eye, and also desirable for gaining wisdom, she took some and ate it. She also gave some to her husband, who was with her, and he ate it. **Then the eyes of both of them were opened**, and they realized that they were naked; so they sewed fig leaves together and made coverings for themselves* (Genesis 3:6-7).

As the Bible says in the above passage, once the natural eyes were opened and activated, human reasoning was triggered into action and unto this day has continued to grow exponentially. Unfortunately, there has been a corresponding dampening of humankind's ability to see into the Spirit realm. However, I believe that the plan and purpose of God concerning our spiritual visual acuity will continue to be:

*...that the God of our Lord Jesus Christ, the glorious Father, may give you the Spirit of wisdom and revelation, so that you may know him better...that **the eyes of your heart may be enlightened** in order that you may know the hope to which he has called you, the riches of his glorious inheritance in the saints, and his incomparably great power for us who believe. That power is like the working of his mighty strength* (Ephesians 1:17-19).

The eye gate receives both from the divine, the devil, and worldly system. The devil's desire is to hijack the eye gate in order to pollute man through this valuable gate. Imagery from the devil and worldly system can stain the "eye lenses" with vile pictures so that it becomes inefficient in receiving from godly sources:

*A person who is pure of heart sees goodness and purity in everything; but a person whose heart is evil and untrusting finds evil in everything, for his dirty mind and rebellious heart **color all he sees and hears*** (Titus 1:15 TLB).

The eye gate is connected to your memory and intellect, and it influences your soul. It is one of the principal ways through which emotions are aroused. When emotions are high, the will of man often succumbs and the human mind will inevitably be dragged along. When this happens, reasoning is thrown to the ground while caution and etiquette are discarded. As a consequence, righteousness takes a pathetic second place.

The power of the eye gate was demonstrated in the beginning of human existence. With his unpolluted and unadulterated eye gate, Adam was able to see, observe, and name the animals:

Now the Lord God had formed out of the ground all the beasts of the field and all the birds of the air. He brought them to the man to see what he would name them; and whatever the man called each living creature, that was its name. So the man gave names to all the livestock, the birds of the air and all the beasts of the field (Genesis 2:19-20).

In this instance, man using the pure state of the eye gate scored 100 percent from God's viewpoint.

Since the eyes can receive both from the natural and the spiritual realms, we should be mindful of what we allow in spiritually and naturally. Most often, we become what we behold. Job said; "I made a covenant with my eyes not to look lustfully at a girl" (Job 31:1). David also said, "I will set before my eyes no vile thing. The deeds of faithless men I hate; they will not cling to me" (Ps. 101:3). What we see can cling to us long after visual exposure has been put off.

Ultimately, we can let in light or darkness. If we give our eyes to the Lord for His Kingdom purposes, we become the light of the world.

NATURAL EYES

Spiritual watchfulness involves the use and possibly the misuse of the natural eyes, and unguarded use of the natural eyes impinges on the functionalities of the spiritual eyes and visual acuity of the person.

The natural eye is the eye sense by which we see things in the natural realm. The natural eyes were not fully operative in the Garden of Eden until Adam and Eve ate from the tree of knowledge of good and evil, when their natural eyes were described as "opened."

> ***Then the eyes of both of them were opened****, and they realized that they were naked; so they sewed fig leaves together and made coverings for themselves" (Genesis 3:7).*

The natural eye is the sense that the Bible describes as the "lamp of the body":

> *The eye is the lamp of the body. If your eyes are good, your whole body will be full of light. But if your eyes are bad, your whole body will be full of darkness, how great is that darkness!* (Matthew 6:22-23)

This is so because man has the inherent ability to control the use of the natural eyes:

> *I will set before my eyes no vile thing. The deeds of faithless men I hate; they shall not cling to me* (Psalm 101:3).

For instance, David became a victim of unguarded and uncontrolled use of his natural eyes:

> *In the spring, at the time when kings go off to war, David sent Joab out with the king's men and the whole Israelite army. They destroyed the Ammonites and besieged Rabbah. But David remained in Jerusalem. One evening David got up from his bed and walked around on the roof of the palace. From the roof he saw a woman bathing. The woman was very beautiful, and David sent someone to find out about her. The man said, "Isn't this Bathsheba, the daughter of Eliam and the wife of Uriah the Hittite?" Then David sent messengers to get her. She came to him, and he slept with her. (She had purified herself from her uncleanness.) Then she went back home. The woman conceived and sent word to David, saying, "I am pregnant"* (2 Samuel 11:1-5).

This is the eyesight that the apostle Paul admonished us about when he says, "So we fix our eyes not on what is seen, but on what is unseen. For what is seen is temporary, but what is unseen is eternal" (2 Cor. 4:18).

Also the wisdom based on the use of the natural eyes is short-lived. As the Bible says, "The things that are not—to nullify the things that are, so that no one may boast before Him" (1 Cor. 1:28b-29).

The natural eyes cannot see into the spiritual realm: "The man without the Spirit does not accept the things that come from the Spirit of God, for they are foolishness to him, and he cannot understand them, because they are spiritually discerned" (1 Cor. 2:14).

SPIRITUAL EYES

Spiritual eyes are the eyes of faith. Also, spiritual eyes are the eyes of the heart or understanding and the eye sense by which we navigate the spirit realm. Unlike the natural eyes, spiritual eyes have multidimensional functionalities and can see into the natural as well as the spiritual realms without the limitation of time, space, and height. This is the eye sense by which prophecy, dreams, and most visions are received. Symbolically, this is the eye sense through which illumination or divine understanding comes in to bring clarity to an issue. The spiritual eye is figuratively also the eye of hope. For some, most of the revelations that they receive are through the spiritual eyes.

I believe this is the eye sense that Adam and Eve used in the Garden Eden before the fall of man, before the Bible records that the eyes of both of them were "opened." This is also the eye sense that the apostle Paul prayed should be enlightened in the lives of the Ephesians:

> *I pray also that **the eyes of your heart** may be enlightened in order that you may know the hope to which he has called you, the riches of his glorious inheritance in the saints, and his incomparably great power for us who believe. That power is like the working of his mighty strength* (Ephesians 1:18-19).

The Bible recorded that Moses in his moment of trial used his spiritual eye to look into the future and saw Him who is invisible to the natural eyes:

> ***By faith** he left Egypt, not fearing the king's anger; he persevered because **he saw Him who is invisible*** (Hebrews 11:27).

The functionality of spiritual eyes is connected to the purity of the heart, being the eye of the heart, and determines whether or not one is able to see God. As the Scriptures say:

> *Blessed are the pure in heart, for they will see God* (Matthew 5:8).

I also call spiritual eyes the eye of understanding because the Bible says:

> *But whoever hates his brother is in darkness...and he does not know where he is going, because the darkness has blinded his eye* (1 John 1:2).

> *But their minds were blinded. For until this day the same veil remains unlifted in the reading of the Old Testament, because the veil is taken away in Christ* (2 Corinthians 3:14).

The god of this age has blinded the minds [understanding] of unbelievers, so that they cannot see the light of the gospel of the glory of Christ, who is the image of God (2 Corinthians 4:4).

THE LIGHT WITHIN US

This is the light of God that exists within every believer: "For God, who said, let light shine out of darkness, **made His light shine in our hearts** to give us the light of knowledge of the glory of God in the face of Christ" (2 Cor. 4:6).

And also "Every good and perfect gift is from above, coming down from the Father of the heavenly lights, who does not change like shifting shadows" (James 1:17).

And that is why the Bible says, "You are the light of the world. A city on a hill cannot be hidden. Neither do people light a lamp and put it under a bowl. Instead they put it on its stand, and it gives light to everyone in the house. In the same way, **let your light shine before men**, that they may see your good deeds and praise your Father in heaven" (Matt. 5:14-16) and also, "**If then the light within you is darkness**, how great is that darkness" (Matt. 6:23).

The Living Bible rendition of the passage is worthy of note:

If your eye is pure, there will be sunshine in your soul. But if your eye is clouded with evil thoughts, and desires, you are in deep spiritual darkness. And oh! How deep that darkness can be! (Matthew 6:22-23 TLB)

ACTIVATION OF THE EYE GATE

As I mentioned previously, I believe that the first recording of the activation of the eye gate dates back to the Book of Genesis in the Garden of Eden. The devil inspired the *opening* of *the natural eyes* of man, contrary to the original intention of God: "Then the eyes of both of them **were opened**, and they realized that they were naked; so they sewed fig leaves together and made coverings for themselves" (Gen. 3:7).

The phrase *the eyes of both of them were opened* implies that something shifted in the functionality of their eyes starting then and continuing to present-day. The Bible says after that point they real-ized they were naked. This shift, therefore, seems to emphasis that they could now see more in the physical realm (natural realm) than they had in the past. They also sewed together fig leaves as coverings, meaning there was a shift toward logics and self-reliance and away from the total dependence they had on God until that point. From then on, man continues to grow in the natural use of the eyes, in log-ics, and in the pursuit of self-reliance. Hidden in this growth and rapid expansion of the natural use of the eye gate was the decline of human eyes in seeing things of the spirit, otherwise known as spiri-tual visual acuity, and sometimes referred to as the "eyes of faith."

Activation of the eye gate is all we need to do to reverse this trend so that man can again sharpen his spiritual visual acuity.

There are other instances in the Bible when God sovereignly inter-vened and opened the eyes of man to see what otherwise would not have been visible. Examples of activation or supernatural opening of the eyes in the Scriptures:

1. The *spiritual eyes* of the Elisha's servant were divinely opened to see the invisible army of God in readiness: "Then the Lord opened the servant's eyes, and he looked and saw the hills full of horses and chariots of fire all round Elisha" (2 Kings 6:17).

2. God temporarily restrained and later opened the spiritual eyes of certain disciples of Jesus Christ: "But their [spiri-tual] eyes were restrained so that they did not know Him" (Luke 24:16 NKJV).

   And, "Then their eyes were opened and they recognized him, and he disappeared from their sight" (Luke 24:31).

3. God opened the light within man to bring understanding to the reading of the Scriptures: *"And He opened their un-derstanding that they might comprehend the scriptures"* (Luke 24:45 NKJV).

FACILITATING THE ACTIVATION OF YOUR EYE GATE

The above Bible passages illustrate the pivotal role of the sovereignty of God in the activation of spiritual eyes. All through the Scriptures we see that people either facilitated or hindered the activation of their spiritual eyes.

Prayers and Fasting. There are many instances of praying and fasting in the Bible, but in particular when Peter was praying and fasting, he fell into a trance in which his eyes were opened and he saw Heaven opened upon him:

> *About noon the following day as they were on their journey and approaching the city, Peter went up on the roof to pray. He became hungry and wanted something to eat, and while the meal was being prepared, he fell into a trance. He saw heaven opened and something like a large sheet being let down to earth by its four corners. It contained all kinds of four-footed animals, as well as reptiles of the earth and birds of the air. Then a voice told him, "Get up, Peter. Kill and eat." "Surely not, Lord!" Peter replied. "I have never eaten anything impure or unclean." The voice spoke to him a second time, "Do not call anything impure that God has made clean." This happened three times, and immediately the sheet was taken back to heaven"* (Acts 10:9-16).

Also when Elisha prayed for his servant, the servant's spiritual eyes were instantly activated:

> *When the servant of the man of God got up and went out early the next morning, an army with horses and chariots had surrounded the city. "Oh, my lord, what shall we do?" the servant asked. "Don't be afraid," the prophet answered. "Those who are with us are more than those who are with them." And Elisha prayed, "O Lord, open his eyes so he may see." Then the Lord opened the servant's eyes, and he looked and saw the hills full of horses and chariots of fire all around Elisha. As the enemy came down toward him, Elisha prayed to the Lord, "Strike these people with blindness." So He struck them with blindness as Elisha has asked* (2 Kings 6:15-18).

A Life of Consecration. I believe the prophet Ezekiel was living a life of consecration in the midst of idolatrous Jewish elders in the land of Babylon when his eyes were opened and he saw the heavens opened upon him and the vision of the throne of God revealed to him;

> *In the thirtieth year, in the fourth month on the fifth day, while I was among the exiles by the Kebar River, the heavens were opened and I saw visions of God. On the fifth of the month—it was the fifth year of the exile of King Jehoiachin—the word of the Lord came to Ezekiel the priest, the son of Buzi, by the Kebar River in the land of the Babylonians. There the hand of the Lord was upon him. I looked, and I saw a windstorm coming out of the north—an immense cloud with flashing lightning and surrounded by brilliant light. The center of the fire looked like glowing metal, and in the fire was what looked like four living creatures. In appearance their form was that of a man, but each of them had four faces and four wings* (Ezekiel 1:1-6).

Spending Time in God's Presence

The Bible says that in the days when Eli was the high priest in Israel there were not many visions because of the prevailing evil at the time, but in the midst of that the boy Samuel stayed with the Ark of God, and as a result the heavens opened upon him. He had a vision with a significant auditory component:

> *The boy Samuel ministered before the Lord under Eli. In those days the word of the Lord was rare; there were not many visions. One night Eli, whose eyes were becoming so weak that he could barely see, was lying down in his usual place. The lamp of God had not yet gone out, and Samuel was lying down in the temple of the Lord, where the ark of God was. Then the Lord called Samuel. Samuel answered, "Here I am." And he ran to Eli and said, "Here I am; you called me." But Eli said, "I did not call; go back and lie down." So he went and lay down. Again the Lord called, "Samuel!" And Samuel got up and went to Eli and said, "Here I am; you called me." "My son," Eli said, "I did not call; go back and lie down." Now Samuel did not yet*

know the Lord: The word of the Lord had not yet been revealed to him. The Lord called Samuel a third time, and Samuel got up and went to Eli and said, "Here I am; you called me." Then Eli realized that the Lord was calling the boy. So Eli told Samuel, "Go and lie down, and if He calls you, say, 'Speak, Lord, for your servant is listening.'" So Samuel went and lay down in his place. The Lord came and stood there, calling as at the other times, "Samuel! Samuel!" Then Samuel said, "Speak, for your servant is listening" (1 Samuel 3:1-10).

Applying the Word of God

The Word of God has the power to transform the soil of your mind and your imagination and prepare your imagination for pictures from God. The Word of God is a potent instrument for the renewing of your mind, and you are transformed by the renewal of our mind. Dwelling on the holy imagery in the Bible helps to prepare your eyes to receive sharply from God as well as sanctify your mind against all vile imagery of the world.

Practicing to Use Your Spiritual Gifts

Hebrews 5:14 admonishes that our spiritual gifts mature by reason of use: "But solid food is for the mature, who by constant use have trained themselves to distinguish good from evil."

Setting Your Mind on Things Above

Being God-focused will help to facilitate the activation of spiritual eyes: "Set your minds on things above, not on earthly things" (Col. 3:2).

The Fear of God

The Bible says God confides in those who fear Him. "The Lord confides in those who fear Him; He makes His covenant known to them" (Ps. 25:14).

An Enlightened Heart

As previously mentioned, Paul prayed for the Ephesians that God would give them wisdom, revelation, and activated eyes of their hearts to live a fulfilled Christian life:

I keep asking that the God of our Lord Jesus Christ, the glorious Father, may give you the Spirit of wisdom and revelation, so that you may know Him better. I pray also that the eyes of your heart may be enlightened in order that you may know the hope to which He has called you, the riches of His glorious inheritance in the saints, and His incomparably great power for us who believe. That power is like the working of His mighty strength (Ephesians 1:17-19).

Walk of Faith

Jesus said to Nathaniel that if he believed, he would see the heavens opened. Faith is important in our walk with God and in navigating the realm of the Spirit. (See John 1:47-51.)

Tithes and Offering

When the windows of the heavens are opened, revelations abound. The Bible says blessings will be poured out when the heavens are opened as God responds to obedience to paying tithes. Following King Solomon's sacrifice, God met him in a dream; and Cornelius had a vision because of his giving to the believers. (See Malachi 3:8-11.)

How the Components of the Eye Gate Work

The three components of the eye gate can work together:

And the end of the time I, Nebuchadnezzar, lift my eyes to heaven, and my understanding returned to me... (Daniel 4:34 NKJV).

Here Nebuchadnezzar lifted up his eyes (the natural eyes) symbolically to Heaven (the spirit realm only via the spiritual eyes) and his understanding (the light within him) returned to him.

In many instances in the Bible, we are reminded that man is responsible for how the eye gate is used. It is, therefore, a matter of determination to keep the eye gate pure.

Turn my eyes away from worthless things; preserve my life according to Your word (Psalm 119:37).

I lift up my eyes to You, to You whose throne is in heaven (Psalm 123:1).

At the end of that time, I, Nebuchadnezzar, raised my eyes toward heaven, and my sanity was restored. Then I praised the Most High; I honored and glorified Him who lives forever. His dominion is an eternal dominion; His kingdom endures from generation to generation (Daniel 4:34).

Let us fix our eyes on Jesus, the Author and Finisher of our faith... (Hebrews 12:2).

EYE GATE RECEPTION

What happens to what is received by the eye gate? In particular, dreams are imparted into the spirit-man, and from hence, visual revelation is fed into the mind. However, the mind also receives from worldly imagery. This dual pathway of reception creates competition in which one path will eventually dominate the other. If you yield your mind to vile worldly images, the mind will become defiled and inefficient in processing holy images. If you yield the mind to holy imagery, the mind becomes sanctified and consecrated, fertile for holy imagination and ready for spiritual encounters.

Functionally, the mind consists of:

- *Memory*, which is a word depository that deals with issues of the past.

- *Contemplation*, which deals with current issues as well as being the arena for conceptualization.

- *Imagination*, which contains the pictorial depository and handles issues of the future, such as planning and conceptualization, and contains the image center.

This pictorial depository of our imagination can also be referred to as our mind's image center. As a pictorial language, dreaming must undergo necessary processing. Our image center should be made conducive to receive pictorial revelations from the spirit and capable of resisting pollution from unholy, worldly images.

How the Image Center Works

The following is an explanation of the role of faith, inner peace, liberty reception, and processing of revelation:

> *Faith.* The level of faith and the busyness of the mind influence the translation of revelations from the spirit to the image center. Faith and the fear of God are two pivotal factors to how much or how deep the revelations you receive from God are experienced. Without faith, a revelation could remain dormant in the spirit. Faith in God enhances the release of the revelation from the spirit to the mind for comprehension.

> *Inner peace.* Visual revelations translate to our image center more successfully when the mind is still. Spend some quiet time after waking up so that the revelations can drift from the spirit into the image center before the day's demands set in. This is one of the reasons why the level of the peace you enjoy determines the height of your spiritual encounters. This is why the pressures and busyness of life can hinder the translation to the mind leading to reduced capability in remembering revelations.

> *Liberty in the spirit.* The processing, understanding, and ability to relate the revelation to the person's life circumstance is dependent on the liberty the seer enjoys in the spirit. This liberty only comes from the presence of the Holy Spirit. Where the Spirit of God is there is liberty.

Conclusion

1. Before the fall of man, the spiritual eyes were originally more active than the natural eyes.

2. Once the natural eyes were opened at the fall of man in the Garden of Eden, the natural eyes have grown exponentially.

3. With this exponential growth in the natural eyes, the spiritual eyes became dampened, tending almost to inactivity,

with only occasioned spells of activities such as in dreams, visions, and other prophetic utterances. However, those who are trained in the use of the spiritual eyes enjoy the true and original benefits of navigating the spirit realm: "but solid food [strong spiritual principle] is for the mature, who by constant use have trained themselves to distinguish good from evil" (Heb. 5:14).

4. There is a subtle struggle of two components of the eye gate that started in the Garden of Eden and continues throughout life.

5. As sin increases, holiness decreases. The activity of spiritual eyes diminishes and for most people becomes completely dormant.

6. The natural eyes take dominance in an era dominated by worldly system.

7. The natural eyes cannot see into the spiritual realm for spiritual things are spiritually discerned.

8. The things or events happening in the natural realm influence the natural eyes. Therefore, the natural eyes are major doorways for the sinfulness and sinful nature to continually gain entrance into people. This is why the Bible says that the eye is the lamp of the soul.

The things we see affect the soil of our minds. The following chart reveals what happens in our minds when we see certain things:

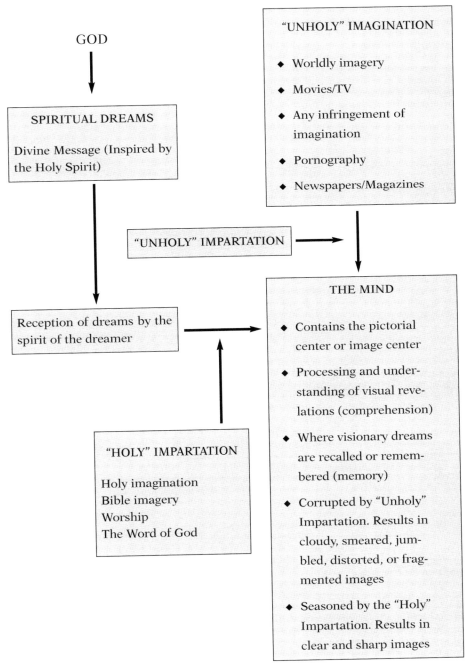

GOD

SPIRITUAL DREAMS

Divine Message (Inspired by the Holy Spirit)

"UNHOLY" IMAGINATION

◆ Worldly imagery

◆ Movies/TV

◆ Any infringement of imagination

◆ Pornography

◆ Newspapers/Magazines

"UNHOLY" IMPARTATION

Reception of dreams by the spirit of the dreamer

THE MIND

◆ Contains the pictorial center or image center

◆ Processing and understanding of visual revelations (comprehension)

◆ Where visionary dreams are recalled or remembered (memory)

◆ Corrupted by "Unholy" Impartation. Results in cloudy, smeared, jumbled, distorted, or fragmented images

◆ Seasoned by the "Holy" Impartation. Results in clear and sharp images

"HOLY" IMPARTATION

Holy imagination
Bible imagery
Worship
The Word of God

PART II

The Ministry of the Watchman

CHAPTER THREE

THE WATCHMAN

THE CALL, THE SPHERE OF INFLUENCE, AND THE FUNDAMENTALS

The watchman ministry operates mostly from the seer's dimension of the prophetic ministry, though the degree and extent to which the seer's anointing operates in the watchman ministry varies. Nevertheless, I believe there is always a substantial slant to receiving by visual revelations in most watchman ministries. The role of the spiritual watchman can be defined as: looking out, to peer in the spirit into the distance, spy, keep watch, scope something out, especially to see approaching danger and warn those who are endangered. As a consequence, this ministry attracts the fury of the enemy. Being a spiritual watchman is to be endowed by God to see things from afar. The watchman's ministry could be regarded as an offshoot of the seer's anointing.

A key distinguishing feature of the watchman is that he is characteristically different from other dreamers in that a great percent of his dreams and other revelations speak of nonpersonal issues. Whereas for other dreamers, it has been estimated that over 90 percent of received dreams or picture revelations are of a personal nature. This distinction is crucial to keep in mind, so that proper integration of this valuable gifting in the Body of Christ can be attained. Just as most dreamers receive volumes of dreams on personal issues, the watchman receives more dreams on nonpersonal matters pertaining mainly to the areas of the watchman's call. When this is not understood, many are led to doubt the validity of the watchman's revelations. When the watchman's revelations are ignored, it leads to loss of valuable resources and unnecessary casualties in the arena of spiritual warfare. Perhaps this is made worse by the fact that the watchman can often fail to see the speck in his own eye, a sequel to the watchman's visual acuity being slanted to the area of his call.

The true spiritual watchman must always be steadfast, always abiding on the side of God, withstanding hostility and religious dogmatism of the people. The Bible says; "The prophet, along with my God, is the watchman over Ephraim, yet snares await him on all his paths, and hostility in the house of his God" (Hos. 9:8).

Watchmen are often timekeepers: "An oracle concerning Dumah: Someone calls to me from Seir, 'Watchman, what is left of the night? Watchman, what is left of the night?' The watchman replies, 'Morning is coming, but also the night. If you would ask, then ask; and come back yet again'" (Isa. 21:11-12).

The sons of Issachar were watchmen who had special understanding of the signs of the times and seasons: "Men of Issachar, who understood the times and knew what Israel should do—200 chiefs, with all their relatives under their command" (1 Chron. 12:32).

Watchmen are also gatekeepers or often work closely with other gatekeepers, as illustrated by King David, the watchman and the gatekeeper in this story:

> While David was sitting between the inner and outer gates, the watchman went up to the roof of the gateway by the wall. As he looked out, he saw a man running alone. The watchman called out to the king and reported it. The king said, "If he is alone, he must have good news." And the man came closer and closer. Then the watchman saw another man running, and he called down to the gatekeeper, "Look, another man running alone!" The king said, "He must be bringing good news, too." The watchman said, "It seems to me that the first one runs like Ahimaaz son of Zadok." "He's a good man," the king said. "He comes with good news" (2 Samuel 18:24-27).

Even in the New Testament, Jesus said:

I tell you the truth, the man who does not enter the sheep pen by the gate, but climbs in by some other way, is a thief and a robber. The man who enters by the gate is the shepherd of the sheep. The watchman opens the gate for him; the sheep listens to his voice... (John 10:1-3).

Thus the gate is closed if the watchman sees and reports coming evil or a dangerous approach. And the gate is then opened at the command of the king by advice based on what the watchman observes.

A Watchman's Report

Most of the time, the prophetic words from the watchman are full of woes, lament, or sadness. This tendency needs to be properly articulated to ensure acceptance by the people and the leadership to avoid the watchman's reports becoming the nuisance that they so easily become. Despite the fact that woes, laments, and sadness are common in most watchman's reports, the watchman ministry has the potential to bring strategic revelations and insightful knowledge of the exact time, name, and place of operation of specific evil forces or principalities that come against the people of God.

For the most part, the watchman has a divinely inspired mandate to warn, which sometimes translates into insatiable urges to give frequent warnings in order for prayers to be offered and calamities averted. Sometimes there is near compulsive urges to warn. This is why the prophet Micah said:

Because of this I will weep and wail; I will go about barefoot and naked. I will howl like a jackal and moan like an owl (Micah 1:8).

And Jeremiah also said:

Whenever I speak, I cry out proclaiming violence and destruction. So the word of the Lord has brought me insult and reproach all day long. But if I say, "I will not mention him or speak any more in his name," his word is in my heart like a fire, a fire shut up in my bones. I am weary of holding it in; indeed, I cannot (Jeremiah 20:8-9).

What we need is a proper understanding and correct handling of this urge to proclaim woes and laments. After all, the ultimate success of a watchman's ministry hinges on the maturity with which these warnings are packaged and made acceptable to the people concerned.

INTERCESSION

Watchmen may not be able to function as effective intercessors, and also, not all intercessors have a watchman's anointing. Nevertheless, intercession should be an integral part of the watchman's ministry. The uniqueness of the watchman ministry is that the watchman actually measures success or effectiveness by not allowing most of his warning prophecies to come to pass. The ultimate goal is that the warning is heeded and judgment averted. Every watchman should strive to become an effective intercessor.

THE CALL

Ezekiel's sphere of influence is shown in his call as a watchman for the house of Israel: "Son of Man, I have made you a watchman for the house of Israel; so hear the word I speak and give them warning from Me" (Ezek. 3:17).

Every watchman is appointed and called by God, and the call of the watchman should come with specifics of the roles and responsibilities of the job. The watchman is called to receive revelations from God and to deliver them to the people. The boundary of the sphere of influence is often well-delineated, as in the case of Ezekiel above, who was called to the house of Israel.

The call of the watchman is typified by the call of Ezekiel. All watchmen should be called by and empowered by the Spirit of God. In the case of Ezekiel, the Spirit of God came upon and imparted to him divine enablement needed for his ministry.

> *As he spoke, the Spirit came into me and raised me to my feet, and I heard him speaking to me. He said: "Son of man, I am sending you to the Israelites, to a rebellious nation that has rebelled against me; they and their fathers have been in revolt*

against me to this very day. The people to whom I am sending you are obstinate and stubborn. Say to them, 'This is what the Sovereign Lord says.' And whether they listen or fail to listen— for they are a rebellious house—they will know that a prophet has been among them. And you, son of man, do not be afraid of them or their words. Do not be afraid, though briers and thorns are all around you and you live among scorpions. Do not be afraid of what they say or terrified by them, though they are a rebellious house. You must speak my words to them, whether they listen or fail to listen, for they are rebellious. But you, son of man, listen to what I say to you. Do not rebel like that rebellious house; open your mouth and eat what I give you" (Ezekiel 2:2-6,8).

Remember these important aspects of the watchman's call:

♦ The call contains the essence of the watchman's assignment, as shown in Ezekiel 2.

♦ God's boldness and confidence for the assignment comes with the call.

♦ God equips and assures him of divine protection.

♦ God clarifies His desire and the need to speak the true message with boldness. Here, God's instruction to Ezekiel was not to allow fear to hinder his message.

♦ The call also makes it clear that obedience to God is a prerequisite, so God warned Ezekiel not to be dissuaded by the circumstances that may come his way.

The watchman must not rebel against the local authority as illustrated by King David, the watchman, and the gatekeeper in the story told in Second Samuel 18:24-27, cited previously.

In Ezekiel's call, God emphasized the need to be grounded in the Word: "Then I looked, and I saw a hand stretched out to me. In it was a scroll" (Ezek. 2:9).

And he said to me, "Son of man, eat what is before you, eat this scroll; then go and speak to the house of Israel." So I opened my mouth, and he gave me the scroll to eat. Then he said to me, "Son of man, eat this scroll I am giving you and fill your stomach with it." So I ate it, and it tasted as sweet as honey in my mouth" (Ezekiel 3:1-3).

Even at the beginning, in this case of Ezekiel, God hints that there would be propensity to the message of lament, mourning, or woes in the watchman's ministry and assignment "which He unrolled before me. On both sides of it were written words of lament and mourning and woe" (Ezek. 2:10). However, this should be handled with maturity to ensure acceptance of the watchman messages.

God's call to Ezekiel also emphasized the need to understand the mission and allow God to order each step of the way.

And he said to me, "Son of man, listen carefully and take to heart all the words I speak to you. Go now to your countrymen in exile and speak to them. Say to them, 'This is what the Sovereign Lord says,' whether they listen or fail to listen" (Ezekiel 3:10-11).

INTIMACY WITH GOD

A watchman should operate from a position of intimacy with God, as the essence of a watchman's ministry is friendship with God. The hallmark of intimacy with God is the expression of imbibed attributes of God such as compassion, slowness to anger, and abounding in love. Both Moses and Daniel operated in this anointing with the love and compassion of God. Yet others like Jeremiah and Jonah, though intimate with God, became judgmental and somehow operated without much love. However, maturity in this ministry is measured by how close the watchman is to God and not by the volume of messages received. Intimacy with God is reliant not only on having the right vertical relationship with God but also on having good relations with other people, as the correct handling of events and circumstances in life is connected with intimacy with God.

PREPARATION FOR MINISTRY

The following fundamentals provide insight into how to prepare for a watchman's ministry:

1. The watchman and the Word of God.

As mentioned previously, prophets Ezekiel and Jeremiah and the apostle John had to eat the Word of God. See Ezekiel 3:1-3, Jeremiah 15:16, and Revelation 10:9-11.

Also, the prophet Samuel had to learn the value of the Word of God early in his life:

> *Now Samuel did not yet know the Lord: The word of the Lord had not yet been revealed to him* (1 Samuel 3:7).

> *The Lord was with Samuel as he grew up, and he let none of his words fall to the ground. And all Israel from Dan to Beersheba recognized that Samuel was attested as a prophet of the Lord. The Lord continued to appear at Shiloh, and there he revealed himself to Samuel through his word* (1 Samuel 3:19-21).

> *And Samuel's word came to all Israel. Now the Israelites went out to fight against the Philistines. The Israelites camped at Ebenezer, and the Philistines at Aphek* (1 Samuel 4:1).

2. The need to be strong physically and emotionally.

Isaiah experienced literal physical pains following the revelation he had received, so the need to ensure physical fitness is paramount for the watchman ministry.

> *A dire vision has been shown to me: The traitor betrays, the looter takes loot. Elam, attack! Media, lay siege! I will bring to an end all the groaning she caused. At this my body is racked with pain, pangs seize me, like those of a woman in labor; I am staggered by what I hear, I am bewildered by what I see. My heart falters, fear makes me tremble; the twilight I longed for has become a horror to me* (Isaiah 21:2-4).

3. The need for spiritual alertness.

Alertness in the spirit is of crucial importance for any effective watchfulness.

An oracle concerning the Desert by the Sea: Like whirlwinds sweeping through the southland, an invader comes from the desert, from a land of terror. They set the tables, they spread the rugs, they eat, and they drink! Get up, you officers, oil the shields! This is what the Lord says to me: "Go, post a lookout and have him report what he sees" (Isaiah 21:1,5-6).

4. The need to strengthen the spirit-man of the watchman.

He who has no rule over his own spirit is like city that is broken down and without walls (Proverbs 25:28 AMP).

To strengthen your spirit means to do that which is necessary to bring your spirit-man into an appropriate relationship with God and into a position of effectiveness, a place of minimal interference from the body and the soul. This is also the place to maximize the watchman's capacity to receive and handle revelations from God.

No man is stronger than his spirit. The most important part of man is the spirit. The spirit of man comes from God and will return to Him. It's the part of man that is created in the likeness and image of God.

5. The need for a solid foundation.

The watchman is stationed on an elevated wall, and if the wall is broken down, the watchman loses that advantage.

When the foundations are being destroyed, what can the righteous do? (Psalm 11:3)

Her [Jerusalem] gates have sunk into the ground; their bars he has broken and destroyed. Her king and her princes are exiled among the nations, the law is no more, and her prophets no longer find visions from the Lord (Lamentations 2:9).

In ensuring a solid foundation, other groups play essential roles. The following groups are coworkers with the watchman:

- ◆ Intercessors cannot be overemphasized; every watchman will need the arm of a prayer ministry.

- Gatekeepers are those who regulate the traffic to and from the domain. The gate is shut when danger approaches and opened when the king or friendly company approach on the advice of the watchman. An enemy allowed in may be difficult to spot.

- Local church leadership (and the local church) ensures that the information from the watchman is put into effective use. A noncompliant leadership will jeopardize the effectiveness of the watchman. The watchman needs to cooperate and submit to local church leadership to attain and maintain credibility.

- Good family life is essential to the watchman. Lack of peace in the home leads to disorganization and incoherency in spiritual duties.

- The role of the peace within the domain. If acrimony exists within the domain, the watchman becomes ineffective.

- Other watchers. There is need for cooperation between other watchers and the watchmen. Those with responsibility to watch over the city will need to cooperate with those with responsibility to watch over the local church. The watchmen's commitment and dedication to watching is their duty that ensures the safety of the people and is of paramount importance.

6. *The watchman needs right-standing with God.*

The psalmist tells us that if God is not watching over a city, the watchmen labor in vain: "Unless the Lord builds the house, its builders labor in vain. Unless the Lord watches over the city, the watchmen stand guard in vain" (Ps. 127:1). Also, the prophet Hosea had this to say, "the prophet, along with my God, is the watchman over Ephraim" (Hos. 9:8a).

The watchman needs to rely on God; by strength shall no man prevail. Also, the psalmist says, the Lord confides in those who fear Him.

7. Satan–the counterfeit watchman.

The watchman needs to be aware of satan. It is important for the watchman to be conscious that the enemy and his agents are watching him. And just as importantly, watchmen need to remember that satan is a counterfeit watchman:

> *The wicked watches the righteous, and seeks to slay him* (Psalm 37:32 NKJV).

> *Do not enter the path of the wicked. And do not walk in the way of evil. Avoid it, do not travel on it; turn away from it and pass on. For they do not sleep unless they have done evil, and their sleep is taken away unless they make someone fall* (Proverbs 4:14-16 NKJV).

> *Be sober, be vigilant; because your adversary the devil walks about like a roaring lion, seeking whom he may devour* (1 Peter 5:8 NKJV).

CHAPTER FOUR

ADDITIONAL ROLES AND RESPONSIBILITIES

Further roles and responsibilities of the spiritual watchman are typified by the roles of the natural watchmen played in the Old Testament. Writing on the role of the natural watchmen in the Old Testament, Dutch Sheets wrote in *Watchman Prayer*, "Watchmen were also posted on the city walls usually near the gate, where they functioned as sentries."[1]

I believe also that the Old Testament often serves as a type and symbol of things that happen in the spirit realm. In the Old Testament there were at least four basic functions and three main watches of four hours each for the watchman, which I will discuss.

THE FOUR BASIC FUNCTIONS

1. To watch out for the enemy without creating rancour and acrimony within the camp.

2. To watch for the king or other members of royal family (the coming of Jesus Christ or divine messenger), and to announce their coming to the city so that they might be received with the proper protocols. When the Ark of God was returned to the Israelites unexpectedly, seventy people were struck down because they did not receive it with the proper protocol:

    Now the people of Beth Shemesh were harvesting their wheat in the valley, and when they looked up and saw the ark, they rejoiced at the sight. The cart came to the field of Joshua of Beth Shemesh, and there it stopped beside a large rock. The people chopped up the wood of the cart and sacrificed the cows as a burnt offering to the Lord. The Levites took down the ark of the Lord, together with the chest containing the gold objects, and placed them on the large rock. On that day the people of Beth Shemesh offered burnt offerings and made sacrifices to the Lord (1 Samuel 6:13-15).

But God struck down some of the men of Beth Shemesh, putting seventy of them to death because they had looked into the ark of the Lord. The people mourned because of the heavy blow the Lord had dealt them, and the men of Beth Shemesh asked, "Who can stand in the presence of the Lord, this holy God? To whom will the ark go up from here?" (1 Samuel 6:19-20)

To encourage the righteous in his righteousness and to warn the wicked to turn from his wickedness (see Ezekiel 33:12-14).

3. The prophetic watchman is also to tell what sort of time it is: "Men of Issachar, who understood the times and knew what Israel should do—200 chiefs, with all their relatives under their command" (1 Chron. 12:32).

4. The watchman anointing and prayer go together—the watch and pray principle. A watchman needs to be prayerful because the elevated spiritual position not only creates a vantage point but also exposes him or her to the radar of surveillance of the enemy.

THE WATCHES

The watches in the Scriptures were time periods of the night assigned for spiritual watchfulness or alertness. There were two systems of nomenclature in Bible days: the "Jew's recording" and the "Old Testament writings" named the watches differently from the "Romans' recording" and the "New Testament writing." The Jews divided the night into three parts of four hours each, and the Romans divided the night into four parts of three hours each. In the Book of Jeremiah, the Bible states, "Arise, cry out in the night, as the watches of the night begins; pour out your heart like water in the presence of the Lord" (Jer. 2:19). The inference from this statement is that watches are for the night season and begins at night or as the night begins.

THE THREE WATCHES—JEW'S RECORDING

As watchmen in the natural world could not watch 24 hours every day, the spiritual watchmen should likewise collaborate with each other in other ministry to avoid fatigue. The periods of watch assigned to a natural watchman, in Bible days, were four hours each and these were regarded as "watches." From the Scriptures, the first watch begins as nighttime starts to set in.

The first watch is the evening watch: "Arise, cry out in the night, **as the watches of the night begin**; pour out your heart like water in the presence of the Lord. Lift up your hands to him for the lives of your children, who faint from hunger at the head of every street" (Lam. 2:19). This watch is for apostolic specification of the mandate to the watchman. It is the watch for impartation, consolidation, and motivation of the specifics of the mission to the watchman.

The middle watch: "Gideon and the hundred men with him reached the edge of the camp at the beginning of the middle watch, just after they had changed the guard. They blew their trumpets and broke the jars that were in their hands" (Judg. 7:19).

This watch is:

- The time of most vulnerability, because this is the period when most people are asleep.

- A time the devil uses to sow weeds among the wheat, during sleep. As the Bible says, "While everyone was sleeping, his enemy [the devil] came and sowed weeds among the wheat" (Matt.13:25).

- A time for intensive spiritual activities—prayers and consecration.

- The midnight hour, when the angel of death passed through Egypt.

- A time the soul and the body are least active; therefore a time of enhanced spiritual receptivity and vulnerability.

- When the angel of the Lord released Paul and Silas.

- A time when the spiritual atmosphere is susceptible to change.

- A time when Gideon destroyed the altars of Baal; therefore a time for spiritual warfare for the destruction of idolatry and other demonic practices.

The last watch: "The next day Saul separated his men into three divisions; during the last watch of the night they broke into the camp of the Ammonites and slaughtered them until the heat of the day. Those who survived were scattered, so that no two of them were left together" (1 Sam. 11:11).

This watch is a time:

- To watch and move in the confidence of what God has done in the previous watches.

- For stirring up people as empowered by the Spirit of God.

- To strategize using the privilege of the revelations received in the previous watches.

- To act out and move out in faith.

- To call for divine validation and intervention.

The Egyptians pursued them, and all Pharaoh's horses and chariots and horsemen followed them into the sea. During the **last watch of the night** *the Lord looked down from the pillar of fire and cloud at the Egyptian army and threw it into confusion. He made the wheels of their chariots come off so that they had difficulty driving. And the Egyptians said, "Let's get away from the Israelites! The Lord is fighting for them against Egypt"* (Exodus 14:23-25).

THE FOUR WATCHES—ROMANS' RECORDING

In Matthew 14:25 and Mark 6:48, the Bible speaks of the fourth watch of the night:

After He had dismissed them, He went up on a mountainside by Himself to pray. When evening came, He was there alone, but the boat was already a considerable distance from land, buffeted by the waves because the wind was against it. During the fourth watch of the night Jesus went out to them, walking on the lake. When the disciples saw Him walking on the lake, they were terrified. "It's a ghost," they said, and cried out in fear. But Jesus immediately said to them: "Take courage! It is I. Don't be afraid" (Matthew 14:23-27).

After leaving them, He went up on a mountainside to pray. When evening came, the boat was in the middle of the lake, and He was alone on land. He saw the disciples straining at the oars, because the wind was against them. About the fourth watch of the night He went out to them, walking on the lake. He was about to pass by them, but when they saw Him walking on the lake, they thought He was a ghost. They cried out, because they all saw Him and were terrified. Immediately He spoke to them and said, "Take courage! It is I. Don't be afraid." Then He climbed into the boat with them, and the wind died down. They were completely amazed (Mark 6:46-51).

THE RIGHT ATTITUDE OF A WATCHMAN

This is revealed in Abraham's response to his divine encounter in the Book of Genesis:

Then the Lord said, "shall I hide from Abraham what I am about to do? Abraham will surely become a great and powerful nation and all nations on earth will be blessed through him. For I have chosen him, so that he will direct his children and his household after him to keep the way of the Lord by doing what is right and just, so that the Lord will bring about for Abraham what He has promised him." Then the Lord said,

"The outcry against Sodom and Gomorrah is so great and their sin so grievous that I will go down and see if what they have done is as bad as the outcry that has reached me. If not, I will know." The men turned away and went toward Sodom, but Abraham remained standing before the Lord. Then Abraham approached Him and said: "Will You sweep away the righteous with the wicked? What if there are fifty righteous people in the city? Will You really sweep it away and not spare the place for the sake of the fifty righteous people in it? Far be it from You to do such a thing—to kill the righteous with the wicked, treating the righteous and the wicked alike. Far be it from You! Will not the Judge of all the earth do right?" The Lord said, "If I find fifty righteous people in the city of Sodom, I will spare the whole place for their sake." Then Abraham spoke up again: "Now that I have been so bold as to speak to the Lord, though I am nothing but dust and ashes, what if the number of the righteous is five less than fifty? Will You destroy the whole city because of five people?" "If I find forty-five there," He said, "I will not destroy it." Once again he spoke to Him, "What if only forty are found there?" He said, "For the sake of forty, I will not do it." Then he said, "May the Lord not be angry, but let me speak. What if only thirty can be found there?" He answered, "I will not do it if I find thirty there." Abraham said, "Now that I have been so bold as to speak to the Lord, what if only twenty can be found there?" He said, "For the sake of twenty, I will not destroy it." Then he said, "May the Lord not be angry, but let me speak just once more. What if only ten can be found there?" He answered, "For the sake of ten, I will not destroy it" (Genesis 18:17-32).

In this account, Abraham typified the correct attitude of an effective watchman. The lessons revealed in the manner in which Abraham handled this extraordinary encounter include the following:

1. A watchman should be in a state of continuous readiness. Abraham was in a state of spiritual alertness, which enabled

him to see the unconventional arrival of the celestial beings in corporal appearance.

2. A watchman should be spiritually sensitive enough to discern when the move of God comes.

3. A watchman should live a life full of kindness. Abraham was prepared to entertain strangers. "Do not forget to entertain strangers, for by so doing some people have entertained angels without knowing it" (Heb. 13:2).

4. A watchman's strength lies in his intimacy with God. God describes Abraham as a friend. Intimacy with God determines what a watchman receives and places him in a position to intercede for others. This is the privilege that Abraham had in order to be allowed to question God.

5. A watchman should be a friend of God.

THE ESSENCE OF A TRUE SPIRITUAL WATCHMAN

A watchman with "volumes of revelations" but who lacks the essence of the will and purpose of God will send mixed and confused signals. We need watchmen such as Daniel, who discovered Jeremiah's prophecy and prayed it through:

> *In the first year of Darius son of Xerxes (a Mede by descent), who was made ruler over the Babylonian kingdom—in the first year of his reign, I, Daniel, understood from the Scriptures, according to the word of the Lord given to Jeremiah the prophet, that the desolation of Jerusalem would last seventy years. So I turned to the Lord God and pleaded with Him in prayer and petition, in fasting, and in sackcloth and ashes* (Daniel 9:1-3).

The watchman should ensure that prophecy and progress should go together. The Bible says:

> *I have posted watchmen on your walls, O Jerusalem; they will never be silent day or night. You who call on the Lord, give yourselves no rest, and give Him no rest till he establishes Jerusalem and makes her the praise of the earth* (Isaiah 62:6-7).

Jesus Christ Himself gave a model of the essence of a true spiritual watchman, He says in John, "I tell you the truth, the Son can do nothing by Himself; He can do only what He sees His Father doing, because whatever the Father does the Son also does" (John 5:19).

Jesus also taught His disciples to pray: "Your kingdom come, Your will be done on earth as it is in heaven" (Matt. 6:10). Unless it exists in Heaven, it cannot be brought into the reality of an earthly existence. So the true essence of the spiritual watchman is to give warnings and other revelations that aligns the earth to the plans and purposes of God.

THE WATCHMAN COULD BRING GOOD NEWS!

The role of the watchman is also to announce the good news of restoration to God.

> *How beautiful on the mountains are the feet of those who bring good news, who proclaim peace, who bring good tidings, who proclaim salvation, who say to Zion, "Your God reigns!" Listen! Your watchmen lift up their voices; together they shout for joy. When the Lord returns to Zion, they will see it with their own eyes* (Isaiah 52:7-8).

These good news announcements are missing in most existing watchman ministries today because they have restricted themselves to operate only in the "warn them" dimension. The watchman ministry should not just be synonymous with bad news. It should also help to create and prepare people to receive the coming of the King with proper protocol.

WATCHING FOR THE WICKED

A watchman is called to minister to both Christians and non-Christians, just as Ezekiel was called to the entire house of Israel. The watchman should also be actively involved in interceding for the wicked so that none will perish and all shall come to the true knowledge of God. Therefore, the role of the watchman includes watching out for the wicked and warning them:

*Son of man, I have made you a watchman for the house of Is-
rael; so hear the word I speak and give them warning from
me. When I say to a wicked man, "You will surely die," and
you do not warn him or speak out to dissuade him from his
evil ways in order to save his life, that wicked man will die for
his sin, and I will hold you accountable for his blood. But if
you do warn the wicked man and he does not turn from his
wickedness or from his evil ways, he will die for his sin; but
you will have saved yourself* (Ezekiel 3:17-19).

WATCHING FOR THE RIGHTEOUS

A watchman becomes restricted if he focuses only on the
wicked—his role also includes ensuring that the righteous do not turn
from their right-standing with God.

*Again, when a righteous man turns from his righteousness
and does evil, and I put a stumbling block before him, he
will die. Since you did not warn him, he will die for his sin.
The righteous things he did will not be remembered and I
will hold you accountable for his blood. But if you do warn
the righteous man not to sin and he does not sin, he will
surely live because he took warning, and you will have saved
yourself* (Ezekiel 3:20-21).

AVOIDING SPIRITUAL BLINDNESS

Seeing is vital to the proper operation of the watchman ministry,
for when it is hindered, the watchman becomes ineffective. The eye is
a major gate for the watchman. To preserve the seer's anointing, the
watchman must live a life of consecration and sanctification and
should be able to resist the lust of the eyes and the cravings of the
flesh. Any of these pollutions will lead to a fragmented visionary reception or blurred images. The prophet Isaiah gave a description of
this state in the Bible:

*Israel's watchmen are blind, they all lack knowledge; they are
all mute dogs, they cannot bark; they lie around and dream,
they love to sleep. They are dogs with mighty appetites; they*

never have enough. They are shepherds who lack understanding; they all turn to their own way, each seeks his own gain. "Come," each one cries, "let me get wine! Let us drink our fill of beer! And tomorrow will be like today, or even far better" (Isaiah 56:10-12).

This Scripture passage is a sad example of degeneration of what a useful ministry should have been.

In Psalm 74:9 the Bible also says, "We do not see our signs; there is no longer any prophet; nor is there any among us who knows how long" (NKJV). A sure sign of spiritual blindness.

ENDNOTE

1. Dutch Sheets, *Watchman Prayer* (Ventura, CA: Regal Books, 2000), 32.

CHAPTER FIVE

ESSENTIAL WATCHMAN ATTRIBUTES

Submission to authority, accountability, and cooperation with leadership as well as other ministries increases the credibility of the watchman. Credibility is earned; and no matter how anointed a watchman is, he will need to work and attain reasonable credibility for his messages to be accepted. Many watchmen have suffered in this area. In general, the watchman has favor from God at the point of call to the ministry. This is important if the watchman is to receive revelations from God. But favor with people, and therefore acceptability by the people, increases with time and maturity, and it is optimal at the point of commission.

SUBMISSION AND COOPERATION

A watchman must work in unity with other ministries—those with the gifts of interpretation and application. The application of revelation should really come from the pastoral level and the interpretations from those who are gifted in interpretation and/or have a Daniel 1:17 anointing: "To these four young men God gave knowledge and understanding of all kinds of literature and learning. And Daniel could understand visions and dreams of all kinds."

Corporately, these three different levels—the watchman, the pastor, and the gifted interpreter—should work together. In Second Samuel 18, the Bible records how the watchman and gatekeeper cooperated with the king who in this instance gave the interpretations (see 2 Sam. 18:24-27).

This was the conclusion of King David based on the revelation given to him by the watchman: "The watchman said, 'It seems to me that the first one runs like Ahimaaz son of Zadok.' 'He's a good man,' the king said. 'He comes with good news'" (2 Sam. 18:27).

Watchmen are also linked with gatekeepers and work closely with them; thus the gate is closed if the watchman sees and reports evil or a dangerous approach. The gate is opened at the command of the king by advice of what the watchman observes.

When this level of cooperation is missing, the watchman's efforts become ineffective and irrelevant, thus allowing the enemy to sneak through these loopholes.

From this example, it can also be seen that the basic role of the watchman is simply to look out and report to the people, even though some watchmen may sometimes lack the understanding of what he receives.

THE ULTIMATE PURPOSE

The fundamental and ultimate purpose of the watchman ministry is to align the people to the purposes of God, expose the plans of the enemy, and to bring God's purposes to the domain:

> *"I looked for a man among them who would build up the wall and stand before me in the gap on behalf of the land so that I would not have to destroy it, but I found none. So I will pour out My wrath on them and consume them with My fiery anger, bringing down on their own heads all they have done, declares the Sovereign Lord"* (Ezekiel 22:30-31).

It is vital to remember that God is the Supreme Watchman. The Bible says:

> *He will not let your foot slip—he who watches over you will not slumber; indeed, He who watches over Israel will neither slumber nor sleep. The Lord watches over you—the Lord is your shade at your right hand; the sun will not harm you by day, nor the moon by night. The Lord will keep you from all harm—He will watch over your life; the Lord will watch over your coming and going both now and forevermore* (Psalm 121:3-8).

The pattern of divine communication with each watchman is unique, as they differ in the way they receive and express their gifting. Watchmen have different personalities, backgrounds, and methods for receiving revelations, as some may be predominantly seers (apostle John) and others nabi prophets (Isaiah). Biblical watchmen had varied methods of presenting their messages to the people. For instance, the prophet Amos was a country man who used country language; Ezekiel was very strange and communicated his messages in bizarre ways; Jeremiah was known as the weeping prophet, his messages being full of woes, laments, and sadness; and Isaiah was a palace prophet who lived with privilege and spoke in sophisticated language.

I believe the following factors influence the uniqueness of the ministry of the watchman: uniqueness of the call or the divine mandate on the watchman; prevailing circumstances in the time of the ministry; whether or not the watchman has an erroneous mind-set that needs correction (internal component); the impending moves of God; and that which He also wants to communicate.

There are features that are special to the ministry of a watchman. I will look at these features using the prophets Ezekiel and Isaiah as examples.

WATCHMAN FEATURES THAT TYPIFY THE MINISTRY OF THE PROPHET EZEKIEL

Lets us examine the life and ministry of Ezekiel, who was called as a watchman to the house of Israel.

Son of Man, I have made you a watchman for the house of Is-rael; so hear the word I speak and give them warning from Me (Ezekiel 3:17).

We can learn the following from the life and ministry of the prophet Ezekiel:

- ◆ The watchman should be accountable to God. "But if the watchman sees the sword coming and does not blow the trumpet to warn the people and the sword comes and takes the life of one of them, that man will be taken away because of his sin, but I will hold the watchman account-able for his blood" (Ezek. 33:6).

- The watchman should be responsible to the people. "Son of man, I have made you a watchman for the house of Israel; so hear the word I speak and give them warning from Me. When I say to the wicked, 'O wicked man, you will surely die,' and you do not speak out to dissuade him from his ways, that wicked man will die for his sin, and I will hold you accountable for his blood. But if you do warn the wicked man to turn from his ways and he does not do so, he will die for his sin, but you will be saved yourself" (Ezek. 33:7-9).

- The watchman should function as a postman and not an enforcer of the warning: "The people to whom I am send-ing you are obstinate and stubborn. Say to them, 'This is what the Sovereign Lord says.' And whether they listen or fail to listen—for they are a rebellious house—they will know that a prophet has been among them. And you, son of man, do not be afraid of them or their words. Do not be afraid, though briers and thorns are all around you and you live among scorpions. Do not be afraid of what they say or terrified by them, though they are a rebellious house. You must speak my words to them, whether they listen or fail to listen, for they are rebellious" (Ezek. 2:4-7).

- The watchman should move with the internationalities of God: "Then the Spirit lifted me up, and I heard behind me a loud rumbling sound—May the glory of the Lord be praised in His dwelling place!" (Ezek. 3:12). "Now the evening before the man arrived, the hand of the Lord was upon me, and He opened my mouth before the man came to me in the morning. So my mouth was opened and I was no longer silent" (Ezek. 33:22).

- The true purpose of the watchman is to change people's lives; the watchman acts as a guard when the enemy ap-proaches and discerns when destructive spirits try to arise from within. "As surely as I live, declares the Sovereign Lord, I take no pleasure in the death of the wicked, but rather that they turn from their ways and live. Turn! Turn from your evil ways! Why will you die, O house of Israel?" (Ezek. 33:11).

WATCHMAN FEATURES THAT TYPIFY THE MINISTRY OF THE PROPHET ISAIAH

An oracle concerning the Desert by the Sea: Like whirlwinds sweeping through the southland, an invader comes from the desert, from a land of terror. A dire vision has been shown to me: The traitor betrays, the looter takes loot. Elam, attack! Media, lay siege! I will bring to an end all the groaning she caused. At this my body is racked with pain, pangs seize me, like those of a woman in labour; I am staggered by what I hear, I am bewildered by what I see. My heart falters, fear makes me tremble; the twilight I longed for has become a horror to me. They set the tables, they spread the rugs, they eat, they drink! Get up, you officers, oil the shields! This is what the Lord says to me: "Go, post a lookout and have him report what he sees. When he sees chariots with teams of horses, riders on donkeys or riders on camels, let him be alert, fully alert." And the lookout shouted, "Day after day, my lord, I stand on the watchtower; every night I stay at my post. Look, here comes a man in a chariot with a team of horses. And he gives back the answer: 'Babylon has fallen, has fallen! All the images of its gods lie shattered on the ground!'" O my people, crushed on the threshing floor, I tell you what I have heard from the Lord Almighty, from the God of Israel. An oracle concerning Dumah: Someone calls to me from Seir, "Watchman, what is left of the night? Watchman, what is left of the night?" The watchman replies, "Morning is coming, but also the night. If you would ask, then ask; and come back yet again" (Isaiah 21:1-12).

The prophet Isaiah saw a dreamlike vision of the fall of Babylon and the possible implications for Judah. In this vision Isaiah was acting as the watchman who was asked to summon the Babylonians, authority to prepare for war! That is what "anointing your shield" means.

- Isaiah was *faithful to his assignment* as a watchman: *"And the lookout shouted, 'Day after day, my lord, I stand on the watchtower; every night I stay at my post'"* (Isa. 21:8).

The Elam that Isaiah saw was a major port of Persia. Dumah was located at the intersection of the east-west trade route between Babylon and Edom and played a vital military and economic role, so that watchfulness of Isaiah transcended into areas of economy and politics.

The prophet Isaiah *declares the night is accompanied by a new day no matter what*. That is to say that salvation will come after darkness.

- Isaiah kept his responsibility to warn people, and he needed to maintain good physical fitness even as his body suffered physical pain during the process of his duty: "At this my body is racked with pain, pangs seize me, like those of a woman in labor; I am staggered by what I hear, I am bewildered by what I see. My heart falters, fear makes me tremble."

SPIRITUAL RECONNAISSANCE, SURVEILLANCE, AND DISCERNMENT

The Bible is full of many instances of the critical roles and values of spiritual reconnaissance, surveillance, and discernment in the conduct of effective war in the spirit. Much has been written about the place of spiritual mapping as a vital strategy in spiritual warfare, but as critical as this step may be, it remains only part of the whole story. Spiritual mapping is in essence the process by which we seek to correctly identify the nature, strength, history, methods of operation, and the legality of the enemy forces in an area. But in reality even as we do this, the enemy is also keeping a watchful eye on us; we are under enemy surveillance. So to put things in their complete and correct perspectives, we need watchmen who know their roles in spiritual reconnaissance, surveillance, and discernment with equal fervency as is watching out for the approaching enemy.

Spiritual Surveillance

Spiritual surveillance is the act of keeping watch over an opposing force, and so it works for us as well as for the enemy. We are being watched, and we should keep watch over the enemy forces as well. By and large, the majority of the unnecessary casualties in spiritual warfare are due to our failure to know that the saints of God are continually under spiritual surveillance by evil forces. Satan is a great watchman with a formidable network of information gathering. When the Lord asked him, "From where do you come?" he answered, "From going to and fro on the earth and from walking back and forth on it" (Job 1:7 NKJV). You should be able to guess what his mission was in this clandestine espionage.

Jesus Christ admonished us that demons walk about looking and watching for places to rest: "When an unclean spirit goes out of a man, he goes through dry places, seeking rest" (Matt. 12:43). And speaking on the same subject, Peter said, "Be of sober spirit, be on the alert. Your adversary, the devil, prowls around like around like a roaring lion, seeking someone to devour." We should be mindful of the fact that the devil's surveillance is formidable, coherent, and can be persistent. This is why the Bible says to give the devil no foothold. We need watchmen to keep ahead of the enemy and to alert the people of the enemy's surveillance, so the people can minimize the loopholes in their midst.

We also take courage in the belief that the Lord watches over the righteous ones, for He who watches over Israel will neither sleep nor slumber. We will do well to keep our mind steadfast on Him, as the Bible teaches, "For the eyes of the Lord range throughout the earth to strengthen those whose hearts are fully committed to him..." (2 Chron. 16:9).

Spiritual Reconnaissance

Spiritual reconnaissance is to make a preliminary survey of the enemy forces for military purposes. This includes what is commonly referred to as spiritual mapping. We should do this if we are to be effective in spiritual warfare, as we see in the story of Moses and the Israelites when God allowed Moses to send men to spy out the Promised Land: "The Lord said to Moses, 'Send some men to explore the land of Canaan, which I am giving to the Israelites. From each ancestral tribe send one of its leaders'" (Num. 13:1-2).

And again Joshua used this strategy:

> *Then Joshua son of Nun secretly sent two spies from Shittim. "Go, look over the land," he said, "especially Jericho." So they went and entered the house of a prostitute named Rahab and stayed there* (Joshua 2:1).

> *Then the two men started back. They went down out of the hills, forded the river and came to Joshua son of Nun and told him everything that had happened to them. They said to Joshua, "The Lord has surely given the whole land into our hands; all the people are melting in fear because of us"* (Joshua 2:23-24).

Good spiritual reconnaissance should be followed by appropriate response to the findings. When Israel did adequate spiritual reconnaissance but failed to discern that God was unhappy with them because of Achan's sin, as a consequence they suffered defeat in the hands of a much smaller force in Ai:

> *Now Joshua sent men from Jericho to Ai, which is near Beth Aven to the east of Bethel, and told them, "Go up and spy out the region." So the men went up and spied out Ai. When they returned to Joshua, they said, "Not all the people will have to go up against Ai. Send two or three thousand men to take it and do not weary all the people, for only a few men are there." So about three thousand men went up; but the men of Ai routed them, who killed about thirty-six of them. They chased the Israelites from the city gate as far as the stone quarries and struck them down on the slopes. At this the hearts of the people melted and became like water. Then Joshua tore his clothes and fell face down to the ground before the ark of the*

Lord, remaining there till evening. The elders of Israel did the same and sprinkled dust on their heads (Joshua 7:2-6).

We also need watchmen who will alert the people of the enemy's reconnaissance. The city of Laish lacked effective spiritual watchmen, and therefore they failed to recognize when they came under Israel's reconnaissance. This story illustrates the fate that could befall a quiet and peaceful city of a people who pay no attention to the danger of the enemy's spiritual mapping.

In the city of Laish were people who were very unsuspecting, so they became easy prey to their enemy:

So the five men left and came to Laish, where they saw that the people were living in safety, like the Sidonians, unsuspecting and secure. And since their land lacked nothing, they were prosperous. Also, they lived a long way from the Sidonians and had no relationship with anyone else (Judges 18:7).

The enemy did a good job in spiritual mapping on Samson's source of power. The Philistines knew they had to discover the secret behind Samson's supernatural power if they were to overcome him.

Some time later, he fell in love with a woman in the Valley of Sorek whose name was Delilah. The rulers of the Philistines went to her and said, "See if you can lure him into showing you the secret of his great strength and how we can overpower him so that we may tie him up and subdue him. Each one of us will give you eleven hundred shekels of silver" (Judges 16:4-5).

It is important to remember that these Old Testament stories are types and symbols of the things of the supernatural.

DISCERNMENT

Spiritual discernment is to perceive clearly something that lies beneath the surface—the real motive or force behind the scene of an outward manifestation. Discernment is a gift of the Holy Spirit and should be distinguished from the outworking of the suspicion of the mind. Discernment is a supernatural ability to know the source, nature, and activities of the Spirit (or spirits) at work in a situation. Discernment can help us to know which spirit is at work, whether it be the Holy Spirit, human spirit, or the spirit of the devil and his agents. One can discern what spirit is in operation by spiritual senses. For instance, one can discern by sight, hearing, smelling, or even by the sense of touch. In this regard, the spiritual principle inherent in Hebrews 5:14 becomes valuable: "But solid food is for the mature, who by constant use have trained themselves to distinguish good from evil." Notice the key operative words in this principle—*solid food*—or strong meat, which means in-depth understanding of deep things. Maturity comes by practice or by the reason of constant use or by exercising our senses, and in that process the spiritual senses are trained to discern good or bad.

Many people have suffered for allowing sentiment to cloud their spiritual discernment. In fact, we should remember that there is no sentiment in spirituality. The key factors are:

- Obedience to the Lord.

- Relying on the truth.

- Allowing the Lord's compassion to consume us.

- Allowing forgiveness to prevail instead of sentiment judged by the flesh.

Remembering these key factors allows us to avoid sentiment. God's compassion is greater than any depth of human sentiment, and man cannot be more compassionate than God. Often I have noticed that the most common hindrance to practicing discernment is when we allow our sentiment to cloud the nudging of the Holy Spirit. The Gibeonites deceived Joshua and the Israelites because they based their decision to covenant with them on their feelings determined by what their natural senses and sentiments of the time dictated. They did not seek the Lord and had no watchmen who could see beyond the surface:

The men of Israel sampled their provisions but did not inquire of the Lord. Then Joshua made a treaty of peace with them to let them live, and the leaders of the assembly ratified it by oath. Three days after they made the treaty with the

Gibeonites, the Israelites heard that they were neighbors, living near them (Joshua 9:14-16).

Many people have suffered severe consequences of allowing their sentiments to compromise adherence to the gentle but clear nudging of God discerned by revelations. The truth that must be said is that God knows the end from the beginning, even when our natural inclination runs contrary to what we discerned.

The value of discernment cannot be overemphasized in the ministry of the watchman. The prophet Isaiah immediately spotted King Hezekiah's lack of discernment when the envoy from Babylon visited him:

> *At that time Merodach-Baladan son of Baladan king of Babylon sent Hezekiah letters and a gift, because he had heard of Hezekiah's illness. Hezekiah received the messengers and showed them all that was in his storehouses—the silver, the gold, the spices and the fine oil—his armory and everything found among his treasures. There was nothing in his palace or in all his kingdom that Hezekiah did not show them. Then Isaiah the prophet went to King Hezekiah and asked, "What did those men say, and where did they come from?" "From a distant land," Hezekiah replied. "They came from Babylon." The prophet asked, "What did they see in your palace?" "They saw everything in my palace," Hezekiah said. "There is nothing among my treasures that I did not show them." Then Isaiah said to Hezekiah, "Hear the word of the Lord: The time will surely come when everything in your palace, and all that your fathers have stored up until this day, will be carried off to Babylon. Nothing will be left, says the Lord. And some of your descendants, your own flesh and blood, that will be born to you, will be taken away, and they will become eunuchs in the palace of the king of Babylon"* (2 Kings 20:12-18).

The apostle Paul and Silas discerned the spirit at work in the slave girl even though what she said was true:

Once when we were going to the place of prayer, we were met by a slave girl who had a spirit by which she predicted the future. She earned a great deal of money for her owners by fortune-telling. This girl followed Paul and the rest of us, shouting, "These men are servants of the Most High God, who are telling you the way to be saved." She kept this up for many days. Finally Paul became so troubled that he turned around and said to the spirit, "In the name of Jesus Christ I command you to come out of her!" At that moment the spirit left her. When the owners of the slave girl realized that their hope of making money was gone, they seized Paul and Silas and dragged them into the marketplace to face the authorities (Acts 16:16-19).

On a personal level, the patriarch Isaac failed to heed the quiet and gentle nudging from the Holy Spirit and acted contrarily to his discernment:

*He went to his father and said, "My father." "Yes, my son," he answered. "Who is it?" Jacob said to his father, "I am Esau your firstborn. I have done as you told me. Please sit up and eat some of my game so that you may give me your blessing." Isaac asked his son, "**How did you find it so quickly, my son?**" "The Lord your God gave me success," he replied. Then Isaac said to Jacob, "Come near so I can touch you, my son, to know whether you really are my son Esau or not." Jacob went close to his father Isaac, who touched him and said, "**The voice is the voice of Jacob, but the hands are the hands of Esau.**" He did not recognize him, for his hands were hairy like those of his brother Esau; so he blessed him. "Are you really my son Esau?" he asked. "I am," he replied. Then he said, "My son, bring me some of your game to eat, so that I may give you my blessing." Jacob brought it to him and he ate; and he brought some wine and he drank. Then his father Isaac said to him, "Come here, my son, and kiss me." So he went to him and kissed him. **When Isaac caught the smell of his clothes, he*** *blessed him and said, "Ah, the smell of my son is like the smell of a field that the Lord has blessed"* (Genesis 27:18-27).

Notice the levels of failure to heed the nudging of spiritual discernment by Isaac:

1. "How did you find it so quickly, my son?" (as he was quickened to ask by the Holy Spirit).

2. "The voice is the voice of Jacob, but the hands are the hands of Esau" (he was nudged by Holy Spirit).

3. "When Isaac caught the smell of his clothes, he blessed him" (his judgment was clouded by his natural perception).

4. Finally, notice he allowed the perception by natural senses to override his inner conviction.

Nehemiah, the rebuilder of the walls of Jerusalem, was ridiculed and threatened by those who opposed his rebuilding of the walls. Then later he came under a new tactic of the enemy—that of psychological warfare, that of intimidation and deception. On several occasions Nehemiah discerned the schemes of the enemy behind the scene:

> *When word came to Sanballat, Tobiah, Geshem the Arab and the rest of our enemies that I had rebuilt the wall and not a gap was left in it—though up to that time I had not set the doors in the gates—Sanballat and Geshem sent me this message: "Come, let us meet together in one of the villages on the plain of Ono." But they were scheming to harm me; so I sent messengers to them with this reply: "I am carrying on a great project and cannot go down. Why should the work stop while I leave it and go down to you?" Four times they sent me the same message, and each time I gave them the same answer* (Nehemiah 6:1-4).

In this instance, Nehemiah discerned that beneath the apparent goodwill suggestion given to him was a ploy to lure him into disobeying God; so he resisted the temptation.

> *One day I went to the house of Shemaiah son of Delaiah, (Shemaiah was said to be receiving messages from God) the*

son of Mehetabel, who was shut in at his home. He said, "Let us meet in the house of God, inside the temple, and let us close the temple doors, because men are coming to kill you— by night they are coming to kill you." But I said, "Should a man like me run away? Or should one like me go into the temple to save his life? I will not go!" (Nehemiah 6:10-11)

DISTINGUISHING DISCERNMENT FROM JUDGMENT

When a watchman discerns a danger or a point of vulnerability as a result of weakness, he warns the people to bring about change. Such warning is known as *admonishment*, and it is an integral part of the watchman's ministry. Technically, when admonishment is not cushioned by inspiration, it amounts to judgment. Whenever a watchman warns or admonishes without giving hope to the people, it amounts to judgment and condemnation. Admonishment itself is to call or warn people to move from a place weakness, vulnerability, or unrighteousness to a place of right standing with God. Motivation can only come when admonishment is followed by inspiration. It is therefore a sign of an immature watchman to warn and then leave the people in condemnation and without hope. Immature watchmen often take the place of judge over the people, but the Bible says mercy triumphs over judgment (see James 2:13). The cardinal purpose of the watchman's ministry is for the calamity or judgment to be avoided.

Distinguishing Discernment From the Suspicious Mind

By and large, the critical issue for most people, watchmen inclusive, is how to differentiate suspicion of their minds and judging by the flesh from the gentle nudging from the Holy Spirit, which is spiritual discernment. I use the following ways to distinguish the difference:

1. By living in the Word of God. The greatest discerner on earth is the Word of God.

    For the word of God is living and active. Sharper than any double-edged sword, it penetrates even to dividing soul and spirit, joints and marrow; it judges [the discerner of] *the thoughts and attitudes of the heart* (Hebrews 4:12).

2. By renewing the mind.

   Do not conform any longer to the pattern of this world, but be transformed by the renewing of your mind. Then you will be able to test and approve what God's will is— His good, pleasing and perfect will (Romans 12:2).

3. By focusing on the things in Heaven rather than on the things on earth.

   Set your minds on things above, not on earthly things. For you died, and your life is now hidden with Christ in God (Colossians 3:2-3).

4. By being of like mind with Jesus Christ.

   If you have any encouragement from being united with Christ, if any comfort from his love, if any fellowship with the Spirit, if any tenderness and compassion, then make my joy complete by being like-minded, having the same love, being one in spirit and purpose. Do nothing out of selfish ambition or vain conceit, but in humility consider others better than yourselves. Each of you should look not only to your own interests, but also to the interests of others. Your attitude should be the same as that of Christ Jesus (Philippians 2:1-5).

5. By keeping a clear and undefiled conscience.

   A person who is pure of heart sees goodness and purity in everything; but a person whose own heart is evil and untrusting finds evil in everything, for his dirty mind and rebellious heart color all he sees and hears (Titus 1:15 TLB).

6. By the transforming hand of the Holy Spirit.

   At that time the Spirit of the Lord will come mightily upon you, and you will prophesy with them and you will feel and act like a different person. From that time on your decisions should be based on whatever seems best under the circumstances, for the Lord will guide you (1 Samuel 10:6-7 TLB).

Every revelation confers some degree of responsibility on the one who receives it. With such responsibilities comes the diminution in the grace of God that accrues from the state of being unaware and innocent about the subject. The onus is on us to make a godly response to the revelations we receive, or are discerned by the Spirit—if we do not, we may suffer the consequences of ignoring it.

CHAPTER SIX

RECLUSE OR RESOURCE?

GROWING AND MATURING IN THE WATCHMAN'S ANOINTING

This is a puzzle that should concern all of us. The loss of any gifted person or any wasted anointing is not only a personal loss but also a loss to the generation to which he was sent. In this regard, we need people with "Epaphra spirit," a people who will not give up until they see the will of God established in the lives of these watchmen: "Epaphras, who is one of you, a bondservant of Christ, greets you, always laboring fervently for you in prayers, that you may stand perfect and complete in all the will of God" (Col. 4:12 NKJV)." Even our watchmen need to be watched over by our prayers.

RECLUSE

The risk of becoming reclusive is a clear and present danger in the life of the watchman! Let us consider the lives of the following watchmen as they related the people of their generation.

Jeremiah

Although Jeremiah had one of the most dramatic lives in Scripture, he never liked his role. For more than four decades Jeremiah gave the leaders of Israel warnings, which they disliked and neglected to heed. As a result, he was arrested on several occasions, imprisoned, and threatened with execution.

Jeremiah was a reluctant messenger, and he remained insecure throughout his life. Though he had great commission given to him, he disliked his role. He spoke hard words to the people, words that were true but also words that reflected the unhappiness that went on in his mind. He quarrelled with God and even hated the life he lived. His messages of gloom were unacceptable to the people, particularly as they came during a miserable period in the history of Israel.

> *Because the Lord revealed their plot to me, I knew it, for at that time he showed me what they were doing. I had been like a gentle lamb led to the slaughter; I did not realize that they had plotted against me, saying, "Let us destroy the tree and its fruit; let us cut him off from the land of the living, that his name be remembered no more." But, O Lord Almighty, you who judge righteously and test the heart and mind let me see your vengeance upon them, for to you I have committed my cause* (Jeremiah 11:18-20).

> *O Lord, you deceived me, and I was deceived; you overpowered me and prevailed. I am ridiculed all day long; everyone mocks me. Whenever I speak, I cry out proclaiming violence and destruction. So the word of the Lord has brought me insult and reproach all day long. But if I say, "I will not mention him or speak any more in his name," his word is in my heart like a fire, a fire shut up in my bones. I am weary of holding it in; indeed, I cannot* (Jeremiah 20:7-9).

It is important to bring a balanced perspective to the divine urgency that is inherent in the revelatory warnings the watchman receives and make such warnings relevant to the practical truths of the realities of the lives of the people.

Micaiah

Not much is written about this prophet, but the king of Israel said of him, "I hate him because he never prophesies anything good about me."

> *So the king of Israel brought together the prophets—about four hundred men—and asked them, "Shall I go to war against Ramoth Gilead, or shall I refrain?" "Go," they answered, "for the Lord will give it into the king's hand." But Jehoshaphat asked, "Is there not a prophet of the Lord here whom we can inquire of?" The king of Israel answered Jehoshaphat, "There is*

*still one man through whom we can inquire of the Lord, but I
hate him because he never prophesies anything good about me,
but always bad. He is Micaiah son of Imlah." "The king should
not say that," Jehoshaphat replied. So the king of Israel called
one of his officials and said, "Bring Micaiah son of Imlah at
once..."* (1 Kings 22:6-27).

The spirit of the word of wisdom is important to make the people
accept even if it is to tell them to repent.

RESOURCE

Becoming a resource for the Body of Christ is a gain to the Body
of Christ. When the gifting of a seer or watchman is well-harnessed
and balanced, it can become very valuable to the Body of Christ in
different ways:

1. Samuel is an example of an exceptional leader who emerged
   in Israel in a transitional time of crisis, a time when they
   needed a leader with foresight and decisiveness, when they
   were required to transit from a period of fragmented tribal
   groupings into a successful monarchy. As a leader, Samuel
   was versatile; he was a judge of outstanding reputation, a
   priest, teacher, and the kingmaker.

   This great leader described himself as a seer:

   *"About this time tomorrow I will send you a man from
   the land of Benjamin. Anoint him leader over my people
   Israel; he will deliver my people from the hand of the
   Philistines. I have looked upon my people, for their cry
   has reached me." When Samuel caught sight of Saul, the
   Lord said to him, "This is the man I spoke to you about;
   he will govern My people." Saul approached Samuel in the
   gateway and asked, "Would you please tell me where the
   seer's house is?" "I am the seer," Samuel replied. "Go up
   ahead of me to the high place, for today you are to eat with
   me, and in the morning I will let you go and will tell you
   all that is in your heart. As for the donkeys you lost three
   days ago, do not worry about them; they have been found.*

*And to whom is all the desire of Israel turned, if not to you
and all your father's family?"* (1 Samuel 9:16-20)

Also the prophet Samuel started the first school of prophets:

*Word came to Saul: "David is in Naioth at Ramah," so
he sent men to capture him. But when they saw a group
of prophets prophesying with Samuel standing there as
their leader, the Spirit of God came upon Saul's men and
they also prophesied* (1 Samuel 19:19-20).

2. Another seer who was a vast in understanding of the mysteries of God is Daniel:

*The queen, hearing the voices of the king and his nobles,
came into the banquet hall. "O king, live for ever!" she
said. "Don't be alarmed! Don't look so pale! There is a
man in your kingdom who has the spirit of the holy
gods in him. In the time of your father he was found to
have insight and intelligence and wisdom like that of the
gods. King Nebuchadnezzar your father—your father
the king, I say—appointed him chief of the magicians,
enchanters, astrologers and diviners. This man Daniel,
whom the king called Belteshazzar, was found to have a
keen mind and knowledge and understanding, and also
the ability to interpret dreams, explain riddles and solve
difficult problems. Call for Daniel, and he will tell you
what the writing means"'* (Daniel 5:10-12).

3. Seers who were great administrators are Daniel and Joseph.

4. Seers who found favor in high places are Daniel and Joseph.

5. Many seasoned seers often enjoy great grace and intimacy
    with God, including Samuel, Zechariah, and Daniel.

GROWING AND MATURING IN WATCHMAN ANOINTING

Growing and maturing in the watchman's anointing involves development on all the aspects of the watchman's personality as well as
in all of the functional aspects of the watchman's ministry. This spans

from the capacity to receive revelations and the ability to increase the scope of what is being received to learning the proper dynamics of how revelation is packaged and delivered to ensure acceptance.

It is perhaps also pertinent to mention that most watchmen start a ministry with a narrow scope of coverage and responsibilities and often only develop over time to its true and wider perspectives. It is therefore not uncommon to find watchmen who started off by being watchmen to their families then gradually mature into their full ministries. The full scope of a watchman's ministry may only become realized at maturity.

The mature watchman's ministry can operate on different levels. For example, a watchman can be called to a local church, a city, a nation, the Body of Christ, or even to a family unit or any combination of these levels.

The following people are among the notable watchmen of our time: Peter Wagner is certainly a watchman to the nations and has special anointing to discern the theme that God is emphasizing to the Body of Christ. Chuck Pierce is also a watchman to the nations with special anointing to direct prophetic intercessory prayers for breakthroughs in the Body of Christ. A few of the many accredited watchmen operating internationally include Dutch Sheets (USA), Cindy Jacobs (USA), Catherine Brown (UK), Emmanuel Ziga (USA), Emmanuel Emmanuel (Nigeria), Obii Pax-Harry (UK), Joy Parrot (USA), and Martha Lucia (USA).

RECEIVING REVELATIONS

To grow in the capacity to receive revelations freely from God, the watchman needs to continuously sharpen his anointing. Intimacy with God is crucial to the capacity to receive divine revelation, as how and what is received is at the prerogative of God. The Lord confides in those who fear Him.

The effectiveness of the watchman's ministry depends on an enhanced capability to receive revelation that is the elevated spiritual pedestal he occupies. This divine positioning also indicates or reflects the vantage point that the watchman occupies in his relationship with God, such that he can receive revelations not obvious to the (ordinary) person. There are factors that would make God want to release revelations to the watchman, and there are equally vital factors that influence how the watchman receives and handles what is being released to him. Otherwise, what is the use of an elevated position if revelations are scanty or poorly understood? Or what use is a revelation if it is not properly received and handled? For this reason, the watchman must position himself to be available to receive an abundance of revelations and become equipped to avail himself of the wisdom inherent in the revelations.

First, let's look at six reasons that make God want to release revelations to a spiritual watchman:

1. God's sovereign choice. Divine revelations come from God. No one can receive revelation unless God gives it.

2. Friendship with God. Before God does anything, the Bible says He tells His servants (friends).

3. Fear of the Lord. God confides in those who fear Him and the fear of the Lord is also the beginning of the wisdom of God. The wisdom of God is the life application of the Word of God in daily living. Living wisely pleases God. Also "the eyes of the Lord are watching over those who fear Him, who rely upon His steady love. He will keep them from death, even in times of trouble" (Ps. 33:18-19 TLB).

4. Correct handling of divine revelations is essential. The watchman should ensure that God receives all the glory. A watchman should not handle revelation from God as though he was the source of the revelation or as though the revelation is his personal opinion.

5. Response to the revelation. The watchman should take the appropriate action in response to the revelation. If the watchman does not take the appropriate action, it means that God may withhold further revelations.

6. The revelatory giftedness of the watchman influences how and what he receives from God. In case of picture revelations, some watchmen are high-volume dreamers, others are low-volume dreamers, and many are in between. God can use the watchman whether he is a low-volume or high-volume dreamer. Ultimately it is what he does with the level of giftedness that counts. God will meet the needs of the watchman at his level of giftedness.

Now let's us look at the factors that will influence how the watchman receives and handles the revelations released to him from God:

- The watchman's level of giftedness is his capacity to receive revelation, and this varies from watchman to watchman, but what he actually receives depends on his intimate relationship with God.

- A watchman with a strong human spirit receives efficiently. The human spirit is described as strong when the body is crucified and the soul (emotion, will, and the mind) is controlled. It is pertinent therefore that the watchman should operate from the spirit and from a strong inner man.

- The watchman can strengthen his spirit in three main ways: (1) by communion with God (He who dwells in the secret place of the Most High shall abide under the shadow of the Almighty; see Psalm 91), (2) by the wisdom of God, which is the life application of the Word of God, and (3) by laying aside personal agendas otherwise referred to as "sanctified conscience." A sanctified conscience is the conscience that is washed by the blood of Jesus Christ, allowing the love of God to prevail at all times.

- The watchman with a strong spirit is one whose spirit is able to bear witness with the Spirit of God because the strength of the human spirit is its capacity to bear witness with the Spirit of God.

- A watchman who is obedient and submitted to the will of God will have an enhanced sowing of revelation in his spirit. Proper sowing and planting of revelations lead to better understanding and effectiveness of the watchman anointing.

- The faith of the watchman in God enhances the release of revelation received or revelation that has remained dormant in the spirit of the watchman (to his mind for comprehension). It is after comprehension that appropriate action can be taken. Faith in God influences how easily the watchman recognizes the prompting of the Holy Spirit as to what he has received.

- The level of the presence of God that the watchman enjoys determines the liberty in God that he has. This is an essential attribute of the indwelling Holy Spirit. This liberty enhances his ability to correlate the revelation and its meaning to relevance in the lives of the people.

- The peace that the watchman enjoys determines and enhances the translation of revelations from his spirit to his mind, and also peace is required for the processing of the revelations in his mind. *So regarding revelation, it is received in the spirit, then faith releases it from the spirit, peace transmits it from the spirit to the mind, and liberty in the Holy Spirit applies it and makes it relevant to the real-life situation.*

INCREASING THE SCOPE OF REVELATIONS RECEIVED

The "scope of the watchman's revelations" could be regarded as the overall coverage of the revelations received. Most watchmen start with a narrow perspective of the call and with maturity the true scope of the call becomes evident to everyone. For instance, a watchman to a local church can mature to become the watchman to the city. The scope of revelations also includes sensitivity of the information and security of its content. A mature watchman should be competent by handling the sensitivity and security content of each revelation.

As mentioned previously, the watchman's visual acuity is slanted to the area of his calling; if that is the case, then a good percentage of the revelation would normally relate to the call. This point is crucial in accepting the value of the watchman ministry in our churches. The watchman may need help managing personal issues, while at the same time be receiving strategic insights into the enemy's plans and the path lying ahead for the church.

The watchman who pays attention to his call and intercedes for it will naturally have the scope of his revelation widened to include God's responses to such intercessory burden. God speaks more or gives further progressive revelation to the watchman about people or on issues for which he shows increasing concern. Perhaps this explains why our immediate family members frequently show up in our dreams. Such concern is called prophetic burden. The importance of increasing the coverage of the prophetic burden carried on behalf of the people cannot be overemphasized either for the watchman's anointing or even in our Christian walk. The prophetic person needs to be in a place where God will give the revelation to him.

Watchmen receive for people for whom they carry a spiritual burden. Ananias was a disciple of Christ, and when God wanted to commission another new disciple in Damascus, he was readily available to God. The prophet Ezekiel was trained as a priest. His burden for the sanctity of the temple of God was evident in his ministry as the watchman of Israel:

> He stretched out what looked like a hand and took me by the hair of my head. The Spirit lifted me up between earth and heaven and in visions of God he took me to Jerusalem, to the entrance to the north gate of the inner court, where the idol that provokes to jealousy stood. And there before me was the glory of the God of Israel, as in the vision I had seen in the plain. Then He said to me, "Son of man, look toward the north." So I looked, and in the entrance north of the gate of the altar I saw this idol of jealousy. And He said to me, "Son of man, do you see what they are doing—the utterly detestable things the house of Israel is doing here, things that will drive me far from my sanctuary? But

you will see things that are even more detestable." Then He brought me to the entrance to the court. I looked, and I saw a hole in the wall. He said to me, "Son of man, now dig into the wall." So I dug into the wall and saw a doorway there. And He said to me, "Go in and see the wicked and detestable things they are doing here." So I went in and looked, and I saw portrayed all over the walls all kinds of crawling things and detestable animals and all the idols of the house of Israel. In front of them stood seventy elders of the house of Israel, and Jaazaniah son of Shaphan was standing among them. Each had a censer in his hand, and a fragrant cloud of incense was rising. He said to me, "Son of man, have you seen what the elders of the house of Israel are doing in the darkness, each at the shrine of his own idol? They say, 'The Lord does not see us; the Lord has forsaken the land.'" Again, He said, "You will see them doing things that are even more detestable." Then He brought me to the entrance to the north gate of the house of the Lord, and I saw women sitting there, mourning for Tammuz (Ezekiel 8:3-14).

As previously said, the watchman's visual acuity is slanted toward his assignment and influenced by how he exercises the prophetic burden carried by the call on his life. Increasing the scope of revelations includes:

- ◆ The listening art, a crucial factor but often a difficult art for many to develop, which is pivotal to the ministry of the watchman.

- ◆ By discernment, where the watchman can pick out the wolves in sheep clothing.

- ◆ Learning to receive by other nonvisual revelations.

- ◆ Prayers/intercession, through which the anointing is sharpened.

AVOIDING ERRORS OF IMMATURE WATCHMANSHIP

The most likely aspect of the watchman responsibilities where immaturity easily shows is in the area of message delivery. Commonly immaturity manifests in personality traits or in the watchman's relational traits. Nowhere is it more critical for the watchman to be able to fulfill his role of alerting the people. Consequently, appropriate delivering of messages is of paramount importance. The watchman needs to appropriately package his message for acceptance, and yet it has to be effective. Among the many factors that are crucial in this regard, four points are particularly worthy to bear in mind:

1. Learning the art of waiting on God and, when appropriate, the art of knowing God's urgency. Allow the Holy Spirit to brood over the revelation.

2. The watchman should not minister to the emotion of the people but aim to see what is at stake in the spirit realm. This means the watchman must not be emotional and should also not let people's emotions influence his message. People often present an emotional front when reacting to situations, yet the watchman should not minister to the emotion but instead go beyond the emotions to the spirit realm. A spiritual message planted in the emotions will not grow. The watchman should help people look into the unseen and not be bogged down by the heat of the day's happening.

3. Militancy and urgency are associated with the reports of woes, laments, and mourning common in the ministry of the watchman, but this should be carefully managed to ensure that the target group receives the messages and the benefits thereof.

4. The closer the message is to what God has said, the better and more effective the message.

Managing Sensitive and Confidential Revelation

It is critical that the watchman manage the sensitivity and the security content of his revelations. The sensitivity and security of the revelation reflects the trust that God has in the watchman. God will trust the watchman with sensitive information concerning his life and possibly his immediate family in these ways:

1. Potential events—things that are likely to happen but are not inevitable in the watchman's life.

2. Decreed events—things that God has ordained to happen, no matter what, in the life of the watchman.

3. The sovereign plan of God for the watchman—the very reason for his life experiences.

Handling sensitive revelation concerning him, the above may seem quite obvious and innocuous, but many watchmen misuse such privileged information by becoming arrogant and judgmental about what was revealed to them. By so doing, they compromise and delay the fulfillment of their commissioning into maturity in the ministry.

The watchman must know that not all revelations are ready for public pronouncement. Timing is a key factor. God Himself told Daniel, *"But you, Daniel, close up and seal the words of the scroll until the time of the end. Many will go here and there to increase knowledge"* (Dan. 12:4) and Nehemiah said,

> *I set out during the night with a few men. I had not told any-one what my God had put in my heart to do for Jerusalem. There were no mounts with me except the one I was riding on. By night I went out through the Valley Gate toward the Jackal Well and the Dung Gate, examining the walls of Jerusalem, which had been broken down, and its gates, which had been destroyed by fire* (Nehemiah 2:12-13).

I believe watchmen evolve along these lines overtly or covertly. If God can trust a watchman with sensitive revelation concerning him-self and the nature of his call, He will progress to trust him with reve-lation about the people group—first regarding their potential events, danger, or blessing; second, their decreed events; and then finally His sovereign plans for them. If these levels are well-managed, God will entrust the watchman with the guarding and protection of the lives of people in the area of his call by revealing warnings about the enemy's plans as well as warnings of the dangers of inherent weaknesses that could lead to vulnerability.

FEATURES OF AN IMMATURE WATCHMAN

Personality traits:

- Lack of integrity, often resulting in a lack of credibility and nonacceptance by the leadership.

- Unnecessary militancy and urgency in handling or delivering warnings, instead of patience.

- Lack of prayer life, lacking in ability to turn every observed warning point into an opportunity to intercede.

- Lack of humility.

Relational traits:

- Too critical.

- Judgmental, passing punishments on people.

- Lack of mercy and grace in delivering messages or warnings. Forgetting God's kindness, love, and redemptive power.

- Disloyal to the leadership and showing lack of submission.

- Self-conceited instead of being committed to the safety of the people.

CHAPTER SEVEN

SPIRITS AGAINST WATCHMEN AND THE LOCAL CHURCH

THE SPIRIT OF STUPOR

The evil of this spirit is the compelling, irresistible urge for intermittent sleepiness, when the person should be awake and alert. This spirit is very dangerous for any person, but it is especially a destructive enemy to the watchman anointing. It is an affliction that wastes great potentials or resources, whether it comes as a result of judgment from God or from the work of the enemy. "As it is written: 'God gave them a spirit of stupor, eyes so that they could not see and ears so that they could not hear, to this very day'" (Rom. 11:8).

> *Be stunned and amazed, blind yourselves and be sightless; be drunk, but not from wine, stagger, but not from beer. The Lord has brought over you a deep sleep. He has sealed your eyes (the prophets). He has covered your heads (the seers). For you the whole vision is nothing but words sealed in a scroll. And if you give the scroll to someone who can read, and say to him "Read this please," he will answer, "I can't, it is sealed." Or if you give the scroll to someone who cannot read, and say, "Read this please," he will answer, "I don't know how to read"* (Isaiah 29:9-12).

Notice that when this spirit is sent from God as judgment, it comes with other limitations that are manifested in a diversity of ways:

- Words sealed in a scroll—meaning the inability to interpret things from God.

- Loss of grace.

- Loss of favor.

◆ Inability to get help or compassion from other people.

Repentance and prayers will overcome this spirit.

A PERVERSE SPIRIT

A perverse spirit causes cloudiness in vision, a lack of understanding, and poor rendering of vision. Often for some watchmen, the problem is not the lack of revelations but poor understanding due to visual cloudiness. Poor understanding results in poor rendering of the messages to the people:

> *The Lord hath mingled a perverse spirit in the midst thereof…* (Isaiah 19:14 KJV).

> *The Lord has sent a spirit of foolishness on them so that suggestions are wrong* (Isaiah 19:14 TLB).

> *And these also stagger from wine and reel from beer: Priests and prophets stagger from beer and are befuddled with wine; they reel from beer, they stagger when seeing visions, they stumble when rendering decisions* (Isaiah 28:7).

The following helps overcome this spirit:

◆ Spending quality time in the presence of God.

◆ Repentance and prayers.

◆ Consistent right-standing with God.

THE SPIRIT OF NONACCEPTANCE BY THE LEADERSHIP

This spirit causes the leaders not to listen to the watchman. However, there are many causes of why the leadership may not listen to the watchman. To be listened to and accepted, the watchman needs credibility and should be accountable to the leadership:

> *When Jeremiah finished telling the people all the words of the Lord their God—everything the Lord had sent him to tell them—Azariah son of Hoshaiah and Johanan son of Kareah and all the arrogant men said to Jeremiah, "You are lying! The Lord our God has not sent you to say, 'You must not go to*

Egypt to settle there.' But Baruch son of Neriah is inciting you against us to hand us over to the Babylonians, so that they may kill us or carry us into exile to Babylon." So Johanan son of Kareah and all the army officers and all the people disobeyed the Lord's command to stay in the land of Judah. Instead, Johanan son of Kareah and all the army officers led away all the remnant of Judah who had come back to live in the land of Judah from all the nations where they had been scattered. They also led away all the men, women and children and the king's daughters whom Nebuzaradan commander of the imperial guard had left with Gedaliah son of Ahikam, the son of Shaphan, and Jeremiah the prophet and Baruch son of Neriah. So they entered Egypt in disobedience to the Lord and went as far as Tahpanhes (Jeremiah 43:1-7).

The following attitudes will help the watchman eliminate this problem:

- ◆ Repentance and prayers.
- ◆ Improving credibility issues.
- ◆ Collaborative work with the leadership.

However, it is important to note that acceptance comes at the point of commission, when God grants the watchman favor with men. At the time of call, watchmen have favor with God so that revelations are abundant, but usually they do not come with a commensurate degree of acceptance. Acceptance comes over time with a good degree of credibility. However, the spirit of nonacceptance described here is different from the nonacceptance inevitable in the training period.

OTHER SPIRITS

In the following passage the prophet Isaiah gives us details about some spirits that can come against watchmen.

Come, wild animals of the field, come, tear apart the sheep; come, wild animals of the forest, devour my people. For the leaders of my people—the Lord's watchmen, His shepherds— are all blind to every danger. They are feather brained and give no warning when danger comes. They love to lie there, love to sleep, to dream. And they are as greedy as dogs, never satisfied, they are stupid shepherds who only look after their own interest each trying to get as much as he can for himself from every possible source (Isaiah 56:9-11 TLB).

Come, all you beasts of the field, come and devour, all you beasts of the forest! Israel's watchmen are blind, they all lack knowledge; they are all mute dogs, they cannot bark; they lie around and dream, they love to sleep. They are dogs with mighty appetites; they never have enough. They are shepherds who lack understanding; they all turn to their own way, each seeks his own gain. "Come," each one cries, "let me get wine! Let us drink our fill of beer! And tomorrow will be like today, or even far better" (Isaiah 56:9-12).

THE SPIRIT OF SPIRITUAL BLINDNESS

The main essence of the ministry of the watchman is to be able to see into the spirit realm and report to the people. If a watchman is blind, he has lost the core of the ministry: "Come, all you beasts of the field, come and devour, all you beasts of the forest! Israel's watchmen are blind, they all lack knowledge."

As watchman, the prophet Isaiah looked into the future and saw where other ungodly nations (beasts) were stirred up to attack Israel. This became simple because the watchmen of Israel were blind, lacking spiritual insights to the plans of the enemy, leaving the nation unprotected. Watchmen can be distracted by worldly desires.

THE SPIRIT OF COVETOUSNESS

Covetousness is a dangerous ploy of the enemy to derail the plans and purposes of God in the life of the watchman. The ministry of the watchman requires singleness of heart and mind to focus on carrying out the assignment. When watchmen have become entangled in the pursuit of worldly pleasures, the anointing is subverted, to say the least: "They are dogs with mighty appetites; they never have enough."

THE SPIRIT OF SELF-CENTEREDNESS

The watchfulness of the watchman's ministry is for the protection and preservation of the people. Therefore, if a watchman becomes self-centered, that purpose is defeated. Unfortunately some watchmen have allowed the devil to lure them into self-centeredness: "They are shepherds who lack understanding; they all turn to their own way, each seeks his own gain."

THE SPIRIT OF DUMBNESS

The main purpose of a watchman is to look ahead and warn the people of any approaching danger or inform the people of the next move of God. If the watchman loses the ability to warn, that watchman has become useless. As the Bible says, "They are all mute dogs, they cannot bark."

DISCERNING SPIRITS AGAINST THE LOCAL CHURCH

The role of the watchman is not only to watch out for the approaching danger or messenger but also to be trained to discern "wolves among the sheep." The apostle Paul warned the Ephesians to guard against this:

> *Keep watch over yourselves and all the flock of which the Holy Spirit has made you overseers. Be shepherds of the church of God, which He bought with His own blood. I know that after I leave, savage wolves will come in among you and will not spare the flock. Even from your own number men will arise and distort the truth in order to draw away disciples after them. So be on your guard! Remember that for three years I never stopped warning each of you night and day with tears* (Acts 20:28-31).

Division, acrimony, and rancour could be remarkably minimized and perhaps even averted in the Body of Christ if our watchmen are alert to spot the moves of the devil and his agents in the midst of God's people. As the apostle Peter also admonished us, "But there were also false prophets among the people, just as there will be false teachers among you. They will secretly introduce destructive heresies, even denying the sovereign Lord who bought them—bringing swift destruction on themselves. Many will follow their shameful ways and will bring the way of truth into disrepute" (2 Pet. 2:1-2).

God Himself commended the church at Ephesus for their vigilance in discerning the false apostles among them: "I know how many good things you are doing. I have watched your hard work and your patience. I know you don't tolerate sin among your members, and you have carefully examined the claims of those who say they are apostles but are not. You have found out how they lie" (Rev. 2:2 TLB).

Now I shift the emphasis to the more subtle challenges that the watchman may have to face from within the Body of Christ such as those that could arise from within the local congregation. I call these challenges "the spirit against the local church." They are the spirits that could arise within the congregation or domain that a watchman should be able to discern and stop from infiltrating the rank and file of the local structure. This problem dates back to the time of the "exodus" of Jews from their slavery in Egypt.

As in the days that Moses led the Israelites out of Egypt, every local congregation is a mixed multitude of people. The Bible says that during the exodus of the Israelites "a mixed multitude went up with them also" (Exod. 12:38 NKJV). Then as now, as we pass through life, things or people get attached to us. Later we see that "The mixed multitudes who were among them yielded to intense craving; so the children of Israel also wept again and said: 'Who will give us meat to eat?'" (Num. 11:4 NKJV). In every multitude of people, there is the diversity of human spirits; therefore, the issue for a local church is not whether diversity of human spirits will arise, but that when they do, these spirits are discerned and properly managed to minimize or curb their unwanted effects.

A Contentious Spirit

Contention is usually about control. Most problems in the church come down to a contention issue—who is in charge. A contentious person can never lead, because he most probably never learned to follow. A true leader should have a servant spirit. Jesus Christ came to earth in order to redeem us, taking on the human experience to save humanity—He was a leader who also knew how to serve.

A contentious spirit is like a malignant cell; if left untreated it can destroy the person and hinder the growth of the church. A person with a contentious spirit is often the door through which satan comes to do his work.

> *For where you have envy and selfish ambition, there you find disorder and every evil practice* (James 3:16).

This spirit will not submit to authority. The apostle John had to deal with it: *"I wrote to the church, but Diotrephes, who loves to be first, will have nothing to do with us"* (3 John 1:9).

> *"For lack of wood the fire goes out, and where there is no whisperer, contention ceases."* (Proverbs 26:20 AMP).

A contentious spirit and the spirit of witchcraft go together. Only love can defeat these spirits.

> *Above all, love each other deeply, because love covers over a multitude of sins"* (1 Peter 4:8).

Every watchman can discern when this spirit is in operation. It is often helpful to also know the psychology of a person with a contentious spirit. In this regard, the following are important to bear in mind. The contentious person believes that:

- When others are set in their ways, they are obstinate; but when he is, he is just "firm."

- When others don't like someone, they are prejudiced; but when he does not, it is "good judgment."

- When others treat someone with care, they are bribing the person; but when he treats this way, he is just being "thoughtful."

- When others take time to do something well, they are lazy or slow; but when he does this, he is "meticulous."

- When others find fault and pick flaws in things, they are critical; but when he does, he is just being "perceptive."

- When others are gentle or mild-mannered, they are weak; but when he is, he is being "gracious."

- When others dress well, they are extravagant; when he does, he is being "tasteful."

- When others say what they think, they are spiteful; when he does, he is being "honest."

- When others take risks, they are reckless; but when he does, he is being "brave."

The way out of this dangerous spirit is found in Philippians 4:8: "Finally, brothers, whatever is true, whatever is noble, whatever is right, whatever is pure, whatever is lovely, whatever is admirable—if anything is excellent or praiseworthy—think about such things."

> ...*try to excel in gifts that build up the church* (1 Corinthians 14:12).

SPIRIT OF WITCHCRAFT

Perhaps the spirit of witchcraft simply refers to any spirit other than the Spirit of God that seeks to manipulate or control others. Most watchmen will attest that the spirit of witchcraft is one of the common spirits that could come against the local church—the spirit of control, manipulation, and intimidation. In the case of Absalom, this spirit manifested as manipulation and Jezebel—the spirit of intimidation and control. In the case of King Saul, it was principally disobedience or rebellion. Samuel said the spirit of rebellion is the spirit of witchcraft: "For rebellion is as the sin of witchcraft" (1 Sam. 15:23 NKJV). As stated previously, it may simply refer to any spirit other than the Spirit of God that seeks to manipulate or control others.

In this generation and in the Western hemisphere, this spirit is predominantly that of manipulation. In Africa, this spirit manifests as the spirit of self-mutilations and destruction. In Asian countries it is the spirit of craftiness, deception, and control.

THE SPIRIT OF ABSALOM

The spirit of Absalom is the spirit that subverts by manipulation. This is a special form of witchcraft spirit that steals the hearts of people by deception and pretence. Absalom flatters and influences people by manipulating human greed and lust for his own personal advantage.

How to deal with the spirit of Absalom: Note that an Absalom spirit will always look for an Ahithophel, so plan to counter the strategy of Ahithophel. An Ahithophel is a person gifted in wisdom and counsel, but is bitter and revengeful. A person with an Absalom spirit will always look for angry and dissatisfied people. We must watch out for these people. Pray to God to overcome any conspiracy. God will turn the counsel of Ahithophel into foolishness.

THE SPIRIT OF SAUL

The spirit of Saul is the spirit of hatred that comes out of envy or jealousy, often as a result of failure in the life of the church leadership. This spirit signifies the dislike of the apprentice and the failure to acknowledge what God is doing in the lives of subordinates. Some spiritual leaders are guilty of the spirit of Saul. This is a politicking spirit that causes division in the church. This spirit has led many great men to becoming unfruitful, murderers, and consumed with hatred.

How to deal with spirit of Saul: continue in the will of God, even if it means serving God at the risk of your life, like David did in facing the ferocity of hatred from Saul toward him. Do not fight back—the battle belongs to God. Wait for God's timing. Touch not the anointed of God, even as David did not touch Saul. Do not rejoice in the fall of God's anointed no matter how mean he becomes. Vengeance belongs to God. Seek the counsel of God.

THE SPIRIT OF GEHAZI

The spirit of Gehazi is the spirit of greed, covetousness, and insubordination, as well as the spirit of self-centeredness. This spirit attacks people with a weak inner man who may have a strong spirit but a soul that is not ruled by the Spirit of God. Regarding Gehazi, I believe his spirit was strong because of his association with the prophet Elisha;

however, he failed to control his emotions (soul). The soul being weak resulted in a weak inner man. A soul that is not controlled by the Spirit leads to perversion despite a strong spirit-man. This spirit led Gehazi to end up with leprosy instead of double portions of anointing:

> *"Go in peace," Elisha said. After Naaman had travelled some distance, Gehazi, the servant of Elisha the man of God, said to himself, "My master was too easy on Naaman, this Aramean, by not accepting from him what he brought. As surely as the Lord lives, I will run after him and get something from him"* (2 Kings 5:19-20).

THE SPIRIT OF MIRIAM

The spirit of Miriam is the spirit of prejudice and separatism or racism in a church. Also, this is the spirit of pride that makes young ministers rise up against the spiritual leader. This spirit despises leadership, and it will always end up as leprosy. Because of the subtlety and the damaging effects of this spirit, God fights this spirit Himself.

> *Miriam and Aaron began to talk against Moses because of his Cushite wife, for he had married a Cushite. "Has the Lord spoken only through Moses?" they asked. "Hasn't he also spoken through us?" And the Lord heard this. (Now Moses was a very humble man, more humble than anyone else on the face of the earth)* (Numbers 12:1-3).

To deal with this spirit of pride, particularly in young ministers, is to teach them how to serve in various capacities within the body of the church, before elevating them to positions of leadership. It is wise to remember what the apostle Paul said regarding aspiring young converts in becoming overseers: "He must not be a recent convert, or he may become conceited and fall under the same judgment as the devil" (1 Tim. 3:6).

THE SPIRIT OF DELILAH

The spirit of Delilah is the spirit of betrayal. This spirit destroys with the kiss of death. Delilah is full of flattery. Delilah betrays trust and friendship. Delilah sows the seeds of distrust and discord. This spirit is relentless. It is always motivated by self-gain. The spirit of Delilah thrives on sexual lust. It targets the seer's anointing of the leadership with the goal of plucking out the eyes of the prophetic, like the spirit of Delilah did to Samson.

> *Some time later, he fell in love with a woman in the Valley of Sorek whose name was Delilah. The rulers of the Philistines went to her and said, "See if you can lure him into showing you the secret of his great strength and how we can overpower him so that we may tie him up and subdue him. Each one of us will give you eleven hundred shekels of silver." So Delilah said to Samson, "Tell me the secret of your great strength and how you can be tied up and subdued"* (Judges 16:4-6).

THE SPIRIT OF JEZEBEL

The spirit of Jezebel is a high-level form of the spirit of witchcraft. This spirit controls by remote manipulation. It is also the power of control from the unseen realm. This spirit is very influential, as it is a major ruling power in the kingdom of darkness. The spectrum of activities of this devious spirit ranges from mild cases when the victims are not aware of being used to deep-rooted evil in people who are basking in the euphoria of this evil spirit's power. Predominantly, females are more commonly involved, but this spirit has no gender preference. The springboard for this evil spirit is sexual exploitation. Jezebel targets spiritual leadership, especially the prophetic and intercessory ministries.

This spirit is named after Queen Jezebel, wife of King Ahab. It represents the character and nature of her demonic influence in the days of King Ahab:

> *He not only considered it trivial to commit the sins of Jeroboam son of Nebat, but he also married Jezebel daughter of Ethbaal king of the Sidonians, and began to serve Baal and worship him* (1 Kings 16:31).

You are to destroy the house of Ahab your master, and I will avenge the blood of my servants the prophets and the blood of all the Lord's servants shed by Jezebel (2 Kings 9:7).

Nevertheless, I have this against you: You tolerate that woman Jezebel, who calls herself a prophetess. By her teaching she misleads My servants into sexual immorality and the eating of food sacrificed to idols (Revelation 2:20).

In present days, this spirit's destructive effects cut across family morality, power plays at the workplace, the entertainment industry, and spiritual leadership. The objective of this spirit is to gain control.

This spirit uses deception, infiltration, manipulation, and sexual laxity as tools to get at its victims. It is relentless in its destruction. A two-pronged strategy is necessary to defeat this spirit. First, for those who are being used, the way out is confession, humility, godly repentance, and submission to the appropriate authority. For leaders who have to confront this spirit, wisdom and discernment is required.

THE SPIRIT OF KORAH

The spirit of Korah is the spirit of rebellion by subversion. This spirit hates the singular authority of the church. This spirit emanates from men of renown and influence. The Korah spirit prevents people from responding to constituted authority by the influence of men in high places in society. This is often the result of hollow and deceptive theology and stems from delusions of grandeur.

Korah son of Izhar, the son of Kohath, the son of Levi, and certain Reubenites—Dathan and Abiram, sons of Eliab, and On son of Peleth—became insolent and rose up against Moses. With them were 250 Israelite men, well-known community leaders who had been appointed members of the council. They came as a group to oppose Moses and Aaron and said to them, "You have gone too far! The whole community is holy, every one of them, and the Lord is with them. Why then do you set yourselves above the Lord's assembly?" (Numbers 16:1-3)

How to deal with the spirit of Korah:

> *He warned the assembly, "Move back from the tents of these wicked men! Do not touch anything belonging to them, or you will be swept away because of all their sins." So they moved away from the tents of Korah, Dathan and Abiram. Dathan and Abiram had come out and were standing with their wives, children and little ones at the entrances to their tents. Then Moses said, "This is how you will know that the Lord has sent me to do all these things and that it was not my idea: If these men die a natural death and experience only what usually happens to men, then the Lord has not sent me. But if the Lord brings about something totally new, and the earth opens its mouth and swallows them, with everything that belongs to them, and they go down alive into the grave, then you will know that these men have treated the Lord with contempt." As soon as he finished saying all this, the ground under them split apart and the earth opened its mouth and swallowed them, with their households and all Korah's men and all their possessions* (Numbers 16:26-32).

Discussion is key in bringing the effect of this spirit to nothing. Also, ask the people to disassociate themselves from Korah, for the spirit of Korah destroys others by association.

THE SPIRIT OF SANBALLAT AND TOBIAH: SPIRIT OF DISTRACTION

The spirit of Sanballat and Tobiah is the spirit of distraction emanating from people of influence. This spirit is propelled by associating with people in high places and thrives on favoritism and corruption. It works its way into people of influence by deceptive association or marriage. Sanballat's family married into the family of the high priest: "One of the sons of Joiada son of Eliashib the high priest **was son-in-law to Sanballat** the Horonite. And I drove him away from me" (Neh. 13:28).

Tobiah also had connections in high places:

Also, in those days the nobles of Judah were sending many letters to Tobiah, and replies from Tobiah kept coming to them. For many in Judah were under oath to him, since he was son-in-law to Shecaniah son of Arah, and his son Jehohanan had married the daughter of Meshullam son of Berekiah. Moreover, they kept reporting to me his good deeds and then telling him what I said. And Tobiah sent letters to intimidate me (Nehemiah 6:17-19).

Before this, Eliashib the priest had been put in charge of the storerooms of the house of our God. He was closely associated with Tobiah (Nehemiah 13:4).

And came back to Jerusalem. Here I learned about the evil thing Eliashib had done in providing Tobiah a room in the courts of the house of God. I was greatly displeased and threw all Tobiah's household goods out of the room. I gave orders to purify the rooms, and then I put back into them the equipment of the house of God, with the grain offerings and the incense (Nehemiah 13:7-9).

Nehemiah faced a daunting task, similar to that in many churches today. In those days, Jerusalem, like the present-day church, was near the state of apostate, and to reverse the trend of desolation there were walls of boundaries and responsibilities to be set in place. Successfully galvanizing the support of the Jews and fending off ridicule within its camp, suddenly Nehemiah is faced with a new strategy of the enemy—that of distractions. Distractions came in the form of Sanballat and Tobiah, who were both influential local politicians with evidence of Jewish ancestry, though they preferred the political status quo and their Jewish identity downplayed.

When Sanballat heard that we were rebuilding the wall, he became angry and was greatly incensed. He ridiculed the Jews and in the presence of associates and the army of Samaria, he said, "What are those feeble Jews doing? Will they restore their wall? Will they offer sacrifices? Will they finish in a day? Can they bring the stone back to life from the heaps of rubble—burned as they are?" Tobiah the Ammonite, who was at his side, said, "What they are building—if even a fox climbed up on it, he would break down their wall of stones!" (Nehemiah 4:1-3)

God Himself, eliminates this spirit. For our part, we need to remain steadfast in righteousness focusing on the things of God. Avoid being lured into the path of distraction.

PART III

The Watchman and the Local Church

CHAPTER EIGHT

HANDLING REVELATIONS

All revelations, including visual ones relating to the local congregation, should be recorded and evaluated by the leadership. Interpretations should be sought and judged. Once the interpretation has been accepted as true, it should be recorded alongside other revelations and only acted upon when it has been confirmed, except when the interpretation itself is a confirmation of a previous revelation. Confirmation is a further revelation on a subject either by prophecy, another dream/vision, or current events.

Periodic review of visual revelations and their interpretation should be done on a regular basis.

Once the meaning of picture revelation is confirmed, it becomes the responsibility of the leadership of the local church to implement it at the right time and in line with the trend of other revelations in the church.

It is not the responsibility of the watchman to police the meaning of the revelation for implementation. Once the watchman has informed the leadership of a revelation that is deemed to pertain to the local congregation, the watchman has completed his role unless the revelation is repeated. Often some watchmen are wrong on this point and take it personally if they think that the revelation's meaning has not been acted on quickly enough. The timing and implementation of any prophecy, including picture revelations relating to the local congregation, rests on the apostolic and pastoral anointing of the leadership. There are several reasons why this should be:

- Every warning revelation, whether in dreams/visions or other forms of revelations, comes with some degree of divinely inbuilt urgency to the recipient that requires apostolic or pastoral moderation.

- ◆ The apostles and pastors usually have access to other prophetic revelations that the individual watchman or prophet may not be aware of. Therefore, the apostles and pastors who oversee many prophets see many parts of the whole but the individual prophet sees only his part.

UNDER PASTORAL COVERING

It is best to handle revelations while under pastoral covering. Abundance of revelation most often leads to spiritual pride if one is not seasoned in the gifting. This was what, apostle Paul referred to when he says, "To keep me from becoming conceited because of these surpassingly great revelations, there was given me a thorn in my flesh, a messenger of Satan, to torment me" (2 Cor. 12:7).

It is spiritual pride to think that the little part God reveals to us is the whole story. Some young prophets have shipwrecked their careers by becoming prideful and not submitting to their pastor because of the abundance of revelations, particularly when the covering pastor is not specifically gifted in the prophetic. We should all know that the first thing that comes with the call to the prophetic ministry is favor with God. Without favor, there will be no abundance of revelations. It is only as one matures that credibility and acceptance becomes obvious and, with it, the favor with man.

We must, therefore, patiently wait for credibility to build up in order for our revelation to become accepted by those to whom the message is intended.

The prophet Samuel is a good example of a seer who remained faithful under a difficult tutelage in the days of Eli as the high priest. Samuel received revelations and even the audible voice of God at a time when "the word of God was rare and there were not many visions," yet he served God under the corrupt priesthood of Eli: "The boy Samuel ministered before the Lord under Eli. In those days the word of the Lord was rare; there were not many visions" (1 Sam. 3:1).

Eventually it was Eli, despite his poor spiritual state, who taught Samuel how to hear the voice of God. At that time Eli could no longer hear God as he used to:

> *Again the Lord called, "Samuel!" And Samuel got up and went to Eli and said, "Here I am; you called me." "My son," Eli said, "I did not call; go back and lie down." Now Samuel did not yet know the Lord: The word of the Lord had not yet been revealed to him. The Lord called Samuel a third time, and Samuel got up and went to Eli and said, "Here I am; you called me." Then Eli realized that the Lord was calling the boy. So Eli told Samuel, "Go and lie down, and if he calls you, say, 'Speak, Lord, for your servant is listening.'" So Samuel went and lay down in his place. The Lord came and stood there, calling as at the other times, "Samuel! Samuel!" Then Samuel said, "Speak, for Your servant is listening"* (1 Samuel 3:6-10).

The prophet Elisha also distinguished himself from the error of the other members of the company of prophets, at least on two distinct occasions. Once Elisha distanced himself from the other members of the company of prophets and persisted in following Elijah before he could attain the double portion of Elijah's anointing:

> *When the Lord was about to take Elijah up to heaven in a whirlwind, Elijah and Elisha were on their way from Gilgal. Elijah said to Elisha, "Stay here; the Lord has sent me to Bethel." But Elisha said, "As surely as the Lord lives and as you live, I will not leave you." So they went down to Bethel. The company of the prophets at Bethel came out to Elisha and asked, "Do you know that the Lord is going to take your master from you today?" "Yes, I know," Elisha replied, "but do not speak of it." Then Elijah said to him, "Stay here, Elisha; the Lord has sent me to Jericho." And he replied, "As surely as the Lord lives and as you live, I will not leave you." So they went to Jericho"* (2 Kings 2:1-4).

Other members of the company of prophets also had revelation that Elijah would be taken away, but I believe they got the application wrong. In this instance, I believe Elisha, out of all the members of the company of prophets, got the correct application of the revelation. As a result, he received the double-portion anointing. The correct application of their revelation was to follow the leadership until God said otherwise and not assume that because it was revealed to them the prophet Elijah was to be taken away, they should abandon him.

The second occasion was when the members of the company of prophets recognized that the anointing of Elijah was resting upon Elisha. Nevertheless, proudly they insisted on a futile search for Elijah, despite the contrary advice of Elisha:

> *The company of the prophets from Jericho, who were watching, said, "The spirit of Elijah is resting on Elisha." And they went to meet him and bowed to the ground before him. "Look," they said, "we your servants have fifty able men. Let them go and look for your master. Perhaps the Spirit of the Lord has picked him up and set him down on some mountain or in some valley." "No," Elisha replied, "do not send them." But they persisted until he was too ashamed to refuse. So he said, "Send them." And they sent fifty men, who searched for three days but did not find him. When they returned to Elisha, who was staying in Jericho, he said to them, "Didn't I tell you not to go?"* (2 Kings 2:15-18)

Though they had recognized Elisha as the new leader, again they failed to heed his advice and engaged in a futile search.

Joshua faithfully served under Moses, though he too must have witnessed and received an abundance of revelation during his service to God under Moses, but he humbly remained submitted to Moses:

> *Then Moses set out with Joshua his aide, and Moses went up on the mountain of God. He said to the elders, "Wait here for us until we come back to you. Aaron and Hur are with you, and anyone involved in a dispute can go to them." When Moses went up on the mountain, the cloud covered it, and the glory of the Lord settled on Mount Sinai. For six days the cloud covered the mountain, and on the seventh day the Lord called to*

Moses from within the cloud. To the Israelites the glory of the Lord looked like a consuming fire on top of the mountain. Then Moses entered the cloud as he went on up the mountain. And he stayed on the mountain forty days and forty nights (Exodus 24:13-18).

As Moses went into the tent, the pillar of cloud would come down and stay at the entrance, while the Lord spoke with Moses. Whenever the people saw the pillar of cloud standing at the entrance to the tent, they all stood and worshiped each at the entrance to his tent. The Lord would speak to Moses face to face, as a man speaks with his friend. Then Moses would return to the camp, but his young aide Joshua son of Nun did not leave the tent (Exodus 33:9-11).

In the end, it was Joshua who led the people of Israel into the Promised Land.

There is danger in becoming conceited. The common sign of being self-conceited is when you think that your little part is the whole story. This evil has led to the fall of many anointed people in the Kingdom of God, and it can come in various forms and shapes. Spiritual pride also involves other attitudes such as looking down on what God is doing through other people, using the power of your spirituality without restraint, or giving your personal opinion as if it is God's opinion. Eli, the high priest, had a proud attitude when the boy Samuel told of the impending judgment on his family: "What was it He said to you?" Eli asked. "Do not hide it from me. May God deal with you, be it ever so severely, if you hide from me anything He told you." So Samuel told him everything, hiding nothing from him. Then Eli said, "He is the Lord; let Him do what is good in His eyes" (1 Sam. 3:17-18).

The disciples of Jesus also had a taste of this evil spirit when they wanted to call down fire on a Samaritan village. However, Jesus rebuked them, saying that they did not know the manner of spirit that they carried.

As the time approached for Him to be taken up to heaven, Jesus resolutely set out for Jerusalem. And He sent messen-

gers on ahead, who went into a Samaritan village to get things ready for Him; but the people there did not welcome Him, because He was heading for Jerusalem. When the disciples James and John saw this, they asked, "Lord, do you want us to call fire down from heaven to destroy them?" But Jesus turned and rebuked them, and they went to another village (Luke 9:51-56).

It is also self-conceitedness to neglect revelatory guidance from God just because you did not personally receive the revelation, even though, for all intents and purposes, such revelations have been properly validated, both in source and content. To disregard your spouse or children's revelations because you are the more acclaimed minister of God and have not personally received the revelation is spiritual pride, and this is dangerous.

We need to be adequately covered and submit to the cover of God over our lives. Most times God uses a difficult leader to develop godly character in us. Remember that Saul was king, David's pastor. Had David killed Saul at the earliest opportunity, David would have become king sooner, but would never have achieved the kingship he eventually attained and never would have been the man after God's own heart.

AVOIDING CORPORATE ERROR OF JUDGMENT

Here Comes the Dreamer Mentality

Visual revelations, especially dreams and visions, have played major roles in the deliverance and the prophetic guidance of many nations. In biblical days, Gideon was strengthened by a dream he heard when on an espionage assignment to the enemy's camp. Gideon went on to deliver God's people from a crippling Midianite bondage (see Judg. 7:9-16). Also, Abraham was given prophetic guidance in a vision to leave his people and move to a place God would show him (see Gen. 12:1-6). Nevertheless, the Bible contains many examples of corporate errors in judgment in the arena of correct understanding of dreams and visions. In some of these cases, there were dire consequences as a result.

One such story is that of Joseph and the household of Jacob. The story of the acrimony that existed in the household of Jacob typifies the kindred feud that exists in some present-day local congregations and the unfortunate approach to relating to seers and watchmen. Kindred feuding is not new; it begins right from the time of Cain and Abel ("Am I my brother's keeper?" Gen. 4:9), through to Joseph and his brothers ("Here comes that dreamer" Gen. 37:19), to Peter and John ("What about him?" John 21:21)—and it continues to thrive. It is important to be on the side of God when the dust settles.

The bone of contention is to ensure proper management of the gifts of the seer and watchman in the local congregation, such as in the case of Joseph. God had singled him out for divine favor. It began as personal favor but later cascaded into the means for his family's survival and eventually evolved into the national salvation of the Jews. Jacob's preferential treatment of Joseph caused his brothers to envy him. To make matters worse, the brothers had a glimpse of the divine favor upon Joseph's life when he told them about his dreams. The result was intensified acrimony in their household.

However, Joseph's dreams and his ability to interpret were special blessings in his life. This gifting later became the very instrument that enabled the family to move to Egypt and escape the famine in Canaan. It was also the means by which God preserved His people from destruction. Whether in the pit, the prison, or the palace, Joseph was remarkable in his ability to remain unwavering in his faith in God.

With the benefit of hindsight, it is easy to see the mistake his brothers made on a collective basis, yet how easy it is for us to repeat the same mistake. We know that they were wrong because they misunderstood the blessings in the dreams that God gave to them through Joseph, and they fought bitterly against the very gift that was meant to save their lives.

Today, however, by despising the seer's and watchman's anointing in our local congregations, we are selling these gifts into reclusive slavery, just like the brothers of Joseph in the days of old. In many respects, the story of the seer in the present-day local church is very similar to the story of Joseph in the household of Jacob:

> *Jacob lived in the land where his father had stayed, the land of Canaan. This is the account of Jacob. Joseph, a young man of seventeen, was tending the flocks with his brothers, the sons of Bilhah and the sons of Zilpah, his father's wives, and he brought their father a bad report about them. Now Israel loved Joseph more than any of his other sons, because he had been born to him in his old age; and he made a richly ornamented robe for him. When his brothers saw that their father loved him more than any of them, they hated him and could not speak a kind word to him. Joseph had a dream, and when he told it to his brothers, they hated him all the more. He said to them, "Listen to this dream I had: We were binding sheaves of corn out in the field when suddenly my sheaf rose and stood upright, while your sheaves gathered round mine and bowed down to it"* (Genesis 37:1-7).

Maybe Joseph did not handle the pronouncement of prophetic dream wisely and perhaps, on his part, he did not know any better:

> *His brothers said to him, "Do you intend to reign over us? Will you actually rule us?" And **they hated him all the more because of his dream and what he had said.** Then he had another dream, and he told it to his brothers. "Listen," he said, "I had another dream, and this time the sun and moon and eleven stars were bowing down to me"* (Genesis 37:8-9).

Perhaps this is the plight of many seers and watchmen in our midst today. As for Joseph's brothers, they misunderstood the dream message from God and in their misconception sold him into slavery:

> *"They have moved on from here," the man answered. "I heard them say, 'Let's go to Dothan.'" So Joseph went after his brothers and found them near Dothan. But they saw him in the distance, and before he reached them, they plotted to kill him. **"Here comes that dreamer!" they said to each other. "Come now, let's kill him and throw him into one of these cisterns and***

say that a ferocious animal devoured him. Then we'll see what
comes of his dreams" (Genesis 37:17-20).

The central issue here is that they did not understand what God revealed to them through Joseph. This remains as relevant now as it was then. Our greatest asset in life is to not only hear the voice of God but to also understand what He says. Our relationship with God is very much dependent on our ability to hear and understand what He says to us.

On a corporate level, we need to understand that revelations are divinely given for God's purposes and that they can come through dreams, visions, trances, impressions, a flash of ideas, word of God, and in many other diverse ways. What is important is that we can ride on revelations that are received by other people, provided it is authenticated as true God-given revelation.

> *And we have the word of the prophets made more certain, and*
> *you will do well to pay attention to it, as to a light shining in*
> *a dark place, until the day dawns and the morning star rises*
> *in your hearts. Above all, you must understand that no*
> *prophecy of Scripture came about by the prophet's own inter-*
> *pretation. For prophecy never had its origin in the will of*
> *man, but men spoke from God as they were carried along by*
> *the Holy Spirit* (2 Peter 1:19-21).

The lesson here is that we should gain proper understanding of all revelation so that we can avail ourselves of God's intended benefits.

CORPORATE VALUE OF OTHER'S DREAMS

This is illustrated by the story of how the enemy's dream and its interpretation strengthened Gideon. Gideon had the desire to obey God, but he lacked the courage to take his people to war; thus God instructed him to take a trip to the enemy's camp. When he heard the dream and its interpretation he was strengthened.

> *During that night the Lord said to Gideon, "Get up, go down*
> *against the camp, because I am going to give it into your hands.*
> *If you are afraid to attack, go down to the camp with your ser-*
> *vant Purah and listen to what they are saying. Afterward, you*

will be encouraged to attack the camp." So he and Purah his servant went down to the outposts of the camp. The Midianites, the Amalekites and all the other eastern peoples had settled in the valley, thick as locusts. Their camels could no more be counted than the sand on the seashore. Gideon arrived just as a man was telling a friend his dream. "I had a dream," he was saying. "A round loaf of barley bread came tumbling into the Midianite camp. It struck the tent with such force that the tent overturned and collapsed." His friend responded, "This can be nothing other than the sword of Gideon son of Joash, the Israelite. God has given the Midianites and the whole camp into his hands." When Gideon heard the dream and its interpretation, he worshipped God. He returned to the camp of Israel and called out, "Get up! The Lord has given the Midianite camp into your hands" (Judges 7:9-15).

I have often gained valuable wisdom keys through listening to other people's dreams.

DESPISING DREAMS AND/OR PROPHESY

There is danger in despising dreams and/or prophesy. The Bible says, "Do not spurn the gifts and utterances of the prophets [**do not depreciate prophetic revelations nor despise inspired instruction or exhortation or warning**] but test and prove all things [until you can recognize] what is good; [to that] hold fast" (1 Thess. 5:20-21 AMP).

King Nebuchadnezzar did not heed the warning in his dream, so the calamity came upon him:

Then Daniel (also called Belteshazzar) was greatly perplexed for a time, and his thoughts terrified him. So the king said, "Belteshazzar, do not let the dream or its meaning alarm you." Belteshazzar answered, "My lord, if only the dream applied to your enemies and its meaning to your adversaries! The tree you saw, which grew large and strong, with its top touching the sky, visible to the whole earth, with beautiful leaves and abundant fruit, providing food for all, giving shelter to the beasts of the field, and having nesting places in its branches for the birds of the air—you, O king, are that tree! You have be-come great and strong; your greatness has grown until it reaches the sky, and your dominion extends to distant parts of the earth. You, O king, saw a messenger, a holy one, coming down from heaven and saying, 'Cut down the tree and destroy it, but leave the stump, bound with iron and bronze, in the grass of the field, while its roots remain in the ground. Let him be drenched with the dew of heaven; let him live like the wild animals, until seven times pass by for him.' This is the inter-pretation, O king, and this is the decree the Most High has is-sued against my lord the king: You will be driven away from people and will live with the wild animals; you will eat grass like cattle and be drenched with the dew of heaven. Seven times will pass by for you until you acknowledge that the Most High is sovereign over the kingdoms of men and gives them to anyone he wishes. The command to leave the stump of the tree with its roots means that your kingdom will be restored to you when you acknowledge that Heaven rules. Therefore, O king, be pleased to accept my advice: Renounce your sins by doing what is right, and your wickedness by being kind to the op-pressed. It may be that then your prosperity will continue." All this happened to King Nebuchadnezzar. Twelve months later, as the king was walking on the roof of the royal palace of Babylon, he said, "Is not this the great Babylon I have built as the royal residence, by my mighty power and for the glory of my majesty?" The words were still on his lips when a voice came from heaven, "This is what is decreed for you, King Neb-uchadnezzar: Your royal authority has been taken from you. You will be driven away from people and will live with the wild animals; you will eat grass like cattle. Seven times will pass by for you until you acknowledge that the Most High is sovereign over the kingdoms of men and gives them to anyone he wishes." Immediately what had been said about Nebuchad-nezzar was fulfilled. He was driven away from people and ate grass like cattle. His body was drenched with the dew of heaven until his hair grew like the feathers of an eagle and his nails like the claws of a bird (Daniel 4:19-33).

According to the Book of Deuteronomy, we assume responsibility for what is revealed to us.

The secret things belong to the Lord our God, but the things revealed belong to us and to our children for ever, that we may follow all the words of this law (Deuteronomy 29:29).

In another instance, we see when the remnant of Judah, after Babylonians defeated them and exiled most of the people, refused to obey the instruction as prophesied by the prophet Jeremiah. As a result, they suffered bitter consequences:

"If you stay in this land, I will build you up and not tear you down; I will plant you and not uproot you, for I am grieved over the disaster I have inflicted on you. Do not be afraid of the king of Babylon, whom you now fear. Do not be afraid of him, declares the Lord, for I am with you and will save you and deliver you from his hands. I will show you compassion so that he will have compassion on you and restore you to your land." However, if you say, "We will not stay in this land," and so disobey the Lord your God, and if you say, "No, we will go and live in Egypt, where we will not see war or hear the trumpet or be hungry for bread," then hear the word of the Lord, O remnant of Judah. This is what the Lord Almighty, the God of Israel, says: "If you are determined to go to Egypt and you do go to settle there, then the sword you fear will overtake you there, and the famine you dread will follow you into Egypt, and there you will die" (Jeremiah 42:10-16).

When Jeremiah finished telling the people all the words of the Lord their God—everything the Lord had sent him to tell them—Azariah son of Hoshaiah and Johanan son of Kareah and all the arrogant men said to Jeremiah, "You are lying! The Lord our God has not sent you to say, 'You must not go to Egypt to settle there.' But Baruch son of Neriah is inciting you against us to hand us over to the Babylonians, so that they may kill us or carry us into exile to Babylon." So Johanan son of Kareah and all the army officers and all the people disobeyed the Lord's command to stay in the land of Judah. Instead, Johanan son of Kareah and all the army officers led away all the remnant of Judah who had come back to live in the land of Judah from all the nations where they had been scattered. They also led away all the men, women and children and the king's daughters whom Nebuzaradan commander of the imperial guard had left with Gedaliah son of Ahikam, the son of Shaphan, and Jeremiah the prophet and Baruch son of Neriah. So they entered Egypt in disobedience to the Lord and went as far as Tahpanhes (Jeremiah 43:1-7).

CHAPTER NINE

INTEGRATION OF WATCHMEN

CORPORATE GUIDELINES FOR INTEGRATION

In general, prophecy can be inspirational or revelatory. Revelatory prophetic messages, no matter how they come, often give direction and may touch on governmental issues. Therefore, those gifted to receive picture revelations on a consistent and frequent basis should be trained to appropriately handle their revelations in a manner beneficial to themselves and the local church. The local church and leadership should provide a framework within a friendly atmosphere for the training, growth, and mentoring of those gifted to receive pictorial revelations. I have found the following guidelines useful as I train and move with many watchmen and church leaders.

The seer/watchman needs to:

- Train his physical body and soul and enhance the spirit to receive adequately from God wisely ministering to the Body of Christ.

- Seek a place of maximal reception of divine revelations.

- Discipline his physical body to be able to withstand and sustain the rigors of seeing into the spirit realm.

- Transform or renew his mind, control his emotions, and yield his human will to God.

- Be strong and discerning in the spirit to pick up things happening in the spirit realm.

- Live a life of love; God is love; love is the hallmark of our discipleship.

- Dwell in the peace of God; the level of peace enjoyed determines the level of experience we have in God.

- Be totally yielded to the will of God.

- Invest in God-given potentials.

- Spend times of intimacy with God; have a worshiping and a prayerful life.

- Know that the place for the richness of the Word of God cannot be overemphasized.

- Avoid undue pressure, tension, and busyness.

- Ensure proper accountability to leadership and responsibility to the local church.

- Avoid the spirit of lawlessness at all cost.

- Avoid using revelations to manipulate others.

The local church needs to:

- Provide secure mentoring support for those in training.

- Provide a forum for prophetic people to learn and develop.

- Meet regularly with those in training.

- Encourage those in training to take responsibility for the outworking of their gift.

- Assist those in training to plan their future moves.

- Create a safe environment that allows for mistakes to be corrected in a brotherly way.

Interactions:

- The seer/watchman receives from God and submits to the leadership with humility.

- The seer/watchman should not police the progress or the implementation of the revelation.

- Both the seer/watchman and the leadership should prayerfully interact to ensure that the essence of the revelation is not lost.

- The leadership should know that most seers or watchmen receive warnings with heavy burdens that often urge them to speak woe. This burden should be carefully managed from both sides, otherwise it can become pervasive, having the capability to drive the seer to a reclusive life if not properly harnessed and managed.

- Both should know that time application of the revelations is often difficult to determine unless in exceptional revelations they come with a clear time frame.

- The apostles and the pastors have better time application than the prophet except for the few instances when God gives the time frame clearly in the revelation. This is because the apostle or pastor can see many parts of the whole as they are in the position to bring together the many parts seen by many prophets. On the other hand, prophets only see in parts.

- For understanding to develop, on a regular basis the leadership should create a forum to meet with the seer and to resolve any unnecessary tension.

- The seer in training needs acceptance, and sometimes correction, to facilitate maturity in the anointing.

- Leaders should give feedback, and the seers should learn to wait for the leadership to make decisions.

THE IMPORTANCE OF A PERSONAL RELATIONSHIP WITH GOD

The enhanced ability to receive revelations positions the watchman into a spiritual place that attracts the fury of satan. The watchman is therefore constantly in peril of the enemy's surveillance and reconnaissance. Therefore, to operate in the watchman's anointing without a personal relationship with the Triune God is to run the risk of allowing the kingdom of darkness to permeate and probably hijack the outworking of the watchman's giftedness for ungodly purposes. The essence of a personal relationship with God in the operation of the watchman's anointing cannot be overemphasized.

Let us examine the lives of two remarkable men, both of whom were remarkably gifted in the seer's and watchman's anointing. One described himself as the "Hebrew of Hebrews," and the other is a Gentile king who once ruled the most powerful and occult nation of his generation. The first man is Paul, who said of himself, "Circumcised on the eighth day, of the people of Israel, of the tribe of Benjamin, a Hebrew of Hebrews; in regard to the law, a Pharisee; as for zeal, persecuting the church; as for legalistic righteousness, faultless" (Phil. 3:5-6).

Paul was a highly gifted man who pursued Judaism with intense passion until he had a compelling encounter with the Lord Jesus Christ, giving his life and giftedness to the Triune God. He went on to receive incredible amounts of revelation from the throne of God, resulting in Paul writing most of the New Testament. He was one of the outstanding watchmen to the Body of Christ.

The other man was King Nebuchadnezzar, who also was gifted to receive revelation by pictures and other forms of visual revelation. Because he received dreams and visions fairly frequently, he could be called a seer. He was the head of the most occult group operating in that time. However, despite being in the midst of occult practices, he had many notable dreams and visions from God, even acknowledging the supremacy of the God of the Hebrews on some occasions. Unfortunately, his gifting was never consecrated to God. His anointing is an example of a wasted anointing.

> As the Bible says, "Every good and perfect gift is from above, coming down from the Father of the heavenly lights, who does not change like shifting shadows" (James 1:17).

This is particularly so in the revelatory gifting, because unless the Lord gives divine revelations, no one can receive them. Unfortunately, many gifted people today are operating outside the Kingdom of God. In most of these instances, these gifted people do not know the Triune God and inadvertently operate with power from the dark side. Without

God, the seer giftedness becomes restricted to operating only in information shifting, because divine revelation comes only from God. The devil cannot tell the future. Any giftedness operating without the fruit of the Holy Spirit will, in time, become perverted and eventually frustrated by God Himself.

The Bible introduced Paul, then known as Saul of Tarsus, as a remarkable young man and one of the most zealous Pharisees of his days:

> *At this they covered their ears and, yelling at the top of their voices; they all rushed at him* [Stephen], *dragged him out of the city and began to stone him. Meanwhile, the witnesses laid their clothes at the feet of **a young man named Saul**. While they were stoning him, Stephen prayed, "Lord Jesus, receive my spirit." Then he fell on his knees and cried out, "Lord, do not hold this sin against them." When he had said this, he fell asleep* (Acts 7:57-60).

The apostle Paul later confirmed this: "I was advancing in Judaism beyond many Jews of my own age and was extremely zealous for the traditions of my fathers. But when God, who set me apart from birth and called me by His grace, was pleased to reveal His son in me so that I might preach Him among the Gentiles, I did not immediately consult any man" (Gal. 1:14-16).

His conversion from Judaism to Christianity gives a fascinating scriptural episode:

> *Meanwhile, Saul was still breathing out murderous threats against the Lord's disciples. He went to the high priest and asked him for letters to the synagogues in Damascus, so that if he found any there who belonged to the Way, whether men or women, he might take them as prisoners to Jerusalem. As he neared Damascus on his journey, suddenly a light from heaven flashed around him. He fell to the ground and heard a voice say to him, "Saul, Saul, why do you persecute me?" "Who are you, Lord?" Saul asked. "I am Jesus, whom you are persecuting," He replied. "Now get up and go into the city, and you will be told what you must do." The men travelling with*

Saul stood there speechless; they heard the sound but did not see anyone. Saul got up from the ground, but when he opened his eyes he could see nothing. So they led him by the hand into Damascus. For three days he was blind, and did not eat or drink anything. In Damascus there was a disciple named Ananias. The Lord called to him in a vision, "Ananias!" "Yes, Lord," he answered. The Lord told him, "Go to the house of Judas on Straight Street and ask for a man from Tarsus named Saul, for he is praying. In a vision he has seen a man named Ananias come and place his hands on him to restore his sight" (Acts 9:1-12).

Later Paul made this remark about how he considered the knowledge of Christ as all surpassing:

But whatever was to my profit I now consider loss for the sake of Christ. What is more, I consider everything a loss compared to the surpassing greatness of knowing Christ Jesus my Lord, for whose sake I have lost all things. I consider them rubbish that I may gain Christ and be found in him, not having a righteousness of my own that comes from the law, but that which is through faith in Christ—the righteousness that comes from God and is by faith. I want to know Christ and the power of his resurrection and the fellowship of sharing in his sufferings, becoming like him in his death, and so, somehow, to attain to the resurrection from the dead (Philippians 3:7-11).

On the other hand we saw King Nebuchadnezzar's ability to spiritually see in the Book of Daniel, where he had a profound revelation regarding the future of his kingdom. However, Nebuchadnezzar had no right-standing with God, coupled with the busyness that rulership demanded of him, so he was unable to remember his dream. In other words, it simply became unfruitful to him, even though the gift or the potential to receive revelations remained in his life. The misplaced divine inbuilt urge to seek a meaning for his dream drove him to excessive compulsion, so much so that he threatened to kill his wise men.

Thus this gifted man suffered perversion of his gifting that was eventually frustrated by God.

King Nebuchadnezzar had some notable visual revelations from God.

- The Dream of a Large Statue

  The king asked Daniel (also called Belteshazzar), "Are you able to tell me what I saw in my dream and interpret it?" Daniel replied, "No wise man, enchanter, magician or diviner can explain to the king the mystery he has asked about, but there is a God in heaven who reveals mysteries. He has shown King Nebuchadnezzar what will happen in days to come. Your dream and the visions that passed through your mind as you lay on your bed are these" (Daniel 2:26-28).

- The Dream of the Tree

  "In the visions I saw while lying in my bed, I looked, and there before me was a messenger, a holy one, coming down from heaven. He called in a loud voice: "Cut down the tree and trim off its branches; strip off its leaves and scatter its fruit. Let the animals flee from under it and the birds from its branches. But let the stump and its roots, bound with iron and bronze, remain in the ground, in the grass of the field. Let him be drenched with the dew of heaven, and let him live with the animals among the plants of the earth. Let his mind be changed from that of a man and let him be given the mind of an animal, till seven times pass by for him. The decision is announced by messengers, the holy ones declare the verdict, so that the living may know that the Most High is sovereign over the kingdoms of men and gives them to anyone He wishes and sets over them the lowliest of men" (Daniel 4:9-17).

- The Apparition in the Fiery Furnace

  Then King Nebuchadnezzar leaped to his feet in amazement and asked his advisers, "Weren't there three men that we tied up and threw into the fire?" They replied, "Certainly, O king." He said, "Look! I see four men walking around in the fire, unbound and unharmed, and the fourth looks like a son of the gods" (Daniel 3:24-25).

However, every divine encounter leaves the recipient with some divine impartation. Nevertheless, how that impartation is put into use is a matter of individual choice. I believe, as a result of this principle, King Nebuchadnezzar received some impartation, despite the evil that surrounded him, as he sporadically made some profound statements in the Scriptures that are worthy of note:

A. *Then Nebuchadnezzar said, "Praise be to the God of Shadrach, Meshach and Abednego, who has sent His angel and rescued His servants! They trusted in Him and defied the king's command and were willing to give up their lives rather than serve or worship any god except their own God. Therefore I decree that the people of any nation or language who say anything against the God of Shadrach, Meshach and Abednego be cut into pieces and their houses be turned into piles of rubble, for no other god can save in this way"* (Daniel 3:28-29).

In a momentary period of repentance and submission to God, this gifted king wrote in chapter 4 of the Book of Daniel:

B. *At the end of that time, I, Nebuchadnezzar, raised my eyes towards heaven, and my sanity was restored.* **Then I praised the Most High; I honored and glorified Him who lives for ever. His dominion is an eternal dominion; His kingdom endures from generation to generation.** *All the peoples of the earth are regarded as nothing. He does as He pleases with the powers of heaven and the peoples of the earth. No one can hold back His hand or say to Him: "What have you done?" At the same time that my sanity was restored, my honor and splendor were returned to me for the glory of my kingdom. My advisers and nobles sought me out, and I was restored to my throne and became even greater than before.*

> *Now I, Nebuchadnezzar, praise and exalt and glorify the King of heaven, because everything He does is right and all His ways are just. And those who walk in pride He is able to humble* (Daniel 4:34-37).

C. *King Nebuchadnezzar, To the peoples, nations and men of every language, who live in all the world: May you prosper greatly! It is my pleasure to tell you about the miraculous signs and wonders that the Most High God has performed for me. How great are His signs, how mighty His wonders! His kingdom is an eternal kingdom; His dominion endures from generation to generation. I, Nebuchadnezzar, was at home in my palace, contented and prosperous* (Daniel 4:1-4).

The central point is that we live in a fallen state and in a world dominated by the prince of the air—the evil one, the devil. However, to consecrate our giftedness to the Triune God, we must make all efforts to avoid demonic influence that may seek to hijack our minds, attitude, and way of life.

Unfortunately, in the end King Nebuchadnezzar never consecrated his gift to God. It is not enough to be gifted and anointed, it is vitally important that we remain in the cover of the glory of God. This is why God said:

> *Let not the wise man boast of his wisdom, or the strong man of his strength, or the rich man boast of his riches, but let him who boasts boast about this: that he understands and know Me that I am the Lord, who exercises kindness, justice and righteousness on earth, for in these I delight...* (Jeremiah 9:23).

It is important to remember that wisdom, giftedness, or other blessings of God only operate effectively within the principles of God and thrive on communion with Him.

> *"And now this admonition is for you, O priests. If you do not listen, and if you do not set your heart to honor My name,"* says the Lord Almighty, *"I will send a curse upon you, and I will curse your blessings..."* (Malachi 2:1-2).

As the priests were admonished in Malachi, we should be aware that though the gift of God is not revocable, if corrupted like the wisdom of Ahithophel, it could be cursed or frustrated by God.

CHAPTER TEN

AVOIDING DEMONIC INFLUENCES

The following steps, when taken in due order, will help the watch-man avoid demonic influences in the operation of his gift.

AVOID DEMONIC PRACTICES

Nebuchadnezzar was involved in numerous demonic practices. The devil and his cohorts can seek to dominate a place spiritually by intensifying their influence and the hold of the second heaven over the place. If the demonic influence and hold over a place is allowed to intensify, the openness of the third heaven over it may become diminished. If this happens, the seer's gifting will be restricted in that place.

AVOID VILE AND UNHOLY IMAGERY

King Nebuchadnezzar lived among the most unholy things and people of the time (see Dan. 2:1-3). There is no doubt that he saw vile things that influenced his thoughts and decisions. On the other hand, Job gave a model example to follow when he said, "I made a covenant with my eyes not to look lustfully at a girl" (Job 31:1). Job was a man who took important steps to ensure a right-standing with God; he regularly performed absolution on behalf of his children, in case they had wrong thoughts concerning God. Therefore, when this man covenanted with his eyes, he certainly knew that the seeing senses were highly vulnerable to seduction by unholy imagery.

The eye gate is a sure way by which people fall into sinful living. We can learn from the life of Israel's greatest king—David:

In the spring, at the time when kings go off to war, David sent Joab out with the king's men and the whole Israelite

151

army. They destroyed the Ammonites and besieged Rabbah. But David remained in Jerusalem. One evening David got up from his bed and walked around on the roof of the palace. From the roof he saw a woman bathing. The woman was very beautiful, and David sent someone to find out about her. The man said, "Isn't this Bathsheba, the daughter of Eliam and the wife of Uriah the Hittite?" Then David sent messengers to get her. She came to him, and he slept with her. (She had purified herself from her uncleanness.) Then she went back home (2 Samuel 11:1-4).

In general, we become what we behold. Vile and unholy images lead to blurred visions and ineffective functioning of the spiritual eyes.

BE MINDFUL WHAT YOU LISTEN TO

Nebuchadnezzar listened to his occult subjects in the matters pertaining to the kingdom (see Dan. 3:8-20). Jesus Christ said we should be mindful what we listen to: "Therefore **consider carefully how you listen**. Whoever has will be given more; whoever does not have, even what he thinks he has will be taken from him" (Luke 8:18).

One of Job's friends had this to say about what we listen to, and if we must listen, then our ears should test what we hear: "Then Elihu said: 'Hear my words, you wise men; listen to me, you men of learning. **For the ear tests words** as the tongue tastes food'" (Job 34:1-3).

AVOID EVIL COMPANY

The Nebuchadnezzar government machinery functioned in the most evil environment and among the most occult people of the time:

A. King Solomon's son, Rehoboam, learned this lesson that bad company corrupts, and he paid dearly for it.

   Three days later Jeroboam and all the people returned to Rehoboam, as the king had said, "Come back to me in three days." The king answered the people harshly. Rejecting the advice given him by the elders, he followed the advice of the young men and said, "My father made

152

your yoke heavy; I will make it even heavier. My father scourged you with whips; I will scourge you with scorpions" (1 Kings 12:12-14).

B. Jacob was disgusted by the violence that once existed in the company of Simeon and Levi.

Simeon and Levi are brothers—their swords are weapons of violence. Let me not enter their council, let me not join their assembly, for they have killed men in their anger and hamstrung oxen as they pleased. Cursed be their anger, so fierce, and their fury, so cruel! I will scatter them in Jacob and disperse them in Israel (Genesis 49:5-7).

Like Jacob we should avoid evil company because evil company corrupts.

DO NOT ASSOCIATE WITH ACCURSED THINGS

The presence of accursed things in the midst of Israel brought reproach on the nation:

The Lord said to Joshua, "Stand up! What are you doing down on your face? Israel has sinned; they have violated my covenant, which I commanded them to keep. They have taken some of the devoted things; they have stolen, they have lied, they have put them with their own possessions. That is why the Israelites cannot stand against their enemies; they turn their backs and run because they have been made liable to destruction. I will not be with you any more unless you destroy whatever among you is devoted to destruction" (Joshua 7:10-12).

When a reproach is brought upon a people from God, no matter the giftedness, one receives fewer revelations.

THE SUSTENANCE OF THE SEER/WATCHMAN ANOINTING

The essence of a personal knowledge of God is the sustenance of the seer and watchman anointing.

The Danger of Corrupt Wisdom

Corruption of the wisdom that propels any giftedness is perhaps more common than we often imagine. Wisdom that drives giftedness becomes corrupt when the original purity of the wisdom becomes perverted through the frailty or hubris of humanity.

The danger of corrupt wisdom is the subtlety with which it creeps into the life of its victim. This is why the Bible says let him who thinks he stands take heed lest he falls (see 1 Cor. 10:12). The Bible says of satan, "Your heart was lifted up [with pride] because of your beauty; you corrupted your wisdom for the sake of your splendor" (Ezek. 28:17 NKJV).

Corrupted wisdom is menacing us every day at an alarming rate. The difficulty is that often the miracles of healings, financial breakthroughs, raising the dead, or other supernatural signs make spectacles of the sovereignty and supremacy of God. That in itself is desirable, for it adds to the effectiveness of reaching out to the unsaved and those God seeks to communicate with. How else would Moses have turned aside if not for the spectacle of a burning bush that was not consumed? But it is also the avenue by which satan lures many into excesses and self-exaltation.

The functionality of giftedness in a person attracts the attention and attacks from the enemy of our soul. King Solomon was described as the wisest king who ever lived; he "was greater in riches and wisdom than all the other kings of the earth. All kings of the earth sought audience with Solomon to hear the wisdom God had put in his heart" (2 Chron. 9:22-23).

Nevertheless, Solomon slid in a very subtle way into disobedience, a cleverly maneuvered pattern that men can not perceive. A passion or giftedness that is not properly harnessed will lead to perversion.

The Bible says of Ahithophel, "For every word Ahithophel spoke seemed as wise as though it has come directly from the mouth of God" (2 Sam. 16:23 TLB).

Through unforgiveness and resentment, his wisdom was corrupted and he made the fatal mistake of joining Absalom's conspiracy.

Because his wisdom had become corrupt, God frustrated his counsel. Ahithophel, in all his wisdom, committed suicide.

AVOIDING SEXUAL WEAKNESS

Sexual desire is easily the most common idol in the hearts of men and women. Time and time again, God allegorized the sin of idolatry with the sin of sexual promiscuity and immorality.

In ancient times, pagan religious worship incorporated adultery into its rituals. Pagans believed that sexual rituals, through occult prostitution, would ecstatically put them in tune with supernatural powers. Somehow, in those times, the people recognized a connection between the intensity of sexual ecstasy and spirituality (operating in the supernatural). These sexual rituals were common at pagan religious shrines, which were located at the high places or hilltops in biblical days. These prostitutes were referred to as "shrine prostitutes." Whenever this practice was entrenched in Israel, it perverted spirituality that became difficult to eradicate. Even the patriarch Judah fell victim to the service of a shrine prostitute:

> *When Tamar was told, "Your father-in-law is on his way to Timnah to shear his sheep," she took off her widow's clothes, covered herself with a veil to disguise herself, and then sat down at the entrance to Enaim, which is on the road to Timnah. For she saw that, though Shelah had now grown up, she had not been given to him as his wife. When Judah saw her, he thought she was a [shrine] prostitute, for she had covered her face. Not realizing that she was his daughter-in-law, he went over to her by the roadside and said, "Come now, let me sleep with you." "And what will you give me to sleep with you?" she asked (Genesis 38:13-16).*

Sexual bondage is peculiar. It creeps in subtly but grips with so much intensity, overwhelming its victims with such a passion that reason and logic are easily thrown into the abyss. This addiction can be traced to the image center of man. The image center is the pictorial depository of our imagination. The grip and enticement of pictures in our imagination is hard to suppress and the addiction difficult to overcome.

Therefore, for those with revelatory giftedness it becomes a snare, because revelations are also translated to our image center for processing and understanding. A sanctified imagination is important for receiving and handling revelations from God, whereas a corrupted imagination, emanating from sexual sin, pollutes the imagination making the watchman's reception blurred and distorted so that the prophets stumble at giving prophecy. Do not allow sexual sin or inordinate sexual indulgence to subvert your walk with God.

The Devil, Religion, and Sexuality

When Israel posed a military threat to Moab, the Moabites, on the advice of Balaam, used this age-long vulnerability to sexual sin to subvert Israel spiritually.

> *While Israel was staying in Shittim, the men began to indulge in sexual immorality with Moabite women, who invited them to the sacrifices to their gods. The people ate and bowed down before these gods. So Israel joined in worshiping the Baal of Peor. And the Lord's anger burned against them* (Numbers 25:1-3).

> *"Have you allowed all the women to live?" he asked them. "They were the ones who followed Balaam's advice and were the means of turning the Israelites away from the Lord in what happened at Peor, so that a plague struck the Lord's people"* (Numbers 31:15-16).

The Moabite women offered sexual favors and then invited the Israelites to their idol worshiping. This strategy of satan continues even to this day and is biting hard at us in an ever-increasing pattern. The news of a minister falling victim to this evil strategy sends shock waves around the world. Yet worse still is the silent evil of pornography and the sexual laxity that are quietly eating deep into the cutting edge of anointed men and women of God.

CHAPTER ELEVEN

STRANGE EVENTS

There is an increasing occurrence of strange events in the last days—most of which are described in the Bible.

The prophet Joel said that strange experiences would be demonstrated on earth and in the sky. The Living Bible translation puts this rather clearly:

> *And I will cause strange demonstrations in the heavens and on the earth* (Acts 2:19 TLB).

> *And put strange symbols in the earth and sky* (Joel 2:30 TLB).

Many contemporary experiences confirm that strange events are indeed on the increase in these last days. It is important that we recognize, understand, and appreciate strange events when they come from God to properly avail ourselves of the intended benefits. God may give send strange spiritual experiences for several reasons. It was because of the strangeness of the burning bush experience that Moses turned aside to hear God and in the process was remantled into his destiny.

Strange spiritual events are occurrences that are curious, extraordinary, unnatural, often bizarre, or mysterious. They are very common in the ministry of seers, and for me they serve to distinguish the seer from other dreamers. These occurrences will increase in the last days. Strange events come in various forms and in varying degrees of strangeness or awesomeness. Most strange events serve to emphasize the sovereignty and supremacy of God, yet in many other instances, the strangeness or bizarre nature of the spiritual encounter seems not to be God's first choice. Some of God's messages may assume strange or bizarre forms, possibly to compel humankind to pay attention to what God might want to say.

This was Moses' experience of strange events: "So Moses thought, 'I will go over and see **this strange sight**—why the bush does not burn up'" (Exod. 3:3).

In this strange encounter, Moses had what most people believe was a "divine sight," the *burning bush encounter*. A divine sight is when the supernatural happening blends into the natural surrounding so that it becomes impossible to tell if it is real or spiritual.

> *Now Moses was tending the flock of Jethro his father-in-law, the priest of Midian, and he led the flock to the far side of the desert and came to Horeb, the mountain of God. There the angel of the Lord appeared to him in flames of fire from within a bush...* (Exodus 3:1-2).

In this divine sight, Moses may have found it difficult to tell whether it was a natural or supernatural occurrence until God spoke to him in the midst of the burning bush.

On the other hand, it is important to remember that strange spiritual experiences do not automatically mean it is of divine origin. As the Bible says: "For false Christs and false prophets **will appear and perform great signs and miracles to deceive even the elect**—if that were possible" (Matt. 24:24). Also in Paul's second letter to the Thessalonians, he says, "This man of sin will come as Satan's tool, full of satanic power and will trick everyone with **strange demonstrations** and will do great miracles" (2 Thess. 2:9 TLB). Satan will empower "this man of sin" to demonstrate compelling but deceptive miracles.

A majority of strange events occur in the "twilight zone." A twilight zone refers to a state that is not clearly defined or demarcated between the spirit and the natural realms. Twilight zone visionary experiences are, therefore, encounters that are difficult to define, whether they occur in the spirit or in the natural realm. It would appear that most of these experiences occur in-between the boundaries of the two realms.

Twilight zone visionary events come in various forms, strangeness, or awesomeness, and they often show differing degrees of involvement of the physical realm. So in some of these experiences, the human body can be variably affected. This is why the apostle Paul was blind for three days following his Damascus-road visionary encounter and why the patriarch Jacob limped the rest of his life after wrestling with the angel of the Lord. In these two instances, their natural bodies were affected.

The apostle Paul had a strange third-heaven encounter, and speaking about this, he says, "I must go on boasting. Although there is nothing to be gained, I will go on to visions and revelations from the Lord. I know a man in Christ who fourteen years ago was caught up to the **third heaven**. Whether it was in the body or out of the body I do not know—God knows. And I know that this man—whether in the body or apart from the body I do not know, but God knows—was caught up to paradise. He heard inexpressible things, things that man is not permitted to tell. I will boast about a man like that, but I will not boast about myself, except about my weaknesses" (2 Cor. 12:1-5).

In Paul's encounter, he describes a very strange experience of a man most people believe to be Paul himself. He was caught up in the third heaven, *whether in body or out of the body he did not know* but he heard many things he was not allowed to talk about. There are times we may receive revelations, which are difficult to recall how they were imparted to us, yet they often carry deep and compelling evidence of their divine origin. Paul finally concluded that the only thing worth boasting about in life is the strength of God that is made manifest in human weaknesses.

BIBLICAL EXAMPLES OF STRANGE EVENTS

Translation

Translation means to transport from one place to another or to convey to Heaven without natural death.

- ◆ *Translation to Heaven.* The following translation to Heaven is recorded in the Bible:

   By faith Enoch was translated that he should not see death; and was not found, because God had translated him: for before his translation he had this testimony, that he pleased God (Hebrews 11:5 KJV).

As they were walking along and talking together, suddenly a chariot of fire and horses of fire appeared and separated the two of them, and Elijah went up to heaven in a whirlwind. Elisha saw this and cried out, "My father! My father! The chariots and horsemen of Israel!" And Elisha saw him no more. Then he took hold of his own clothes and tore them apart (2 Kings 2:11-12).

◆ *Translation from one place to another.*

In one instance, Ezekiel was *lifted by his hair and then translated to the temple* in Jerusalem. In this description, the Bible records that the Spirit of God lifted the prophet Ezekiel by the hair into the celestial expanse between the earth and the heavens. The expanse between the earth and the heavens is the celestial expanse, which includes the second heaven. This is also the zone of interaction and conflict between the agents of God and the agents of the devil. In this vision of God, Ezekiel was translated to the temple in Jerusalem.

In the sixth year, in the sixth month on the fifth day, while I was sitting in my house and the elders of Judah were sitting before me, the hand of the Sovereign Lord came upon me there. I looked, and I saw a figure like that of a man. From what appeared to be his waist down he was like fire, and from there up his appearance was as bright as glowing metal. He stretched out what looked like a hand and took me by the hair of my head. The Spirit lifted me up between earth and heaven and in visions of God he took me to Jerusalem, to the entrance to the north gate of the inner court, where the idol that provokes to jealousy stood. And there before me was the glory of the God of Israel, as in the vision I had seen in the plain. Then he said to me, "Son of man, look toward the north." So I looked, and in the entrance north of the gate of the altar I saw this idol of jealousy. And he said to me, "Son of man, do you see what they are doing—the utterly detestable things the house of Israel is doing here,

*things that will drive me far from my sanctuary? But you
will see things that are even more detestable." Then he
brought me to the entrance to the court. I looked, and I
saw a hole in the wall* (Ezekiel 8:1-7).

There are other strange but holy transportations in the Bible:

The Spirit of God transported Philip away from the Ethiopian eunuch to another earthly location.

*When they came up out of the water, the Spirit of the Lord
suddenly took Philip away, and the eunuch did not see him
again, but went on his way rejoicing* (Acts 8:39).

By divine empowerment, Elijah outran the chariot by the Spirit
of God.

*The seventh time the servant reported, "A cloud as small as a
man's hand is rising from the sea." So Elijah said, "Go and tell
Ahab, 'Hitch up your chariot and go down before the rain stops
you.'" Meanwhile, the sky grew black with clouds, the wind rose,
a heavy rain came on and Ahab rode off to Jezreel. The power of
the Lord came upon Elijah and, tucking his cloak into his belt,
he ran ahead of Ahab all the way to Jezreel* (1 Kings 18:44-46).

In the Book of Acts, the apostle Paul described a vision in which a
man from Macedonia appeared to him and begged him to come and help
the saints in Macedonia. I believe this was not an angel but a divinely instigated translation of the spirit of a prayerful man, resident in Macedonia. The man shown to Paul in the vision was probably a man who was
praying for spiritual reenforcement to come to the saints in Macedonia.
Hence, in this vision, he symbolically asks for the apostle Paul to join
with the saints in Macedonia to push back the evil principality in that region. Paul believes the message and obeys God; this eventually allows for
the entrance of the Gospel of Christ to the Western hemisphere:

*Paul and his companions traveled throughout the region of
Phrygia and Galatia, having been kept by the Holy Spirit from
preaching the word in the province of Asia. When they came to
the border of Mysia, they tried to enter Bithynia, but the Spirit*

of Jesus would not allow them to. So they passed by Mysia and went down to Troas. During the night Paul had a vision of a man of Macedonia standing and begging him, "Come over to Macedonia and help us." After Paul had seen the vision, we got ready at once to leave for Macedonia, concluding that God had called us to preach the gospel to them (Acts 16:6-10).

APPARITIONS

An apparition is another form of strange events; it is a visionary encounter in which a supernatural happening becomes perceptible to the natural eyes. An apparition can only happen because the supernatural event has sufficiently involved and permeated the physical realm to the extent that it makes it possible to be seen by the natural eyes. Examples of apparitions:

- When an angel assumes temporal appearance, the process involves a sufficient degree of the physical realm to make angels perceptible by the natural eyes.

- *The fourth man in the burning furnace* is an example of temporal appearance of the angel of the Lord or preincarnate appearance of Jesus Christ.

  ...and commanded some of the strongest soldiers in his army to tie up Shadrach, Meshach and Abednego and throw them into the blazing furnace. So these men, wearing their robes, trousers, turbans and other clothes, were bound and thrown into the blazing furnace. The king's command was so urgent and the furnace so hot that the flames of the fire killed the soldiers who took up Shadrach, Meshach and Abednego, and these three men, firmly tied, fell into the blazing furnace. Then King Nebuchadnezzar leaped to his feet in amazement and asked his advisers, "Weren't there three men that we tied up and threw into the fire?" They replied, "Certainly, O king." He said, "Look! **I see four men walking around in the fire, unbound and unharmed, and the fourth looks like a son of the gods"** *(Daniel 3:20-25).*

◆ *The mysterious handwriting on the wall* came in full view of all the people present at the king's banquet and is another example of strange biblical events:

> *Suddenly the fingers of a human hand appeared and wrote on the plaster of the wall, near the lampstand in the royal palace. The king watched the hand as it wrote. His face turned pale and he was so frightened that his knees knocked together and his legs gave way. The king called out for the enchanters, astrologers and diviners to be brought and said to these wise men of Babylon, "Whoever reads this writing and tells me what it means will be clothed in purple and have a gold chain placed around his neck, and he will be made the third highest ruler in the kingdom"* (Daniel 5:5-7).

CARRYOVERS

A carryover is said to occur when an event or occurrence in the spiritual encounter is carried over into the physical realm. Examples:

◆ Jacob limped for the rest of his life after a visionary encounter:

> *That night Jacob got up and took his two wives, his two maidservants and his eleven sons and crossed the ford of the Jabbok. After he had sent them across the stream, he sent over all his possessions. So Jacob was left alone, and a man wrestled with him till daybreak. When the man saw that he could not overpower him, he touched the socket of Jacob's hip so that his hip was wrenched as he wrestled with the man. Then the man said, "Let me go, for it is daybreak." But Jacob replied, "I will not let you go unless you bless me." The man asked him, "What is your name?" "Jacob," he answered. Then the man said, "Your name will no longer be Jacob, but Israel, because you have struggled with God and with men and have overcome." Jacob said, "Please tell me your name." But he replied, "Why do you ask my name?" Then he blessed him*

there. So Jacob called the place Peniel, saying, "It is because I saw God face to face, and yet my life was spared." The sun rose above him as he passed Peniel, and he was limping because of his hip. Therefore to this day the Israelites do not eat the tendon attached to the socket of the hip, because the socket of Jacob's hip was touched near the tendon (Genesis 32:22-32).

◆   Daniel became pale after a visionary encounter:

This is the end of the matter. I, Daniel, was deeply troubled by my thoughts, and my face turned pale, but I kept the matter to myself (Daniel 7:28).

DREAMLIKE STATE VISIONARY ENCOUNTER

The following story is recorded in the Book of Acts when Peter was miraculously released from the jail. He walked out of the jail and passed through the iron gate before he came into his natural senses:

Now behold an angel of the Lord stood by him, and a light shone in the prison; and he struck Peter on the side and raised him up, saying, "Arise quickly!" And his chain fell off his hands. Then the angel said to him, "Gird yourself and tie on your sandals"; and so he did. And he said to him, "Put on your garment and follow me." So he went out and followed him, and did not know that what was done by the angel was real, but thought he was seeing a vision. When they were past the first and the second guard posts, they came to the iron gate that leads to the city which opened to them of its own accord; and they went out and went down one street, and immediately the angel departed from him. And when Peter had come to himself… (Acts 12:7-12 NKJV).

Personal Testimony

This type of strange experience is perhaps commoner than often appreciated, or if appreciated they are not publicly acknowledged. This is my personal experience with this type of strange event:

This event happened many years ago immediately following the birth of our last child, who had to be delivered by caesarean section.

Before the delivery, I was booked to travel to the United States for a conference. My wife and baby had returned home and were doing well just a few days before my scheduled trip. I seriously considered cancelling the trip, but my wife insisted that she was able to cope on her own and that I should go ahead with the plans for the trip. Two nights before I traveled, I had this strange encounter:

> In a dreamlike state, some gentlemen came to the house and asked me to show them around our home. In particular they wanted to know where the gas and electricity meters were located. I showed them around the house and left them seated in our sitting room. The next scene I can remember was that I was walking down our staircase to join them in the sitting room. Halfway down the stairway I came to my natural consciousness and I woke up.

I knew from then on that the Lord had sent His angels to my house to reassure me and to remind me of His faithfulness.

TRANSFIGURATION

Most people associate transfiguration with what happened on the mountain of transfiguration. However, Jesus Himself described the event as a visionary encounter in which the select disciples were privileged to see His earthly body assume a heavenly transformation.

Transfiguration is when an earthly vessel transforms to take on a temporary heavenly appearance. Thus the Bible speaks of the heavenly appearance that once came upon Jesus, in His humanity, during His earthly ministry.

Transfiguration of Jesus

> *There He was transfigured before them. His face shone like the sun and His clothes became as white as the light. And behold, Moses and Elijah appeared to them talking with Him. ...While he [Peter] was still speaking, behold a bright cloud overshadowed then and suddenly a voice came out of the cloud saying, "This is my beloved Son in whom I am well pleased. Hear*

*Him." Now as they came down from the mountain, **Jesus** commanded them, saying, "Tell the vision to no one until the Son of man is risen from the dead"* (Matthew 17:2-9).

The Transfiguration of Steven

The Bible also describes the remarkable transformation of Steven during his martyrdom.

All who were sitting in the Sanhedrin looked intently at Steven and they saw that his face was like the face of an angel (Acts 6:15).

At this point everyone in the council chamber saw Stephen's face become as radiant as an angel (Acts 6:15 TLB).

CHAPTER TWELVE

SIGNS, WONDERS, AND MIRACLES

DISCERNING THE SOURCE OF STRANGE EVENTS

The Bible says that God will show forth wonders in heavens and signs on earth. However, as mentioned previously, signs and wonders are not seals of divinity. Important considerations:

♦ A *miracle* is an event that appears to be unexplained by the laws of nature and so is held to be supernatural in origin or an act of God.

♦ A *wonder* is defined as that which arouses awe, astonishment, admiration, or something strange.

♦ A *sign* is a pointer, like a signpost, confirming the Word of God and directing man's attention to Christ.

♦ Whether a sign, a wonder, or a miracle, they all transcend the limits of natural logic and may serve to confirm the supernaturalness, supremacy, and sovereignty of God. The Bible says, "How great are His signs; how mighty His wonders!" (Dan. 4:3). In Exodus we are told, "And it shall come to pass, if they will not believe thee, neither hearken to the voice of the first sign, that they will believe the voice of the latter sign" (Exod. 4:8 KJV). From this passage, the inference is that a sign from God has "voice," and clearly God's objective in giving the sign is to speak to us. Though signs are supernatural signals from Heaven, they happen in the natural and are therefore easily missed.

Beware! Satan and His Cohorts Can Do Strange Things

As the Bible says, *"This man of sin will come as Satan's tool, full of satanic power and will trick everyone with strange demonstrations and will do great miracles"* (2 Thess. 2:9 TLB).

So then miracles, signs, and wonders are not always of God. We need to be alert and have a discerning spirit as satan's ability to pretend is probably far beyond human comprehension: *"And no wonder, for Satan himself masquerades as an angel of light"* (2 Cor. 11:14). Also the Bible admonishes us to *"Be of sober spirit, be on the alert. Your adversary, the devil, prowls around like a roaring lion, seeking someone to devour"* (1 Pet. 5:8 NASB).

The Sons of Sceva (Acts 19:11-20)

In this strange occurrence in the Book of Acts concerning the sons of Sceva, the demonic spirits actually physically beat up the sons of Sceva because they lacked the spiritual legal rights to challenge them. In the last days there will be a generation of sons of Sceva mentality. These are those who will profess to walk in apostolic and prophetic anointing but without the legitimate divine authority to back them up.

The Witch of Endor

When Saul saw the Philistine army, he was afraid; terror filled his heart. He inquired of the Lord, but the Lord did not answer him by dreams or Urim or prophets. Saul then said to his attendants, "Find me a woman who is a medium, so that I may go and enquire of her." "There is one in Endor," they said. So Saul disguised himself, putting on other clothes, and at night he and two men went to the woman. "Consult a spirit for me," he said, "and bring up for me the one I name." But the woman said to him, "Surely you know what Saul has done. He has cut off the mediums and spiritists from the land. Why have you set a trap for my life to bring about my death?" Saul swore to her by the Lord, "As surely as the Lord lives, you will not be punished for this." Then the woman asked, "Whom shall I bring up for you?"

"Bring up Samuel," he said. When the woman saw Samuel, she cried out at the top of her voice and said to Saul, "Why have you deceived me? You are Saul!" The king said to her, "Don't be afraid. What do you see?" The woman said, "I see a spirit coming up out of the ground." "What does he look like?" he asked. "An old man wearing a robe is coming up," she said. Then Saul knew it was Samuel, and he bowed down and prostrated himself with his face to the ground. Samuel said to Saul, "Why have you disturbed me by bringing me up?" "I am in great distress," Saul said. "The Philistines are fighting against me, and God has turned away from me. He no longer answers me, either by prophets or by dreams. So I have called on you to tell me what to do." Samuel said, "Why do you consult me, now that the Lord has turned away from you and become your enemy? The Lord has done what he predicted through me. The Lord has torn the kingdom out of your hands and given it to one of your neighbours—to David. Because you did not obey the Lord or carry out his fierce wrath against the Amalekites, the Lord has done this to you today. The Lord will hand over both Israel and you to the Philistines, and tomorrow you and your sons will be with me. The Lord will also hand over the army of Israel to the Philistines" (1 Samuel 28:5-19).

Let us examine the many schools of thoughts on this event:

♦ One school of thought says that the witch of Endor made up the story. In other words she did not actually see Samuel because there is no evidence in the narrative that King Saul himself saw the prophet Samuel.

♦ Another school of thought believes it was not the prophet Samuel who came out but an evil entity.

♦ Yet some from another school believe that God used the opportunity and broke through the occurrence and spoke His divine will. This argument is based on the fact that the witch was surprised to see Samuel come up.

My Thoughts on This Event

The Bible says that the devil had the keys of "Hades and Death" before the death and resurrection of Jesus Christ:

> *In as much then as the children have partaken of flesh and blood, He Himself likewise shared in the same, that through death, He might destroy him who had **the power of death, that is the devil*** (Hebrews 2:14 NKJV).

However, a situational change occurred after the resurrection of Jesus Christ, as implied in the passage in Hebrews 2:14 and also confirmed in the Book of Revelation:

> *I am He who lives, and was dead, and behold, I am alive forevermore. Amen. And **I have the keys of Hades and of Death*** (Revelation 1:18 NKJV).

The *New Spirit Filled Bible Commentary* on the above Bible passage is very helpful:

> *Jesus is now Lord over the realms of life and death. The power of **satanic prerogatives**, because of man's original rebellion is now curbed.*[1]

Satan had the *power of prerogatives* over the realm of the dead before the death and resurrection of Jesus Christ. It is important to remember that death was only instituted after satan instigated Adam and Eve to disobey God. Following this disobedience, man fell from the heightened level of spirituality he enjoyed with God and satan usurped the dominion of the earth from man. Fear and the power of death came upon man. Thus "the prince of the air," satan, gained the dominion of the earth and keys of death temporarily.

It is quite conceivable that satan, who had the keys of the realm of death, could release any "body" held in *captivity of the temporary abode of the realm of the death*. Some people believe that God brought Samuel up during the encounter of Saul and the witch of Endor. But the truth is, at this time, satan still had the keys of death. We also know that God will not violate His Word and by inference the usurped authority of satan.

The temporary abodes of death were *Hades* for the wicked and *Abraham's bosom* for the righteous. Perhaps the body of prophet Samuel was thus released from Abraham's bosom but as in all things God had the ultimate power and prevailed over what the prophet had to say. The prophet Samuel himself found this event unpleasant: "Now Samuel said to Saul, 'Why have you disturbed me by bringing me up?'" (1 Sam. 28:15).

This is reminiscent of how Balaam was compelled to bless Israel contrary to King Balak's evil intention (see Num. 23:1-12). On that occasion, God spoke His infallible words, despite the fact that the whole occasion was initiated at the divination of Balaam. Perhaps it was for this same reason that God did not allow satan to have access and control over Moses' body:

> *But even the archangel Michael, when he was disputing with the devil about the body of Moses did not dare to bring a slanderous accusation against him, but said "The Lord rebuke you"* (Jude 19).

> *And Moses the servant of the Lord died there in Moab, as the Lord had said. He buried him in Moab, in the valley opposite Beth Peor, but to this day* **no one knows where his grave is** (Deuteronomy 34:5-6).

Immediately after the resurrection of Jesus Christ, many righteous people who were dead were released from the temporary abode of the death and they were seen in the city:

> *And Jesus cried out again with a loud voice, and yielded up His spirit. Then behold, the veil of the temple was torn in two from top to bottom; and the earth quaked, and the rocks were split. And the graves were opened; and many bodies of the saints who had fallen asleep were raised; and coming out of the graves after His resurrection. They went into the holy city and appeared to many* (Matthew 27:50-53 NKJV).

It is also noteworthy that the Bible describes the ascension of the righteous, after Jesus had ascended, as leading the captives. This is why the Bible says in the Book of Ephesians, "When He ascended on high, He led captives in His train and gave gifts to men" (Eph. 4:8). These captives referred to those who were being held at the temporary abode of death.

COUNTERFEIT ILLUSIONS AND MANIFESTATIONS

The Lord said to Moses and Aaron, "When Pharaoh says to you, 'Perform a miracle,' then say to Aaron, 'Take your staff and throw it down before Pharaoh,' and it will become a snake." So Moses and Aaron went to Pharaoh and did just as the Lord commanded. Aaron threw his staff down in front of Pharaoh and his officials, and it became a snake. Pharaoh then summoned the wise men and sorcerers, and the Egyptian magicians also did the same things by their secret arts: Each one threw down his staff and it became a snake. But Aaron's staff swallowed up their staffs. Yet Pharaoh's heart became hard and he would not listen to them, just as the Lord had said (Exodus 7:8-13).

In the days of Pharaoh, as in many parts of the world today, the level of delusion was such that magic was allowed to flourish. Magicians are those who through the use of magic can influence or harness powers from gods. By occult art, by operating through illusion, and by demonic powers, they achieved a temporary demonstration of miracles and wonders as they muttered magic formulas and incantations. These miracles can mimic divine miracles. However, only those whose hearts are not yielded to God will become ease prey to this deception.

RECOGNIZING DIVINE STRANGE EVENTS

The first and most important factor that influences whether a person is able or not to recognize a divinely orchestrated strange event, is the state of person's heart. Those whose hearts are not yielded to the truth of Christ are less likely to distinguish divine from satanic strange events: "And in every sort of evil that deceives those who are perishing. They perish because they refused to love the truth and so be saved. For this reason God sends then a powerful delusion so that they will believe the lie" (2 Thess. 2:10-11).

- Divine strange events reveal the glory of God—"This, the first of His miraculous signs, Jesus performed in Cana of Galilee. He thus revealed His glory, and His disciples put their faith in Him" (John 2:11)—but magic miracles and wonders do not, they draw people away from God.

- Divine events draw attention to something God is doing that otherwise might have been missed.

- Divine strange events increase our faith in God and draw us closer to Him as exemplified by what happened to the disciples. "After **He was raised from the dead**, His disciples recalled what He had said. **Then they believed** the Scripture and the words that Jesus had spoken" (John 2:22).

- These divine events establish the authority or the sovereignty of God as illustrated by the demand of the Jews. "Then the Jews demanded of Him, '**What miraculous sign can You show us to prove Your authority** to do all this?'" (John 2:18). On the one hand, magic miracles create fear and binds people to the bonds of the gods and their evil covenants.

- Divine strange events bring people to the knowledge of God; the apostle Paul says, "I will not venture to speak of anything except what Christ has accomplished through me in leading the Gentiles to obey God by what I have said and done—**by the power of signs and miracles, through the power of the Spirit**. So from Jerusalem all the way round to Illyricum, I have fully proclaimed the gospel of Christ" (Rom. 15:18-19).

- They draw people to the majesty of God.

- They exalt the name of God.

- They bring reverence to God.

- They bring reassurance of the character of God; love, kindness, compassion, mercy, and forgiveness.

- Divine strange events are often a one-time occurrence, divinely made for the particular situation.

- The focus is never on the human being even though the divine strange happening may be distinctively associated with the person; for example, the healing power of God in the crusade of an evangelist associated with healing anointing may manifest even before the evangelist arrives at the crusade arena.

THE RETURN OF SPIRITUAL "URIM AND THUMMIM"

God's Signs Accompanied by the Word of Knowledge

I have met some people who are especially gifted in the ability to see into the spirit realm and discern signs, often in the form of "lights" accompanied by a word of knowledge. Because of the instant word of knowledge, these people are often able to immediately interpret these signs. Therefore I feel the main purpose of this emerging special group of spiritual watchmen is discernment for quick determination of the mind of God on urgent matters such as Urim and Thummim were in the olden days.

Urim is derived from the Hebrew word meaning light, flame, shine daybreak or fire. *Thummim* is from the Hebrew word meaning true knowledge, perfection or perfect knowledge or complete truth. These were two gemstones that Moses was inspired to place in the pocket formed by the joining of Ephod and the "breastplate of judgment":

> *Then Moses brought Aaron and his sons forward and washed them with water. He put the tunic on Aaron, tied the sash around him, clothed him with the robe and put the ephod on him. He also tied the ephod to him by its skillfully woven waistband; so it was fastened on him. He placed the breastpiece on him and put the Urim and Thummim in the breastpiece* (Leviticus 8:6-8).

The pocket was part of the priestly garment that Aaron, the high priest, worn when going into the Holy of Holies:

> ...*connecting it to the waistband, so that the breastpiece will not swing out from the ephod. "Whenever Aaron enters the Holy Place, he will bear the names of the sons of Israel over his heart on the breastpiece of decision as a continuing memorial before the Lord. Also put the Urim and the Thummim in the breastpiece, so they may be over Aaron's heart whenever he enters the presence of the Lord. Thus Aaron will always bear the means of making decisions for the Israelites over his heart before the Lord* (Exodus 28:28-30).

Urim and Thummim symbolized the belief that God would reveal His true judgment on the issue and also expresses the confidence of the people that God would bring perfect knowledge or true judgment. That is why the breastplate was called the breastplate of judgment. The exact description of Urim and Thummim was probably lost in antiquity, but they were stones thought to be marked in some way that enabled the high priest to determine God's yes or no on urgent matters. Nobody knows how exactly the stones were used; perhaps they were drawn from the pocket to determine God's will or answer. Most likely one stone indicated yes and the other no, and whichever one the priest pulled out is taken to mean a direct answer from God.

Why are lights significant? Because light is contrary to everything the devil stands for. The devil is darkness, and darkness is the absence of light. The Bible says Jesus Christ is the light of this world: "I am the Light of the world. Whoever follows Me will never walk in darkness but will have the light of life" (John 8:12); and that God is the Father of lights: "Every good gift and every perfect gift is from above, and comes down from the Father of lights, who does not change like shifting shadows" (James 1:17); and that we are the children of light (see Eph. 5:8-11).

Why perfect knowledge? Because satan will increase the level of falsehood and amount of counterfeit words of knowledge in the last days. The devil is the father of lies, and when he speaks lies, he speaks his native language and the truth is not in him. The devil is a liar (see

John 8:44) and his strategy is to deceive people (see 2 Cor. 11:3-4). God is releasing spiritual Thummim (true knowledge) from His throne to overcome this onslaught from the devil.

Word of knowledge is the ability to know something by supernatural means that is beyond human mind and reasoning: "But the manifestation of the Spirit is given to each one for the profit of all; for one is given the word of wisdom through the Spirit, to another the word of knowledge through the same Spirit" (1 Cor. 12:7-8 NKJV). As Paul mentions, the Holy Spirit helps the believer detect counterfeit words of knowledge when he encounters one (see Acts 16:16).

Perfect knowledge or word of knowledge should be coupled with the word of wisdom to make the revelation relevant to the real-life situation. So the word of knowledge should come with word of wisdom to ensure its relevant application.

The word of wisdom is the wisdom of God made relevant or applicable for a given situation. The word of wisdom is not resident on any person but it is an instantaneous expression of the spirit of wisdom that springs up at the time of need. The word of wisdom is an offshoot of the indwelling spiritual wisdom (wisdom from the On High) in the person. I believe the Bible refers to the expression of the word of wisdom when Jesus says, "But make your mind not to worry beforehand how you defend yourselves. For I will give you words and wisdom that none of your adversaries will be able to resist or contradict" (Luke 21:14-15).

The need for precision and accuracy in the things of the spirit is increasing exponentially. The era of trial and error can no longer stand the test of time as the magnitude and deceptiveness of satan increase in these last days.

When signs from God are accompanied by a word of knowledge, it can facilitate a quick determination of the will of God in urgent issues. But when signs are actually accompanied by explanatory word of knowledge and wisdom, it takes the process to new high in speed and finality. Discerning of signs is important in our walk with God.

The Bible says in the Book of Acts:

In the last days, God says, I will pour out my Spirit on all people. Your sons and daughters will prophesy, your young men will see visions, your old men will dream dreams. Even on my servants, both men and women, I will pour out my Spirit in those days, and they will prophesy. I will show wonders in the heaven above and signs on the earth below, blood and fire and billows of smoke. The sun will be turned to darkness and the moon to blood before the coming of the great and glorious day of the Lord (Acts 2:17-20).

Wonders in Heaven will be mirrored on earth by divine signs. Just as dreams, visions, and prophecy will be on the increase in the last days, so will signs or the ability to discern divine signs increase. Signs are things or occurrences that draw our attention to what is happening that we might otherwise have missed. God is releasing signs that are to help us judge and to lead us to the resolution of urgent matters in the Kingdom of God. God gives these special signs in parallel to the wonders in Heaven; perhaps that is why wonders and signs are often mentioned together in the Bible.

"The return of Urim and Thummim," so to say, will not be the physical stones as in the olden days but will come in the form of the ability to determine the will of God on urgent matters. The cardinal features of this gifting will be the discerning signs, especially lights (symbolized by Urim in olden days), accompanied with the manifestation of the word of wisdom and word of knowledge (symbolized by Thummim in the olden days). Other signs may often manifest in the midst of these but usually not without the background of these features. These other signs include discerning of various types of sounds and trances.

Essentially this gifting involves a quickening of the Holy Spirit in a form of divine enablement that allows the gifted person to determine the will of God, particularly in deciding between two options, such as whether or not to or whether it is godly or of the devil.

In the Old Testament, Urim (light) and Thummim (perfect knowledge) were used for determining the will of God in urgent situations when decisions needed to be made swiftly: "He is to stand before Eleazar the priest, who will obtain decisions for him by inquiring of the Urim before the Lord. At his command he and the entire community of the Israelites will go out, and at his command they will come in" (Num. 27:21).

Now in the dispensation of the Holy Spirit, the emerging use of signs manifested by the light of God (Urim) accompanied by the word of wisdom and of knowledge (Thummim) will take a leading role to guide us in urgent matters that require the need to know the will of God. The Bible says of King Saul in his darkest days of reign that he needed to know the will of God about going to war: "When Saul saw the Philistine army, he was afraid; terror filled his heart. He inquired of the Lord, but the Lord did not answer him by **dreams or Urim or prophets**" (1 Sam. 28:5-6). In the Old Testament, the priestly anointing was distinctively separate from the prophetic ministry. Urim and Thummim probably constitute the only official and accepted prophetic role for the Old Testament priests.

In the Old Testament, Moses recommended that Urim and Thummim should be symbolically placed close to Aaron's heart maybe to indicate a heart connection with God. In the same way, the Holy Spirit wells up in the saints of God—"but whoever drinks the water I give him will never thirst. Indeed, the water I give him will become in him a spring of water welling up to eternal life" (John 4:14)—and may express Himself through signs accompanied by the word of knowledge: "And there are diversities of activities, but it is the same God who work all in all. But the manifestation of the Spirit is given to each one for the profit of all: for to one is given the word of wisdom through the Spirit, to another the word of knowledge through the same Spirit" (1 Cor. 12:6-8 NKJV). Therefore, a heart connection with God is essential for the operation of these signs (lights and perfect knowledge).

As in the olden days, a background of holiness and righteousness is important for the recipient of such a gift and he should be a person chosen, favored, and consecrated unto God: "About Levi he said: 'Your Thummim and Urim belong to the man you favored. You tested him at Massah; you contended with him at the waters of Meribah'" (Deut. 33:8).

In general, events, types, and symbols in the Old Testament are often shadows of the things to come in the dispensation of the Holy Spirit. Without the indwelling of the Holy Spirit, men of old were carried or propelled along as the Spirit of God occasionally came upon them. Therefore in some urgent determination of the will of God, they had to rely on physical means with the hope that it would be backed up by God. Hence they cast lots at their period of uncertainty, a method used in the Old Testament to discern God's will. However, after the Pentecost, the believers now rely directly on the Holy Spirit for guidance.

Our time is different because the Holy Spirit dwells in us at all times and our spirits bear witness with the Spirit of God that we are the children of God (see Rom. 8:16). And also "as many as are led by the Spirit of God they are the sons of God" (Rom. 8:14 NKJV).

We see the operation of signs from Heaven accompanied by the word of knowledge in the ministry of Jesus Christ on earth: "Then John gave this testimony: '**I saw the Spirit come down from heaven as a dove [sign]** and remain on Him. I would not have known Him, except that **the One who sent me to baptize with water told me [word of knowledge]**, The man on whom you see the Spirit come down and remain is He who will baptize with the Holy Spirit.' I have seen and I testify that this is the Son of God" (John 1:32-34).

ENDNOTE

1. Thomas Nelson Bible, 2002, 1818.

Conclusion

In conclusion, I would like to borrow a leaf from one of the greatest watchmen that ever existed in the Body of Christ—the apostle Paul. Writing from his lonely abandonment in jail, Paul reflects as life closes up on him. He writes in the first epistle to the Thessalonians words of edification, exhortation, and comforting in more than five places:

> *For our exhortation did not come from error or uncleanness nor was it in deceit* (1 Thessalonians 2:3 NKJV).

> *As you know how we exhorted and comforted and charged everyone of you as father does his own children* (1 Thessalonians 2:11 NKJV).

> *Therefore comfort one another with these words* (1 Thessalonians 4:18 NKJV).

> *Therefore comfort each other and edify one another just as you also are doing* (1 Thessalonians 5:11).

> *Now we exhort you brethren, warn those who are unruly, comfort the fainthearted, uphold the weak, be patient with all* (1 Thessalonians 5:14).

Why did Paul go this length to underpin the importance of edification, exhortation, and comforting? The answer is found in an earlier part of the letter. As a watchman, Paul foresaw danger looming over the Thessalonians: "**...lest by some means the tempter had tempted you, and our labor might be in vain**" (1 Thess. 3:5).

Edification, exhortation, and comforting are essential pillars of an effective watchman ministry. Unfortunately, for the most part the watchman anointing has been narrowed down to "warn-them ministry" without these other essential features. Change is inevitable if we are to realize the full power of this valuable ministry and bring it to its crucial relevance in this century.

The watchmen should move in edification, exhortation, and comforting in a new and fresh way. The twenty-first-century watchman ministries need to have a widened perspective. It is time that the conservative, narrow, and restricted perspectives of the watchman's ministry break out into the reality of its great potentials, values, and visions.

The Bible says the key components of prophecy involve edification, comforting, and exhortation. I believe that these components have essential roles in the watchman's ministry. Let us examine how these factors play out in the ministry of the watchman.

EDIFICATION

Edification entails identifying a weakness and helping to build up that area. For the most part this is an essential function of the watchman. The watchman should carry a reasonable burden for intercession. This is an inevitable consequence of the prophetic privilege inherent in the watchman's ministry. In time past, the watchman ministry has by and large been restricted to these functions: to identify dangers, to intercede for the identified danger, and to warn the people concerned.

Edification is a basic rule of life for corporate existence. It is the process by which one helps to build or strengthen an area identified mostly by revelation. Therefore, there is a twofold expression of this process. First, to be able to peep beyond the surface or the natural realm into the supernatural sphere and prophetically identify any area in a person or group of people or in an institution that is weak. Second, to help in strengthening that area so that it meets what is required of it. This is one of the roles of a watchman's ministry.

Edification involves the following steps:

1. Identification of the area of weakness. Either spontaneously revealed by God or by the prophet intentionally, asking God to reveal the area that needs building up.

2. Asking God to give His divine instruction and details of the nature of the weakness.

3. Determining the nature of God that would be opposite to the weakness identified.

4. Asking God for Scripture that would help strengthen the person, group of people, or church in that nature of the weakness.

5. Praying that God would give the follow-up instructions that would nurture the person, group, or church in that area of weakness after the initial building up.

6. By prayerfully considering the level of elevation that God would want the person, group, or church to attain after the strengthening or restoration.

> *"But you, O Israel, my servant, Jacob, whom I have chosen, you descendants of Abraham my friend, I took you from the ends of the earth, from its farthest corners I called you. I said, 'You are my servant'; I have chosen you and have not rejected you. So do not fear, for I am with you; do not be dismayed, for I am your God. I will strengthen you and help you; I will uphold you with my righteous right hand. All who rage against you will surely be ashamed and disgraced; those who oppose you will be as nothing and perish. Though you search for your enemies, you will not find them. Those who wage war against you will be as nothing at all. For I am the Lord, your God, who takes hold of your right hand and says to you, Do not fear; I will help you. Do not be afraid, O worm Jacob, O little Israel, for I myself will help you," declares the Lord, your Redeemer, the Holy One of Israel. "See, I will make you into a threshing sledge, new and sharp, with many teeth. You will thresh the mountains and crush them, and reduce the hills to chaff"* (Isaiah 41:8-15).

EXHORTATION

Besides edification, the watchman should tap into the principles of exhortation. *Exhortation* involves turning the people in the direction of God to a place where the power of God is deliberately celebrated, no matter what, rather than pay undue attention to the magnitude of the onslaught of the enemy. The Bible is full of instances of this principle in action, and the prophet Ezekiel, the watchman of Israel, applied the principles of exhortation at a critical moment in the history of Israel:

> *"This is what the Sovereign Lord says: The enemy said of you, 'Aha! The ancient heights have become our possession.'"* ...*"'But you, O mountains of Israel, will produce branches and fruit for my people Israel, for they will soon come home. I am concerned for you and will look on you with favor; you will be ploughed and sown, and I will multiply the number of people upon you, even the whole house of Israel. The towns will be inhabited and the ruins rebuilt'"* (Ezekiel 36:2, 8-10).

The watchman should be cognizant of the various steps of exhortation as he engages them in his ministry:

- ◆ *Commendation.* Commending the people to God by entreating them. This step means commending people to the all sufficiency of God's nature. Terms such as "I urge you"; "I entreat you"; and "I encourage you" are phrases used for this purpose in the Bible.

> ***Therefore, I urge you, brothers, in view of God's mercy,*** *to offer your bodies as living sacrifices, holy and pleasing to God— this is your spiritual act of worship. Do not conform any longer to the pattern of this world, but be transformed by the renewing of your mind. Then you will be able to test and approve what God's will is—His good, pleasing and perfect will* (Romans 12:1-2).

> *I plead with Euodia and I plead with Syntyche to agree with each other in the Lord. Yes, and I ask you, loyal*

yokefellow, help these women who have contended at my side in the cause of the gospel, along with Clement and the rest of my fellow workers, whose names are in the book of life (Philippians 4:2-3).

*By the meekness and gentleness of Christ, **I appeal to you**—I, Paul, who am "timid" when face to face with you, but "bold" when away! I beg you that when I come I may not have to be as bold as I expect to be toward some people who think that we live by the standards of this world. For though we live in the world, we do not wage war as the world does. The weapons we fight with are not the weapons of the world. On the contrary, they have divine power to demolish strongholds. We demolish arguments and every pretension that sets itself up against the knowledge of God, and we take captive every thought to make it obedient to Christ* (2 Corinthians 10:1-5).

- *Persuasion.* This is consistently persuading people to see things from God's perspectives and, if necessary, to repeat the prophetic promise.

- *Admonishment.* This is to call the people from a place that is not good to a place of righteousness or a place where God would want them to be. Admonishment is also to warn the people to move away from stagnation and toward a fresh relationship with God. People need to move into a place of increased sensitivity to the Holy Spirit, a place where they can hear the gentle, continual discipline or warning of God. The watchman should avoid judgment. Admonishing should be followed by inspiration so that stimulation or motivation can occur. Admonishing without inspiration is judgment.

In general, exhortation creates an impetus for motivation. This is amply exemplified by the speech given by the apostle Peter in the Book of Acts:

"Therefore let all Israel be assured of this: God has made this Jesus, whom you crucified, both Lord and Christ." When the people heard this, they were cut to the heart and said to Peter and the other apostles, "Brothers, what shall we do?" Peter replied, "Repent and be baptized, every one of you, in the name of Jesus Christ for the forgiveness of your sins. And you will receive the gift of the Holy Spirit. The promise is for you and your children and for all who are far off—for all whom the Lord our God will call." With many other words he warned them; and he pleaded with them, "Save yourselves from this corrupt generation." Those who accepted his message were baptized, and about three thousand were added to their number that day (Acts 2:36-41).

In addition to edification and exhortation, the watchman should be conversant with how to bring people to a place of comfort and peace in times of trouble.

COMFORT

♦ *Comforting* is about calming people down, so that they retreat into the spirit to find peace and obtain divine strategy to face the challenges. Again let us look at how Ezekiel applied this in his ministry:

*"Therefore prophesy concerning the land of Israel and say to the mountains and hills, to the ravines and valleys: 'This is what the Sovereign Lord says: I speak in my jealous wrath because you have suffered the scorn of the nations. Therefore this is what the Sovereign Lord says: I swear with uplifted hand that **the nations around you will also suffer scorn. But you, O mountains of Israel, will produce branches and fruit for my people Israel, for they will soon come home. I am concerned for you and will look on you with favor; you will be ploughed and sown, and I will multiply the number of people upon you, even the whole house of Israel. The towns will be inhabited and the ruins rebuilt. I will increase the number of men and***

animals upon you, and they will be fruitful and become numerous. I will settle people on you as in the past and will make you prosper more than before. Then you will know that I am the Lord. I will cause people, my people Israel, to walk upon you. They will possess you, and you will be their inheritance; you will never again deprive them of their children. This is what the Sovereign Lord says: Because people say to you, "You devour men and deprive your nation of its children"' (Ezekiel 36:6-13).

The key steps in comforting are:

◆ Distributing a measure of peace to the people.

◆ Enabling them to avoid worrying.

◆ Encouraging them to practice calmness in the midst of trouble.

◆ Teaching them to have absolute dependency on the majesty of God.

◆ Strengthening them to reenforce the power of God.

◆ Praying them into a place of security in God.

The prophet Jahaziel comforted Israel in a moment of utter despair and hopelessness. He saw beyond the prevailing circumstance and peeped into the spirit realm to see the arm of Lord, the God of their salvation fighting their battle. This is what he said:

*All the men of Judah, with their wives and children and little ones, stood there before the Lord. Then the Spirit of the Lord came upon Jahaziel son of Zechariah, the son of Benaiah, the son of Jeiel, the son of Mattaniah, a Levite and descendant of Asaph, as he stood in the assembly. He said: "Listen, King Jehoshaphat and all who live in Judah and Jerusalem! **This is what the Lord says to you: 'Do not be afraid or discouraged because of this vast army. For the battle is not yours, but God's.** Tomorrow march down against them. They will be climbing up by* *the Pass of Ziz, and you will find them at the end of the gorge in the Desert of Jeruel. You will not have to fight this battle. Take up your positions; stand firm and see the deliverance the Lord will give you, O Judah and Jerusalem. Do not be afraid; do not be discouraged. Go out to face them tomorrow, and the Lord will be with you."' Jehoshaphat bowed with his face to the ground, and all the people of Judah and Jerusalem fell down in worship before the Lord* (2 Chronicles 20:13-18).

In the words of the apostle Paul: "Rejoice in the Lord always. I will say it again: Rejoice! Let your gentleness be evident to all. The Lord is near. **Do not be anxious about anything, but in everything, by prayer and petition, with thanksgiving, present your requests to God. And the peace of God, which transcends all understanding, will guard your hearts and your minds in Christ Jesus.** Finally, brothers, whatever is true, whatever is noble, whatever is right, whatever is pure, whatever is lovely, whatever is admirable—if anything is ex-cellent or praiseworthy—think about such things. Whatever you have learned or received or heard from me, or seen in me—put it into practice. And the God of peace will be with you" (Phil. 4:4-9). These words are comforting in whatever circumstance you may find yourself.

When a watchman operates these pivotal components, his ministry will shift from a predominantly warn-them ministry to its full potential in Christ Jesus. I hope as you have read this book that you now know who you really are as a watchman, your nature and how to administer the grace of your giftedness, and even the kindness of the Giver of the gift in a new way. As the Bible says, "The people who know their God shall be strong and carry out great exploits" (Dan. 11:32).

GLOSSARY OF TERMS

Adept in understanding the mysteries of God. To be highly skilled and proficient in understanding the hidden things of God.

Angelic interactions. The appearance and involvement of angels in spiritual experiences.

Apparition. A visionary encounter in which the visionary encounter has become perceptible with the natural eyes.

Celestial expanse. The invisible realm of the heavens.

Church. The word *church* means belonging to the Lord. The local church is thus the tribe of Jesus, called out of all tribes and nations. Church (uppercase *c*) also means the global Body of Christ.

Concerted approach. An organized and joint method, or the way that is mutually contrived.

Corrupt wisdom. Wisdom originating from God that has become perverted.

Counterfeit watchman. One who has capacity to watch in the spirit but is powered by the evil spirit.

Dark speeches and mysteries of God. The things of God that have hidden meaning and, unless unfolded by God, the human mind on its own cannot grasp the true and complete perspective.

Distinguishing feature. That which sets something apart from others and helps identify it.

Divine messenger. God's messenger sent to bring a message or perform an assignment on earth.

Dreamer of dreams. The people who are also called high-volume dreamers.

Elevated spiritual position. A pedestal in the spirit realm that is high up and enables the occupant to see far in the spirit.

Errors of presumption. Mistakes as a result of assuming the knowledge of something without first ascertaining its truthfulness.

Farmer's vocabulary. The limits and capacity of the farmer reservoir of vocabulary.

General misconception. Widespread belief that is based on falsity or wrong premises.

Gift of intercession. The burden to pray for another given by God.

Heavenly places. The realm of the spirit that is invisible to the naked eyes.

Heavenly realm. That which pertains to the spirit sphere.

High-volume dreamers. High-volume dreamers are those dreamers who dream two or more dreams most nights on a consistent basis.

Human spirit. The immaterial part of man that originates from the breath of God; it will return back to God when the human body dies.

Idolatry in the temple. The worship of other gods within the temple of the living God.

Interactive dream. A dream in which the dreamer experiences direct exchange with God.

Intercessor. One who has been gifted by God to carry the burden to pray for others.

Interpret riddles, enigmas, and knotty situations. To bring elucidations, the puzzles, difficult, and not easily understood things of God.

Judgment Throne Room. The part of the throne room of God that is used for judgment or courtlike audiences.

Ministry of the watchman. The call, anointing, and manifestation of the gifting of spiritual watchfulness.

Nabi prophet. The nabi (meaning *spokesman*) prophet receives mainly by hearing things in the spirit realm. Nabi prophets receive by inspiration of the Spirit of God, and their utterances are propelled by faith.

Paranoia. A delusion that one is being persecuted, or excessive fear or distrust of people or situations, or exaggerated sense of one's importance.

Period of silence. A period of lack of the ability to speak, or a period when God is not releasing revelation to the person.

Pictorial revelations. Revelations in dreams or visions that come in picture form.

Preincarnate appearance of Jesus. The appearance of Jesus Christ before His earthly ministry.

Prophetic pitfall. A danger in the operation of the prophetic gifting that is not easily anticipated or may be difficult to see ahead of time or avoided.

Prophetic privilege of intercession. Using the privilege of the benefits of the revelations received to intercede on behalf of others.

Receive revelation, capacity for. The ability of the person to receive revelation which is predicated on the person's giftedness and the personal relationship with God.

Receptive seer's dimension. The aspect of the seer's anointing that deals with the capacity to receive, reflect on, and process revelations.

Retained consciousness. The degree of awareness of one's real identity or one's natural standing during the dream or vision encounter.

Right-standing with God. Doing what is right and in line with God's rules, or righteousness before God.

Scope of reception, increase. To widen one's range and the reach of one's revelation.

Second heaven. The part of celestial expanse that is invisible and occupies the interface between the first and the third heaven. It is the zone of conflict between the evil and righteous agents.

Seer. Those gifted with visions and dreams and other forms of picture revelations on a consistent basis and operate mainly from the receptive dimension of the prophetic ministry. Seers are those whose eyes have been divinely unveiled to see and understand things that are not open to the ordinary person.

Seer's anointing. The powerful expression of the gift of the Holy Spirit in the person that enables the person to function as a seer.

Seer's unique message. This means each seer's anointing is expressed from the background of their character and cultural disposition.

Sentiment. Thought which originates from emotion, mostly not spiritual.

Sovereignty and supremacy of God. The power and self-governing nature of God's rulership.

Sphere of influence. The degree of being able to impart to others.

Spiritual cockiness. To be proud or arrogant because of what God is doing in one's life.

Spiritual strategist. One who is able to plan wisely and effectively in the spirit realm with good results.

Spirits against a local church. Spirits that come against the local church originating from the devil.

Spirits against the watchmen. The contrary spirits that are against the watchman's anointing and function.

Strange spiritual experiences. Occurrences that are curious, extraordinary, unique, unnatural, bizarre, or mysterious.

Strength of the human spirit. The capacity of the human spirit to bear witness with the Spirit of God.

Strong country language. A language that is characteristic of country people.

Sun worship. The worship of the sun as a god.

Temporal appearance of angel. When an angel assumes a body to enable it to relate to this world or time.

Third heaven. The abode of God and the future home of believers.

Translation. The act of moving from one place to another, particularly in the spirit.

Vision, long and vivid. A long and clear vision or dream.

Warfare, ineffective and sometimes unnecessary. Engaging in warfare that is not in line with the will of God and therefore not backed up by the Spirit of God.

Warn, near-compulsive urge. A sometimes inbuilt drive to give messages with woes and lamentations.

Watchman's report, often full of woes, laments, and sadness. The inherent tendency of the watchman to warn people of impending danger and that failure to avert the danger will result in dire consequences.

THE SECOND BOOK

THE ILLUSTRATED BIBLE BASED
DICTIONARY
OF
DREAM
SYMBOLS

HOW TO UNDERSTAND THE
LANGUAGE OF THE WATCHMAN

PART I

Symbols

CHAPTER ONE

INTRODUCTION TO SYMBOLS

A symbol is an image that stands for something in addition to its literal meaning. It therefore has more meaning than just its simple literal meaning on its own in the natural run of things. In practical terms, symbols are things that represent or stand for something else, or are used to typify something else, either by association, resemblance, or convention.A symbol can also mean a material object used to represent something invisible, such as an idea (e.g., the dove as a symbol of peace).

HOW SYMBOLS DERIVE THEIR MEANING

A message that is given in symbols automatically switches your thinking to symbolism. Every parable needs to be symbolically interpreted and the meaning should be drawn for each symbol. (A parable language is when symbols are used to represent things.) Symbols are not real entities; they are simply representations of the real entities. The meaning of a symbol is drawn first of all from the reservoir of the Word of God, then from the inherent meaning of the symbol or its association to the dreamer's experience, or from the culture and colloquial expressions in society.

In general terms, interpretation is the deciphering of a parable language that involves:

- Bringing meaning to the symbols in the dream and then gaining understanding of the message in the dream. Deriving the meanings for symbols should first of all be hinged on the Word of God; this process also brings understanding to the symbolic actions in the dream.

- Expounding on the relevance of the symbols and the message of the dream to the dreamer's life circumstance. Exposition is bringing understanding to the symbols and events as they relate to the dreamer's personal experience. Exposition centers on the dreamer's experience.

- The deriving of the meaning for the symbols and the exposition must go together to truly interpret a dream or vision.Therefore, the true and complete interpretation must incorporate the two phases as well as be drawn in the following order:
  * The Scriptures.
  * The inherent meaning of the symbol.
  * The dreamer's personal experience.
  * The social influences of the dreamer (the culture and the colloquial expressions the dreamer is used to).

A symbol does not mean the same thing all the time and therefore the meaning of a symbol must be drawn for each dream. Remember, the true meaning of a symbol in a dream does not come from human reasoning or intellectualism, but by allowing the meaning to flow into our hearts or subconscious mind from the Holy Spirit.This inflow into our hearts occurs by being quiet and still in the inner being.The choice of symbols in the dream is very specific and purposeful, and it is the prerogative of God. A dream is therefore the truest representation of the situation because it is God's perspective of it; a dream addresses the issue more frankly than human illustration.

Why God Uses Symbols

- They help us to see the real thing from God's perspective because the symbol shows God's thinking.
- Striking features of symbols help the impartation and interpretation.

- The hidden meaning of the symbol allows God to clarify things in stages.

- Humility is the key, as it increases your dependence on the Holy Spirit. *"To keep me from becoming conceited **because of these surpassingly great revelations,** there was given me a thorn in my flesh, a messenger of satan, to torment me. Three times I pleaded with the Lord to take it away from me. But He said to me, 'My grace is sufficient for you, for My power is made perfect in weakness.' Therefore I will boast all the more gladly about my weaknesses, so that Christ's power may rest on me"* (2 Corinthians 12:7-9, emphasis added).

- The Lord will relate to a person in symbolism that has meaning to him/her. Dreams are a form of communication, an intimate language between the dreamer and the Lord.

- They secure the message from the enemies.

- They make you want to search out the meaning.

- The language of symbols is deep and powerful; at the same time it's the most elementary language of men and therefore available to all ages.

- The human mind understands or reads in pictures.

CHAPTER TWO

UNDERSTANDING THE LANGUAGE OF SYMBOLS

(THE LANGUAGE OF THE SPIRIT)

The language of the spirit is the language of symbolism and no other book speaks in symbols more than the Bible. Symbolism is also the language of dreams and in several ways the language pattern in dreams is akin to the pattern of speech used in the Bible. Some people have described the Old Testament as the New Testament concealed because of the extensive use of symbolism.

The language of reason is limited whereas the language of symbols is infinite. Though a symbol may be identified by one word, it may also take volumes to be comprehensively described. There is great depth and power to the language of symbols and symbolic actions. As the saying goes, a picture is worth a thousand words. Children learn the language of pictures and symbols before they learn the language of words and reason. Man thinks and processes information in pictures.

God Himself described His pattern of speech to the prophets in Numbers:

He said, "Listen to My words: When a prophet of the Lord is among you, I reveal Myself to him in visions, I speak to him in dreams. But this is not true of My servant Moses; he is faithful in all My house. With him I speak face to face, clearly and not in riddles; he sees the form of the Lord. Why then were you not afraid to speak against My servant Moses?" (Numbers 12:6-8)

Key points from the above passage are:

- God does not speak to everyone the same way.
- He speaks in dreams and visions.
- He speaks in clear language.
- He speaks in riddles or parables.
- He speaks in dark speeches.
- He speaks in similitude.

He is God; therefore, He may choose how He speaks to us.

Jesus Christ revealed the secrets of the Kingdom of God only to the disciples and He also explained why He spoke and taught in parables:

> The disciples came to Him and asked, "Why do You speak to the people in parables?" He replied, "The knowledge of the secrets of the kingdom of heaven has been given to you, but not to them. Whoever has will be given more, and he will have abundance. Whoever does not have, even what he has will be taken from him. This is why I speak to them in parables: 'Though seeing, they do not see; though hearing, they do not hear or understand' " (Matthew 13:10-13).

Notice from the passage that parables were available to all people. Just as it was in those days the parable language of God (dreams) is available to everyone today, but the heathen will "see and hear" without gaining understanding of the dreams.

Jesus taught in parables and used symbols to illustrate His message:

> With many similar parables Jesus spoke the word to them, as much as they could understand. **He did not say anything to them without using a parable.** But when He was alone with His own disciples, He explained everything (Mark 4:33-34, emphasis added).

Jesus also described the role of the Holy Spirit in the understanding of what God says; that is, the Holy Spirit will explain the dark speeches, similitude, and parables of God to us (see Jn. 14:25-27).

Let us look at this passage and the wisdom keys inherent in them:

All this I have spoken while still with you. But the Counselor, the Holy Spirit, whom the Father will send in My name, will teach you all things and will remind you of everything I have said to you. Peace I leave with you; My peace I give you. I do not give to you as the world gives. Do not let your hearts be troubled and do not be afraid (John 14:25-27).

From this passage it is clear to see that the Holy Spirit helps us by explaining parable language to us; without this, we will be unable to understand the mind of God on the issue.

CHAPTER THREE

THE POWER OF THE
LANGUAGE OF SYMBOLS

Those who have understood the tremendous power of symbols have gained incredible insight into the mysteries of God, because God's ways are wrapped up in the language of symbolism. Human beings think in pictures and people need visual appreciation in order to grasp the essence of a concept. Symbols evoke powerful emotion and elicit strong passion; from generation to generation, politicians, philosophers, and religious leaders have used them to illustrate their points. For example, national commitment is symbolized in the pride and honor that is accorded to the national symbol in the form of a flag. Many would be outraged to see their flag dishonored, and public hatred is often demonstrated by the burning of an enemy's national flag.

DAVID—A BIBLICAL EXAMPLE

Symbolism brought the seriousness of David's adulterous act to him. Nathan's message to King David could have easily been a perfect setting for the plotting of a dream and God could have chosen to send King David the same message through a dream. Nathan narrated the message to David in a dream format, in parable, to bring home the gravity of the sin.

The Lord sent Nathan to David. When he came to him, he said, "There were two men in a certain town, one rich and the other poor. The rich man had a very large number of sheep and cattle, but the poor man had nothing except one little ewe lamb he had bought. He raised it, and it grew up with him and his children. It shared his food, drank from his cup and even slept in his arms. It was like a daughter to him. Now a traveler came to the rich man, but the rich man refrained from taking one of his own sheep or cattle to prepare a meal for the traveler who had come to him. Instead, he took the ewe lamb that belonged to the poor man and prepared it for the one who had come to him." David burned with anger against the man and said to Nathan, "As surely as the Lord lives, the man who did this deserves to die! He must pay for that lamb four times over, because he did such a thing and had no pity." Then Nathan said to David, "You are the man! This is what the Lord, the God of Israel, says: 'I anointed you king over Israel, and I delivered you from the hand of Saul. I gave your master's house to you, and your master's wives into your arms. I gave you the house of Israel and Judah. And if all this had been too little, I would have given you even more. Why did you despise the word of the Lord by doing what is evil in His eyes? You struck down Uriah the Hittite with the sword and took his wife to be your own. You killed him with the sword of the Ammonites'" (2 Samuel 12:1-9).

ANATOMY OF NATHAN'S STATEMENT TO DAVID

SYMBOL / ACTION	MEANING	THE POWER OF IMAGERY
Rich man.	David.	Important personality
Poor man.	Uriah.	A person who is vulnerable because he lacks the necessities of life.
Little ewe, like a daughter.	Uriah's wife—precious to him.	Something precious to the dreamer.
Arrival of traveler.	A need arises.	A potential need is imminent or at hand.
Refrain from using his own.	Selfishness.	Spirit of self-centeredness, or inconsiderate of others.
David's anger burned against the injustice of the man in Nathan's story.	Then David came to a realization that the sin was his, therefore realizing the true gravity of the sin.	Holy anger stirred by spirit of righteousness or coming to one's senses after a period of attack of carnality.

CHAPTER FOUR

HOW TO DERIVE MEANING FROM PARABLE LANGUAGE

THE PARABLE OF THE SOWER

Then He told them many things in parables, saying:"A farmer went out to sow his seed. As he was scattering the seed, some fell along the path, and the birds came and ate it up. Some fell on rocky places, where it did not have much soil. It sprang up quickly, because the soil was shallow. But when the sun came up, the plants were scorched, and they withered because they had no root. Other seed fell among thorns, which grew up and choked the plants. Still other seed fell on good soil, where it produced a crop—a hundred, sixty or thirty times what was sown. He who has ears, let him hear" (Matthew 13:3-9).

THE INTERPRETATION

Listen then to what the parable of the sower means: When anyone hears the message about the kingdom and does not understand it, the evil one comes and snatches away what was sown in his heart. This is the seed sown along the path. The one who received the seed that fell on rocky places is the man who hears the word and at once receives it with joy. But since he has no root, he lasts only a short time. When trouble or persecution comes because of the word, he quickly falls away. The one who received the seed that fell among the thorns is the man who hears the word, but the worries of this life and the deceitfulness of wealth choke it, making it unfruitful.

213

But the one who received the seed that fell on good soil is the man who hears the word and understands it. He produces a crop, yielding a hundred, sixty or thirty times what was sown (Matthew 13:18-23).

THE ANATOMY OF THE PARABLE OF THE SOWER

SYMBOL	MEANING	DERIVED DREAM SYMBOL
Seed.	Word of God.	Word of God; God's promises, (something capable of multiplication).
Soil.	Heart of Man.	Potential for multiplication, either good or bad; the essence of life.
Farmer.	Jesus Christ.	God, pastor, spiritual leaders.
"Sown along the paths."	No understanding, taken away by the devil.	Unprotected, easily taken by the devil.
"Seeds fell on rocky places."	Receives the Word with joy, but lacks depth and stolen by trouble and persecution of the world.	"Walking on rocky places," = times of trouble, persecution, and lack of depth in the matter.
"Seeds fell on thorns."	The Word of God is heard, but choked by worries of life or the attraction of worldly riches.	Thorns = worries of life, distraction by worldly riches.
"Seeds on good soil."	Hears the Word, understands and becomes fruitful.	Well prepared for life expectancy, conducive for growth.

BENEFITS OF A PARABLE LANGUAGE

- Economy—a picture is worth a thousand words.

- It shows the essence—you apply the specifics to your situation; gives the principle so that the essence can be applicable at other times.

- A parable allows God to code messages for the dreamer.

- Is protected by hiding the promise from the enemy.

- Allows God to package and unfold His message according to the areas of priority.

  The disciples came to Him and asked, "Why do You speak to the people in parables?" He replied, "The knowledge of the secrets of the kingdom of heaven has been given to you, but not to them. Whoever has will be given more, and he will have abundance. Whoever does not have, even what he has will be taken from him. This is why I speak to them in parables: 'Though seeing, they do not see; though hearing, they do not hear or understand'" (Matthew 13:10-13).

  I spoke to the prophets, gave them many visions and told parables through them (Hosea 12:10).

- The mind speaks in the language of reason and concepts, but dreams speak in the language of riddles and parables.

- The language of pictures and symbols is universal and has no age barrier.

- Allows God to give the best possible picture or the truest perspective of the situation.

- A dream parable often shows the present condition and what will happen if we continue to go in the same direction.

  *The proverbs (truths obscurely expressed, maxims, and **parables**) of Solomon son of David, king of Israel: That people may know skillful and godly wisdom* *and instruction, discern and comprehend the words of understanding and insight.Receive instruction in wise dealing and the discipline of wise thoughtfulness, righteousness, justice, and integrity.That prudence may be given to the simple,and knowledge, discretion, and discernment to the youth. The wise also will hear and increase in learning and the person of understanding will acquire skill and attain to sound counsel [so that he may be able to steer his course rightly]. That people may understand a proverb* **[parable]** *and a figure of speech or an enigma with its interpretation, and the words of the wise and their dark saying or riddles* (Proverbs 1:1-6 AMP, emphasis added).

Chapter Five

How to Use the Dictionary of Dream Symbols

A seer receives in the language of symbols. However, in order to be relevant to the contemporary world, the seer should communicate the revelations with wisdom in language that people will understand. A seer should therefore be a student of the language of symbols and be able to communicate in simple terms with the people.

In general, when one sees a picture and switches to symbolic thinking, two questions should arise in the mind: What is the literal meaning of the picture? And what does the picture evoke? The answer to the first question will usually be the most obvious meaning for the symbol. In order to capture or broaden it to include the complete perspective of all the possible meanings, the second question must then be asked. This will help to explore the connotations and overtones in addition to the literal or most obvious meaning. If either of these two aspects is not well understood, the understanding of pictorial language is impoverished and not complete.

Example: The word *wife* is ordinarily understood to mean female, woman. This word also evokes some lateral thinking (connotations)—mother, home keeper, the Church, Bride of Christ.

Types of Symbol

A metaphor is a symbol with implied comparison (for example, the tongue as the pen of a ready writer; or Jesus, the Lion of the tribe of Judah). A simile, on the other hand, compares one thing to another and it makes the comparison explicit by using formula as "like" or "as." For example, "As the deer pants for water, so my soul pants for You." A motif is a pattern that appears in written text or a mental picture that has emerged from a written text. We allow the motif to develop wherever the Bible says, "Selah," i.e., pause and think.

EZEKIEL—A BIBLICAL EXAMPLE

God described Ezekiel as the watchman to the house of Israel and He used extensive symbolism in most of His communications with the Prophet Ezekiel. Let us see how the above principles can help us understand the multiple dimensions to the symbolism in Ezekiel's vision of the valley of dry bones.

The hand of the Lord was upon me, and He brought me out by the Spirit of the Lord and set me in the middle of a valley; it was full of bones. He led me back and forth among them, and I saw a great many bones on the floor of the valley, bones that were very dry. He asked me, "Son of man, can these bones live?" I said, "O Sovereign Lord, You alone know." Then He said to me, "Prophesy to these bones and say to them, 'Dry bones, hear the word of the Lord! This is what the Sovereign Lord says to these bones: I will make breath enter you, and you will come to life. I will attach tendons to you and make flesh come upon you and cover you with skin; I will put breath in you, and you will come to life. Then you will know that I am the Lord.'" So I prophesied as I was commanded. And as I was prophesying, there was a noise, a rattling sound, and the bones came together, bone to bone. I looked, and tendons and flesh appeared on them and skin covered them, but there was no breath in them. Then He said to me, "Prophesy to the breath; prophesy, son of man, and say to it, 'This is what the Sovereign Lord says: Come from the four winds, O breath, and breathe into these slain, that they may live.' " So I prophesied as He commanded me, and breath entered them; they came to life and stood up on their feet—a vast army (Ezekiel 37:1-10).

The interpretation given by God:

Then He said to me:"Son of man, these bones are the whole house of Israel. They say, 'Our bones are dried up and our hope is gone; we are cut off.' Therefore prophesy and say to them:'This is what the Sovereign Lord says: O My people, I am going to open your graves and bring you up from them; I will bring you back to the land of Israel. Then you, My people, will know that I am the Lord, when I open your graves and bring you up from them. I will put My Spirit in you and you will live, and I will settle you in your own land. Then you will know that I the Lord have spoken, and I have done it, declares the Lord"' (Ezekiel 37:1-14).

THE ANATOMY OF EZEKIEL'S VISION

SYMBOL	MEANING	THE POWER OF IMAGERY
A collection of dry bones littering a valley floor.	A state of hopelessness; extreme hardship; impossibility.	
Scattered.	Jews scattered in the nations.	
The bones (the hopeless situation) came together and assembled into skeletons (bone to his bones).	Coming together as predestined, each bone identified the exact skeleton to which it originally belonged.	Coming together of the Jews to a state of their own as prophesied.
As he observed flesh and skin grew on the skeleton.	This speaks of comfort and protection from God that will eventually emerge, particularly during the process.	

SYMBOL	MEANING	THE POWER OF IMAGERY
The bodies stayed dead, until a dramatic moment when God put breath into them.	Not filled with the spirit of God until the time appointed for this to happen.	After the restoration and recovery from the dead situation, the people remained spiritually dead. Their old souls needed to be renewed. The word "breath" also means spirit and the vision is reminiscent of Genesis 2:7 where God breathed life into the first man.
Come from the four winds.	The role of the four corners of the world in the eventual salvation of Israel.	God is saying that it would take a miracle to bring the remnants of Israel back together from many locations or nations where they are scattered. Israel will need an even greater miracle to be spiritually born-again with the spirit of God.
Vast army.	The eventual strength of the army of Israel, as it shall be like the army of the Lord.	

USING THE DICTIONARY

This dictionary has been designed to assist the reader in broadening lateral thinking and to prevent or resist the tendency to become fixed on the meaning of a symbol. If you are fixed on the meaning of a symbol, you become limited in the benefits that can be obtained from a dream.

The following points are important to bear in mind when using the dictionary of symbols:

- Interpretation belongs to God. Therefore, attempting to use this dictionary without the help of the Holy Spirit is a futile exercise.

- This dictionary is not a carte blanche for dream interpretation.

- The true meaning of a symbol must be drawn within the context of each dream; do not be fixed on the meaning of a symbol as it could vary from dream to dream and from person to person.

- The Bible says that God expresses spiritual truth in spiritual words; the derived meaning for a symbol must therefore be largely dependent on the Word of God.

- The reader must bear in mind at all times that what is personally descriptive should not be taken as generally prescriptive. God deals with each one of us uniquely.

PART 2

Dictionary of Dream Symbols
Understanding What The Watchman Receives

ACID: Something that eats from within. Keeping offense or hatred or malice.

> *See to it that no one misses the grace of God and that no bitter root grows up to cause trouble and defile many* (Hebrews 12:15).

ADULTERY: Unfaithfulness regarding things of the spirit or of the natural, or actual adultery; lust for the pleasures of this world; sin.

> *The acts of the sinful nature are obvious: sexual immorality, impurity and debauchery; idolatry and witchcraft; hatred, discord, jealousy, fits of rage, selfish ambition, dissensions, factions* (Galatians 5:19-20).

> *You adulterous people, don't you know that friendship with the world is hatred toward God? Anyone who chooses to be a friend of the world becomes an enemy of God* (James 4:4).

AIRPLANE: A personal ministry or a church; capable of moving in the Holy Spirit. Flowing in high spiritual power. Holy spirit-powered ministry.

Crashing: The end of one phase or change of direction.

High: Fully-powered in the Spirit.

Low: Only partially operative in the Spirit.

Soaring: Deep in the Spirit or moving in the deep things of God.

Warplane: Call to intercessory ministry; things of present or spiritual warfare.

AIRPORT: This often refers to the ministry that sends out missionaries; high-powered spiritual church capable of equipping and sending out ministries; ministry in preparation or capable of providing or nourishing others in readiness for service.

ALLIGATOR: Large-mouthed enemy; verbal attacks.

ALTAR: A place set apart for spiritual rituals or prayers/worship; place of sacrifice; call to repentance; place for meeting with God or the devil.

David built an altar to the Lord there and sacrificed burnt offerings and fellowship offerings. Then the Lord answered prayer in behalf of the land, and the plague on Israel was stopped (2 Samuel 24:25).

Then Noah built an altar to the Lord, taking some of all the clean animals and clean birds, he sacrificed burnt offerings on it (Genesis 8:20).

There he built an altar, and he called the place El Bethel, because it was there that God revealed Himself to him when he was fleeing from his brother (Genesis 35:7).

Destroy completely all the places on the high mountains and on the hills and under every spreading tree where the nations you are dispossessing worship their gods. Break down their altars, smash their sacred stones and burn their Asherah poles in the fire; cut down the idols of their gods and wipe out their names from those places (Deuteronomy 12:2-3).

ANCHOR: The pillar that something or person hangs on; something that hope is built on.

We have this hope as an anchor for the soul, firm and secure. It enters the inner sanctuary behind the curtain (Hebrews 6:19).

ANKLES: Little faith, early stages.

As the man went eastward with a measuring line in his hand, he measured off a thousand cubits and then led me through water that was ankle-deep (Ezekiel 47:3).

ANOINT: Equipping with the Holy Spirit for service. The power of Holy Spirit to do something; sanctification; setting apart for something; a call to a particular responsibility.

Is any one of you sick? He should call the elders of the church to pray over him and anoint him with oil in the name of the Lord (James 5:14).

Also, anoint Jehu son of Nimshi king over Israel, and anoint Elisha son of Shaphat from Abel Meholah to succeed you as prophet (1 Kings 19:16).

ANT: Industrious, ability to plan ahead; conscious of seasons of life; unwanted guest.

> *Go to the ant, you sluggard; consider its ways and be wise! It has no commander, no overseer or ruler, yet it stores its provisions in summer and gathers its food at harvest* (Proverbs 6:6-8).

> *Ants are creatures of little strength, yet they store up their food in the summer* (Proverbs 30:25).

ANTIQUES: Something relating to the past; an inherited thing.

> *This is what the Lord says: "Stand at the crossroads and look; ask for the ancient paths, ask where the good way is, and walk in it, and you will find rest for your souls." But you said, "We will not walk in it"* (Jeremiah 6:16).

APPLES: Spiritual fruit, something precious like the apple of God's eyes, something dear to God.

> *When the woman saw that the fruit of the tree was good for food and pleasing to the eye, and also desirable for gaining wisdom, she took some and ate it. She also gave some to her husband, who was with her, and he ate it* (Genesis 3:6).

> *In a desert land he found him, in a barren and howling waste. He shielded him and cared for him; He guarded him as the apple of His eye* (Deuteronomy 32:10).

> *For this is what the Lord Almighty says: "After he has honored Me and has sent Me against the nations that have plundered you—for whoever touches you touches the apple of his eye"* (Zechariah 2:8).

ARK: Something relating to God's presence. Something of strength or a symbol of God's authority.

> *Place the cover on top of the ark and put in the ark the Testimony, which I will give you. There, above the cover between the two cherubim that are over the ark of the Testimony, I will meet with you and give you all my commands for the Israelites* (Exodus 25:21-22).

ARM: Power and strength whether for or against the dreamer; superior assistance, the spirit of might.

But his bow remained steady, his strong arms stayed limber, because of the hand of the Mighty One of Jacob, because of the Shepherd, the Rock of Israel (Genesis 49:24).

Therefore, say to the Israelites: "I am the Lord, and I will bring you out from under the yoke of the Egyptians. I will free you from being slaves to them, and I will redeem you with an outstretched arm and with mighty acts of judgment" (Exodus 6:6).

With him is only the arm of flesh, but with us is the Lord our God to help us and to fight our battles. And the people gained confidence from what Hezekiah the king of Judah said (2 Chronicles 32:8).

Who has believed our message and to whom has the arm of the Lord been revealed? (Isaiah 53:1).

ARMIES: Spiritual warriors—good or bad.

ARMOR: Spiritual covering that protects the dreamer. Divine protection. The truth of God.

Finally, be strong in the Lord and in His mighty power. Put on the full armor of God so that you can take your stand against the devil's schemes (Ephesians 6:10-11).

ARROWS: Powerful words whether for or against the dreamer. Word of God or curses from the devil. Spiritual children. Good or bad intentions. Arrows with poisonous tip equals words capable of much damage. Modern sign for direction.

Sons are a heritage from the Lord, children a reward from Him. Like arrows in the hands of a warrior are sons born in one's youth (Psalm 127:3-4).

They sharpen their tongues like swords and aim their words like deadly arrows (Psalm 64:3).

Like a club or a sword or a sharp arrow is the man who gives false testimony against his neighbor (Proverbs 25:18).

"Open the east window," he said, and he opened it. "Shoot!" Elisha said, and he shot. "The Lord's arrow of victory, the

arrow of victory over Aram!" Elisha declared. "You will completely destroy the Arameans at Aphek" (2 Kings 13:17).

He made my mouth like a sharpened sword, in the shadow of His hand He hid me; He made me into a polished arrow and concealed me in His quiver (Isaiah 49:2).

ASHES: Signs of repentance or sorrow. To humble oneself. A memorial. Aftermath of God's consuming fire (see Ezek. 28:18; 2 Pet. 2:6).

Your maxims are proverbs of ashes; your defenses are defenses of clay (Job 13:12).

My ears had heard of you but now my eyes have seen you. Therefore I despise myself and repent in dust and ashes (Job 42:5-6).

Tamar put ashes on her head and tore the ornamented robe she was wearing. She put her hand on her head and went away, weeping aloud as she went (2 Samuel 13:19).

ATOM BOMB: Something capable of great destruction. Something of great suddenness or quick in occurring.

ATTIC: The mind-zone; thought process. The spirit realm. Memories/past issues/stored up materials.

About noon the following day as they were on their journey and approaching the city, Peter went up on the roof to pray. He became hungry and wanted something to eat, and while the meal was being prepared, he fell into a trance. He saw heaven opened and something like a large sheet being let down to earth by its four corners (Acts 10:9-11).

AUTOGRAPH: Prominence or fame.

AUTUMN: Transition. The close of harvest season or entering difficult times. End of something and beginning of another.

They do not say to themselves, "Let us fear the Lord our God, who gives autumn and spring rains in season, who assures us of the regular weeks of harvest" (Jeremiah 5:24).

AUTOBIKE: A spirit-powered ministry that has either one or two-person involvement. Single man ministry with a lot of exhibitionism.

AUTOMOBILE: Means of getting to a destination or achieving the desired goal.

The chariots storm through the streets, rushing back and forth through the squares. They look like flaming torches; they dart about like lightning (Nahum 2:4).

Air-conditioning: If in good working condition, indicates adequate comfort for situation; if not working, indicates faulty provision for comfort.

Brakes: Slowing down; to stop; compelled to stop; hindrance.

Convertible: Capable of open-heaven ministration; indicative of revelatory ministry.

Driver's seat: Indicates leadership.

Engine: Holy Spirit power, supernatural empowerment

Four-wheel drive: A powerful ministry; ground breaking; capable of global influence.

Junkyard: Ministries that are abandoned or in need of repairs.

Rear-view mirror: Looking back, focusing on things in the past; warning to look ahead; warning to watch your back.

Seatbelt: Something that ensures safety; fastened means prepared/prayers; unfastened means prayerlessness/carelessness.

Steering: The controlling and leading part, the means by which leadership is affected.

Tires: Symbolic of the spiritual conditions of the ministry; flat means needing spiritual enabling, needing more prayers; full means powered by the Spirit.

Topless van: Not having adequate anointing for the occasion; vulnerable or transparent.

Van: Goods—delivering, group-ministering.

Vehicle key: Authority in the ministry.

Wreck: Crashing, clash, end of one phase, change of direction. Danger. Contention or confrontation or offense.

AWAKENING: To be alert/watchfulness; to be stirred into action. Rousing the dreamer or being aroused in order to take action. Aroused from passivity and vulnerability to initiatives and progression or aggression (see Isa. 52).

> *Then the Lord awoke as from sleep, as a man wakes from the stupor of wine* (Psalm 78:65).

> *Awake, awake! Clothe yourself with strength, O arm of the Lord; awake, as in days gone by, as in generations of old. Was it not you who cut Rahab to pieces, who pierced that monster through?* (Isaiah 51:9).

> *"Awake, O sword, against My shepherd, against the man who is close to Me!" declares the Lord Almighty. "Strike the shepherd, and the sheep will be scattered, and I will turn My hand against the little ones"* (Zechariah 13:7).

> *Wake up, wake up Deborah! Wake up wake up, break out in song! Arise, O Barak! Take captive your captives, O son of Abinoam* (Judges 5:12).

AX: The Word of God. To encourage by kind word. Issue that needs to be settled.

> *The ax is already at the root of the trees, and every tree that does not produce good fruit will be cut down and thrown into the fire* (Matthew 3:10).

BABY: The beginning of something new. Beginning to be productive. New Christians. Something in its infancy or early stages.

> *Like newborn babies, crave pure spiritual milk, so that by it you may grow up in your salvation* (1 Peter 2:2).

> *Brothers, I could not address you as spiritual but as worldly— mere infants in Christ. I gave you milk, not solid food, for you were not yet ready for it. Indeed, you are still not ready* (1 Corinthians 3:1-2).

BACK: Pertaining to the past. Something behind or hidden; out of view. Concealed thing.

Answer me, O Lord, answer me, so these people will know that You, O Lord, are God, and that You are turning their hearts back again (1 Kings 18:37).

Let no one in the field go back to get his cloak (Mark 13:16).

Jesus replied, "No one who puts his hand to the plow and looks back is fit for service in the kingdom of God" (Luke 9:62).

BACKSIDE: Something in the past or behind the dreamer. Something concealed from view or understanding. Evocative image for rejection, a time of pruning, e.g., Moses at the backside of desert.

BADGER: Underground dwellers.

BAKER: One who instigates or originates something.

BAKING: Making provision for feeding people. Preparation for welfare ministry; God's provision; hospitality; preparing for tomorrow.

BALANCES: Something reflecting both sides of the matter. Something waiting to tilt one way or the other. Judgment. Need to objectively look at things.

BALD HEAD: Lacking wisdom.

BALM: Healing, anointing; something to relieve pain, stress, or agony.

Is there no balm in Gilead? Is there no physician there? Why then is there no healing for the wound of My people? (Jeremiah 8:22).

Babylon will suddenly fall and be broken. Wail over her! Get balm for her pain; perhaps she can be healed (Jeremiah 51:8).

Judah and Israel traded with you; they exchanged wheat from Minnith and confections, honey, oil and balm for your wares (Ezekiel 27:17).

BANK: Heavenly account. God's favor for a future season. A place of safety/security. A dependable place or source; God's provision.

Not that I am looking for a gift, but I am looking for what may be credited to your account (Philippians 4:17).

But store up for yourselves treasures in heaven, where moth and rust do not destroy, and where thieves do not break in and steal (Matthew 6:20).

BANNER OR FLAG: The covering to which everyone belongs or is committed to. Something that brings unity, love, or purpose; a unifying object or circumstance; victory.

Moses built an altar and called it The Lord is my Banner (Exodus 17:15).

BANQUET: God's provision. A full cup. Plentiful/affluence/abundance. Satisfaction. Blessing. Celebrations. Structured teaching of the Word of God.

He has taken me to the banquet hall, and his banner over me is love (Song of Solomon 2:4).

King Belshazzar gave a great banquet for a thousand of his nobles and drank wine with them...As they drank the wine, they praised the gods of gold and silver, of bronze, iron, wood and stone. Suddenly the fingers of a human hand appeared and wrote on the plaster of the wall, near the lampstand in the royal palace. The king watched the hand as it wrote (Daniel 5:1,4-5).

BAPTIZING: A change in spiritual life; transformation from the natural to Christ-likeness. A change from the natural to the spiritual. Dying to self, expression of the new man.

He went into all the country around the Jordan, preaching a baptism of repentance for the forgiveness of sins (Luke 3:3).

We were therefore buried with him through baptism into death in order that, just as Christ was raised from the dead through the glory of the Father, we too may live a new life (Romans 6:4).

Having been buried with Him in baptism and raised with Him through your faith in the power of God, who raised Him from the dead (Colossians 2:12).

BARBERSHOP: Time, place, period of changing beliefs or customs or habits. A church where these can take place; a place of correction.

BARENESS: Unproductive, difficult time or period.

BARN: A place of provision. A church. Stored spiritual wealth.

Let both grow together until the harvest. At that time I will tell the harvesters: First collect the weeds and tie them in bundles to be burned; then gather the wheat and bring it into my barn (Matthew 13:30).

Is there yet any seed left in the barn? Until now, the vine and the fig tree, the pomegranate and the olive tree have not borne fruit. From this day on I will bless you (Haggai 2:19).

BASEMENT: The unseen part of something. Storage zone. Related to the foundation. Hidden. Bloodline-related issue.

BASKET: A measure of something; A measure of God's provision. A measure of judgment.

This is what the Sovereign Lord showed me: a basket of ripe fruit. "What do you see, Amos?" He asked. "A basket of ripe fruit," I answered. Then the Lord said to me, "The time is ripe for My people Israel; I will spare them no longer" (Amos 8:1-2).

Then the angel who was speaking to me came forward and said to me, "Look up and see what this is that is appearing." I asked, "What is it?" He replied, "It is a measuring basket." And he added, "This is the iniquity of the people throughout the land." Then the cover of lead was raised, and there in the basket sat a woman! He said, "This is wickedness," and he pushed her back into the basket and pushed the lead cover down over its mouth. Then I looked up—and there before me were two women, with the wind in their wings! They had wings like those of a stork, and they lifted up the basket between Heaven and earth. "Where are they taking the basket?" I asked the angel who was speaking to me. He replied, "To the country of Babylonia to build a house for it. When it is ready, the basket will be set there in its place" (Zechariah 5:5-11).

BAT: Creature of darkness. Satanic instrument, related to witchcraft. A nighttime creature. Could represent association with the dark side of life.

BATHING: What you do on the outside or outwardly to prevent unclean or unholy attitude from sticking to you; outward repentance.

BATHROOM: A period of cleansing/entering a time of repentance. A place of voluntary nakedness or vulnerability or facing reality in one's life.

BEAM: Power or illumination coming from God or the heavenly. A time of exposure or spotlight. A supporting frame. God is the Father of lights and Christians are the children of lights.

BEAR: Danger; wicked person or spirit; vindictiveness. Evil, something that is after what you possess.

> *But David said to Saul, "Your servant has been keeping his father's sheep. When a lion or a bear came and carried off a sheep from the flock, I went after it, struck it and rescued the sheep from its mouth. When it turned on me, I seized it by its hair, struck it and killed it. Your servant has killed both the lion and the bear; this uncircumcised Philistine will be like one of them, because he has defied the armies of the living God. The Lord who delivered me from the paw of the lion and the paw of the bear will deliver me from the hand of this Philistine." Saul said to David, "Go, and the Lord be with you"* (1 Samuel 17:34-37).

> *You know your father and his men; they are fighters, and as fierce as a wild bear robbed of her cubs. Besides, your father is an experienced fighter; he will not spend the night with the troops* (2 Samuel 17:8).

> *It will be as though a man fled from a lion only to meet a bear, as though he entered his house and rested his hand on the wall only to have a snake bite him* (Amos 5:19).

BEARD: To have respect for authority.

Messy: Insane.

Trimmed: Sane.

BEAUTY SHOP: A place of preparation with emphasis on outward appearance, tending toward vanity. See also *Barber's Shop.*

BED: Revelations, rest, contentment. Becoming relaxed or lax.

BEDROOM: A place of intimacy. A place of rest, sleep, or dreams. A place of covenant, a place of revelation.

BEES: That which makes offensive noise. More noisy than effective. A double-edged situation capable of going bad or producing sweetness. Stinging words, gossip.

> *Some time later, when he went back to marry her, he turned aside to look at the lion's carcass. In it was a swarm of bees and some honey* (Judges 14:8).

BELLS: Call to attention or action. To bring to alertness. To say it loudly; public warning.

BELLY: Feelings, desires, spiritual well-being, sentiment.

BICYCLE: A ministry depending on much human effort. One-man ministry.

BINOCULARS: Looking ahead, looking into the future. Prophetic ministry.

BIRD: Symbol of leader, evil or good at different levels. Agents of authority.

> ***Dove:*** Holy Spirit, peace, a seal of approval from Heaven. May mean spiritual naivety.

> ***Eagle:*** Personality or spirit capable of soaring in the Spirit. Good focus/swiftness powerful. A prophet of God.

> ***Owl:*** A watchful eye that monitors; spirit of craftiness.

> ***Raven:*** Symbol of unclean spirit.

> ***Sparrow:*** Divine provision and food. Symbol of God's desire to provide for us.

Vulture: Evil spirit, opportunistic person. Night creature or something that preys on dead things (human weaknesses). Unclean spirit. A loner.

Feathers: A protective covering, a shield or instrument for flying or moving in the spirit.

Wings: A place of refuge. God's presence. Safety/something that provides escape from danger.

Fowler: A person or spirit that entraps. Fowler's net.

BLACK: Lack, famine. Evil, demonic spirit. Darkness.

May darkness and deep shadow claim it once more; may a cloud settle over it; may blackness overwhelm its light (Job 3:5).

They are wild waves of the sea, foaming up their shame; wandering stars, for whom blackest darkness has been reserved forever (Jude 1:13).

I clothe the sky with darkness and make sackcloth its covering (Isaiah 50:3).

BLEEDING: Hurting. To lose spiritually; verbal accusation. Traumatic.

BLIND: Lack of understanding, ignorance. Not able to see into the spirit world.

BLOOD: Atonement, to appease. Something that testifies.

BLOOD TRANSFUSION: Getting new life, rescuing situation.

BLUE: Heaven-related or something related to the Holy Spirit. Spiritual.

BOAT: A ministry that is capable of influencing many people.

BODY ODOR: Unclean spirit, after-effect of fleshy actions.

BONES: The substance of something. The main issue. Long-lasting.

Skeleton: Something without flesh/substance. Something without details.

BOOK: Gaining understanding/knowledge. Scriptures. Revelation. Promise from God. Message based on the title of the book.

BOTTLE: Something relating to the body as the container of anointing.

BOW, ARROW or GUN: Source from which attacks come. The power of a nation or person. Verbal attacks. The tongue.

But his bow remained steady, his strong arms stayed limber, because of the hand of the Mighty One of Jacob, because of the Shepherd, the Rock of Israel (Genesis 49:24).

"They make ready their tongue like a bow, to shoot lies; it is not by truth that they triumph in the land. They go from one sin to another; they do not acknowledge Me," declares the Lord (Jeremiah 9:3).

This is what the Lord Almighty says: "See, I will break the bow of Elam, the mainstay of their might" (Jeremiah 49:35).

BOWL: A container; measure of something.

His offering was one silver plate weighing a hundred and thirty shekels, and one silver sprinkling bowl weighing seventy shekels, both according to the sanctuary shekel, each filled with fine flour mixed with oil as a grain offering (Numbers 7:13).

You drink wine by the bowlful and use the finest lotions, but you do not grieve over the ruin of Joseph (Amos 6:6).

And the Lord Almighty will shield them. They will destroy and overcome with slingstones. They will drink and roar as with wine; they will be full like a bowl used for sprinkling the corners of the altar (Zechariah 9:15).

And that is what happened. Gideon rose early the next day; he squeezed the fleece and wrung out the dew—a bowlful of water (Judges 6:38).

BRACELET: Pertaining to pride. Valuable but of the world, means identity if it has a name.

BRANCHES: God's people, churches. Church split.

I am the vine; you are the branches. If a man remains in Me and I in him, he will bear much fruit; apart from Me you can do nothing (John 15:5).

I am the true vine, and my Father is the gardener. He cuts off every branch in Me that bears no fruit, while every branch that does bear fruit He prunes so that it will be even more fruitful (John 15:1-2).

BRASS: Hardness, hard covering. Judgment/captivity/hard to break out from. Strength. Negative stronghold. Resistance.

Do I have the strength of stone? Is my flesh bronze? (Job 6:12).

The sky over your head will be bronze, the ground beneath you iron (Deuteronomy 28:23).

They killed the sons of Zedekiah before his eyes. Then they put out his eyes, bound him with bronze shackles and took him to Babylon (2 Kings 25:7).

I will break down your stubborn pride and make the sky above you like iron and the ground beneath you like bronze (Leviticus 26:19).

BREAD: Jesus Christ; Bread of life; Word of God; source of nourishment; God's provision.

Then she arose with her daughters-in-law that she might return from the country of Moab: for she had heard in the country of Moab that the Lord had visited His people by giving them bread (Ruth 1:6 NKJV).

At this the Jews began to grumble about him because He said, "I am the bread that came down from Heaven" (John 6:41).

Then at last they understood that He wasn't telling them to guard against the yeast used in bread, but against the teaching of the Pharisees and Sadducees (Matthew 16:12).

A man ought to examine himself before he eats of the bread and drinks of the cup (1 Corinthians 11:28).

Give us today our daily bread (Matthew 6:11).

Fresh: New word from God.

Moldy: Something that is not new. Unclean.

Unleavened: Showing lack of sin, something prepared in haste.

BREAST: Source of milk for new Christians. Object of enticement. Source of sustenance.

Because of your father's God, who helps you, because of the Almighty, who blesses you with blessings of the heavens above, blessings of the deep that lies below, blessings of the breast and womb (Genesis 49:25).

Why were there knees to receive me and breasts that I might be nursed? (Job 3:12).

A loving doe, a graceful deer—may her breasts satisfy you always, may you ever be captivated by her love (Proverbs 5:19).

BREASTPLATE: God's protective shield. Covering or the anointing which covers one. Preparing to give judgment. Protective of vital human organs or issues.

He put on righteousness as his breastplate, and the helmet of salvation on his head; he put on the garments of vengeance and wrapped himself in zeal as in a cloak (Isaiah 59:17).

He placed the breastpiece on him and put the Urim and Thummim in the breastpiece (Leviticus 8:8).

Stand firm then, with the belt of truth buckled around your waist, with the breastplate of righteousness in place (Ephesians 6:14).

BREATH: Means Spirit; spirit of man. Breath of life. Sign of life. Revive to life.

The Lord God formed the man from the dust of the ground and breathed into his nostrils the breath of life, and the man became a living being (Genesis 2:7).

His breath sets coals ablaze, and flames dart from His mouth (Job 41:21).

Topheth has long been prepared; it has been made ready for the king. Its fire pit has been made deep and wide, with an abundance of fire and wood; the breath of the Lord, like a stream of burning sulphur, sets it ablaze (Isaiah 30:33).

Then he said to me, "Prophesy to the breath; prophesy, son of man, and say to it, 'This is what the Sovereign Lord says: Come from the four winds, O breath, and breathe into these slain, that they may live'" (Ezekiel 37:9).

BRICK: A building unit. Something that is man-made or designed to be durable. Something used for personality building.

They said to each other, "Come, let's make bricks and bake them thoroughly." They used brick instead of stone, and tar for mortar (Genesis 11:3).

The bricks have fallen down, but we will rebuild with dressed stone; the fig trees have been felled, but we will replace them with cedars (Isaiah 9:10).

A people who continually provoke Me to My very face, offering sacrifices in gardens and burning incense on altars of brick (Isaiah 65:3).

BRIDE: The Church relationship to Jesus. Special to Jesus. Covenant or relationship.

"Lift up your eyes and look around; all your sons gather and come to you. As surely as I live," declares the Lord, "you will wear them all as ornaments; you will put them on, like a bride" (Isaiah 49:18).

The bride belongs to the bridegroom. The friend who attends the bridegroom waits and listens for him, and is full of joy when he hears the bridegroom's voice. That joy is mine, and it is now complete (John 3:29).

One of the seven angels who had the seven bowls full of the seven last plagues came and said to me, "Come, I will show you the bride, the wife of the Lamb" (Revelation 21:9).

BRIDGE: Something that takes you across an obstacle, e.g., faith. The connection between two things/circumstances. Something that holds you up in times of difficulty.

BRIDLE: Put control over, e.g., self-control over the use of the tongue. Something imposed by some higher authority to affect control

> *A whip for the horse, a bridle for the ass, and a rod for the fool's back* (Proverbs 26:3 KJV).

> *If anyone among you thinks he is religious, and does not bridle his tongue but deceives his own heart, this one's religion is useless* (James 1:26 NKJV).

> *I said, "I will watch my ways and keep my tongue from sin; I will put a muzzle on my mouth as long as the wicked are in my presence"* (Psalm 39:1).

> *Because your rage against Me and your tumult have come up to My ears, Therefore I will put My hook in your nose and My bridle in your lips, and I will turn you back by the way which you came* (Isaiah 37:29 NKJV).

BRIERS: Something "wild and thorny" that needs to be trimmed. Something uncultivated or false.

BRIGHTNESS: Presence of God. Revelation. Solution. End of difficult period.

> *I looked, and I saw a figure like that of a man. From what appeared to be His waist down He was like fire, and from there up His appearance was as bright as glowing metal* (Ezekiel 8:2).

> *Those who are wise will shine like the brightness of the heavens, and those who lead many to righteousness, like the stars for ever and ever* (Daniel 12:3).

> *You looked, O king, and there before you stood a large statue—an enormous, dazzling statue, awesome in appearance* (Daniel 2:31).

> *The Son is the radiance of God's glory and the exact representation of His being, sustaining all things by His powerful word. After He had provided purification for sins, He sat down at the right hand of the Majesty in heaven* (Hebrews 1:3).

BRIMSTONE: Judgment of God. Punishment. Trial period.

BROKEN: Loss of strength, authority, or influence. Open. Heart; wounded.

> *Like a city whose walls are broken down is a man who lacks self-control* (Proverbs 25:28).

> *I will seek what was lost and bring back what was driven away, bind up the broken and strengthen what was sick; but I will destroy the fat and the strong, and feed them in judgment* (Ezekiel 34:16 NKJV).

BROOK: A provision of God. Something that brings refreshment, wisdom, prosperity from God. If dirty, means corrupted or contaminated. A source of defense.

> *The rivers will turn foul; the brooks of defense will be emptied and dried up; the reeds and rushes will wither* (Isaiah 19:6 NKJV).

> *Get away from here and turn eastward, and hide by the Brook Cherith, which flows into the Jordan. And it will be that you shall drink from the brook, and I have commanded the ravens to feed you there* (1 Kings 17:3-4 NKJV).

> *My brothers have dealt deceitfully like a brook, like the streams of the brooks that pass away* (Job 6:15 NKJV).

BROOM: Something, or in the process of, getting rid of sins. Symbol of witchcraft.

BROTHER: Christian brother (spiritual brother); biological brother. Someone with similar qualities.

> *Whoever does God's will is My brother and sister and mother* (Mark 3:35).

BROTHER-IN-LAW: Same as a brother, but under special obligation. Spiritual brother without in-depth love. A person of another church who is also Christian. Actual brother-in-law. Someone with similar qualities.

BROWN/TAN: Life; change of season; born again.

BRUISE: Event or circumstance that leaves a hurt feeling with one. In need of healing. Suffering of Jesus on our behalf. Inner hurting of spirit.

This is what the Lord says: "Your wound is incurable, your injury beyond healing" (Jeremiah 30:12).

But He was wounded for our transgressions, He was bruised for our iniquities; The chastisement for our peace was upon Him, and by His stripes we are healed (Isaiah 53:5 NKJV).

BUCKET: A measure of something. Used for service. Supplies life.

Surely the nations are like a drop in a bucket; they are regarded as dust on the scales; he weighs the islands as though they were fine dust (Isaiah 40:15).

Water will flow from their buckets; their seed will have abundant water. Their king will be greater than Agag; their kingdom will be exalted (Numbers 24:7).

BUILDING: Symbolic of the spiritual and emotional being of the place, person, or church. Life of the person, church, or office.

And I tell you that you are Peter, and on this rock I will build My church, and the gates of Hades will not overcome it (Matthew 16:18).

He is like a man building a house, who dug down deep and laid the foundation on rock. When a flood came, the torrent struck that house but could not shake it, because it was well built (Luke 6:48).

Therefore everyone who hears these words of Mine and puts them into practice is like a wise man who built his house on the rock. The rain came down, the streams rose, and the winds blew and beat against that house; yet it did not fall, because it had its foundation on the rock. But everyone who hears these words of Mine and does not put them into practice is like a foolish man who built his house on sand (Matthew 7:24-26).

BULL: Threatening situation. Warfare. Opposition. A source of economy.

BUNDLE: Measure of harvest. Grouping for judgment or reward. Fullness.

Then it happened as they emptied their sacks, that surprisingly each man's bundle of money was in his sack; and when they and their father saw the bundles of money, they were afraid (Genesis 42:35 NKJV).

Even though someone is pursuing you to take your life, the life of my master will be bound securely in the bundle of the living by the Lord your God. But the lives of your enemies He will hurl away as from the pocket of a sling (1 Samuel 25:29).

BURIAL: Memorial to mark the end of something.

Uzziah rested with his fathers and was buried near them in a field for burial that belonged to the kings, for people said, "He had leprosy." And Jotham his son succeeded him as king" (2 Chronicles 26:23).

He will have the burial of a donkey—dragged away and thrown outside the gates of Jerusalem (Jeremiah 22:19).

When she poured this perfume on My body, she did it to prepare Me for burial (Matthew 26:12).

BURIED: A permanent end to something. To bring to final end.

We were therefore buried with Him through baptism into death in order that, just as Christ was raised from the dead through the glory of the Father, we too may live a new life (Romans 6:4).

having been buried with Him in baptism and raised with Him through your faith in the power of God, who raised Him from the dead (Colossians 2:12).

BURN: To consume. To heat up or stir up. To set aflame. To kindle. Sign of fervency. Total change of something by a drastic action.

Now the people complained about their hardships in the hearing of the Lord, and when he heard them his anger was aroused. Then fire from the Lord burned among them and consumed some of the outskirts of the camp (Numbers 11:1).

I will enslave you to your enemies in a land you do not know, for My anger will kindle a fire that will burn against you (Jeremiah 15:14).

Command the Israelites to bring you clear oil of pressed olives for the light so that the lamps may be kept burning (Exodus 27:20).

BUS: A big ministry.

School bus: A teaching ministry.

BUTTER: Something that brings soothing, smooth words. Encouragement.

He will eat curds [butter] *and honey when he knows enough to reject the wrong and choose the right* (Isaiah 7:15).

His speech is smooth as butter, yet war is in his heart; his words are more soothing than oil, yet they are drawn swords (Psalm 55:21).

BUY: To prepare, take, acquire, or obtain something good or bad.

"Fields will be bought for silver, and deeds will be signed, sealed and witnessed in the territory of Benjamin, in the villages around Jerusalem, in the towns of Judah and in the towns of the hill country, of the western foothills and of the Negev, because I will restore their fortunes," declares the Lord (Jeremiah 32:44).

Buy the truth and do not sell it; get wisdom, discipline and understanding (Proverbs 23:23).

For a hundred pieces of silver, he bought from the sons of Hamor, the father of Shechem, the plot of ground where he pitched his tent (Genesis 33:19).

CAFETERIA: A place or period of spiritual nourishment—good or bad. A church. Structural teaching of the Word of God. Celebration.

CAGE: To restrict. Limited mobility. Negatively—captivity. Positively—to guard or watch.

Like cages full of birds, their houses are full of deceit; they have become rich and powerful (Jeremiah 5:27).

CAKE, BREAD: Provisions from Heaven. Nourishment from God.

The people went around gathering it, and then ground it in a hand mill or crushed it in a mortar. They cooked it in a pot or made it into cakes. And it tasted like something made with olive oil (Numbers 11:8).

CALF: A young cow or bull. Increase in prosperity.

CAMEL: Having a servant heart. Capable of bearing other people's burdens. Intercessory spirit.

CAMP: Temporary settlement; a transit situation. Something intended for traveling or for temporary residence, not permanent building.

> *Jacob also went on his way, and the angels of God met him. When Jacob saw them, he said, "This is the camp of God!" So he named that place Mahanaim* (Genesis 32:1-2).

> *They left the Red Sea and camped in the Desert of Sin. They left the Desert of Sin and camped at Dophkah. They left Dophkah and camped at Alush. They left Alush and camped at Rephidim, where there was no water for the people to drink. They left Rephidim and camped in the Desert of Sinai. They left the Desert of Sinai and camped at Kibroth Hattaavah. They left Kibroth Hattaavah and camped at Hazeroth. They left Hazeroth and camped at Rithmah* (Numbers 33:11-18).

CANDLE: Word of God. Symbolic of man's spirit. If not lit, could mean lack of God's presence. Jesus is also source of light. Conscience.

> *The lamp of the Lord searches the spirit of a man; it searches out his inmost being* (Proverbs 20:27).

> *At that time I will search Jerusalem with lamps and punish those who are complacent, who are like wine left on its dregs, who think, "The Lord will do nothing, either good or bad"* (Zephaniah 1:12).

> ***Lamp and electricity:*** Symbolic of man's spirit. If not lit, it could mean lack of God's presence. (Jesus is also source of light.) Conscience.

CANDLESTICK: People who carry the light of God. The lamp stand, Spirit of God. Church.

CARPENTER: Jesus. Someone who makes or amends things. A preacher.

CAT: Deceptive situation/person. Something or a person who is self-willed. Not a teachable spirit. A sneaky, crafty, and deceptive spirit. Witchcraft, waiting to attack. A personal pet. A precious habit that could be dangerous.

CAVE: Safe hiding place. Secret place of encountering God.

CHAIN: Bondage or captivity. To be bound in the spirit or in the natural.

CHAIR: Authority over something; coming to position of authority or a place of respite; throne of God.

CHANNEL: A way out. A process of time. Difficult period leading to the next stage.

CHASE: Cause to flee. Get rid of something. To pursue. To go after something.

CHECK/CHEQUE: The seal of promise. Promise that is guaranteed.

CHEEK: Vulnerable part, beauty.

CHEESE: To comfort. To soothe.

CHEETAH: Unclean spirit.

CHEW: To meditate. To ruminate. To cut off.

CHICKEN: An evangelist. Gifting, caring spirit. Gathering.

> *O Jerusalem, Jerusalem, you who kill the prophets and stone those sent to you, how often I have longed to gather your children together, as a hen gathers her chicks under her wings, but you were not willing* (Matthew 23:37; Luke 13:34).

Rooster: Boasting.

Chick: Defenseless.

CHILDHOOD HOME: Influence from the distant past, whether good or bad.

CHOKING: Biting more than you can chew. Too fast, too much in the wrong way.

CHRISTMAS: New thing in Christ. Tradition of men. Spiritual gift. Season of gifts/love. A period of joy and humanitarianism. Celebration of Christ. False or pretend celebration or hypocrisy.

CIRCLE: Something endless signifies agreement or covenant. If making a circle, relating to the universe; Ring, round.

> *He sits enthroned above the circle of the earth, and its people are like grasshoppers. He stretches out the heavens like a canopy, and spreads them out like a tent to live in* (Isaiah 40:22).

CIRCUMCISION: Cutting off fleshy things/coming to liberty. Covenanting with God. Blood relationship. New levels of spiritual walk, born again. New level of maturity.

> *You are to undergo circumcision, and it will be the sign of the covenant between Me and you* (Genesis 17:11).

> *Circumcise yourselves to the Lord, circumcise your hearts, you men of Judah and people of Jerusalem, or My wrath will break out and burn like fire because of the evil you have done—burn with no one to quench it* (Jeremiah 4:4).

> *Then He gave Abraham the covenant of circumcision. And Abraham became the father of Isaac and circumcised him eight days after his birth. Later Isaac became the father of Jacob, and Jacob became the father of the twelve patriarchs* (Acts 7:8).

CITY: The makeup of the person. All that has been inputted in the person or people. The city or what the city is known for. Group or church.

CLASSROOM: A time of spiritual preparation. A person with a gifting to teach others.

CLAY: Something that refers to frailty of man; delicate and fragile; not secure.

> *I am just like you before God; I too have been taken from clay* (Job 33:6).

> *Its legs of iron, its feet partly of iron and partly of baked clay. While you were watching, a rock was cut out, but not by human hands. It struck the statue on its feet of iron and clay and smashed them. …As the toes were partly iron and partly*

clay, so this kingdom will be partly strong and partly brittle (Daniel 2:33-34,42).

CLEAN: To make holy, pure; to make righteous; to make ready and acceptable.

CLEANSE: To put right something. To put away what is bad.

CLEAR: To bring light to the situation; to bring understanding. To be set free from something.

CLOCK: Timing is important in the situation. Time to do something is revealed. May refer to Bible passages. Running out of time.

CLOSE: To shut up, to keep silent, or to be hedged or walled up.

For the Lord has poured out on you the spirit of deep sleep, and has closed your eyes, namely, the prophets; and He has covered your heads, namely, the seers (Isaiah 29:10 NKJV).

For this people's heart has become calloused; they hardly hear with their ears, and they have closed their eyes. Otherwise they might see with their eyes, hear with their ears, understand with their hearts and turn, and I would heal them (Matthew 13:15).

CLOSET: Hidden, confidential, personal, or exclusive. A place of prayer. A place of fellowship with God.

Gather the people, sanctify the congregation, assemble the elders, gather the children, and those that suck the breasts: let the bridegroom go forth of his chamber, and the bride out of her closet (Joel 2:16 KJV).

But thou, when thou prayest, enter into thy closet, and when thou hast shut thy door, pray to thy Father which is in secret; and thy Father which seeth in secret shall reward thee openly (Matthew 6:6 KJV).

Therefore whatsoever ye have spoken in darkness shall be heard in the light; and that which ye have spoken in the ear in closets shall be proclaimed upon the housetops (Luke 12:3 KJV).

CLOTHING: Covering whether pure or impure. Your standing or authority in a situation. Covering God is providing to us.

Tearing cloths: Signifies grief, sorrow.

CLOUDS: Heavenly manifestation; glory, presence of God. Dark time of travel, fear, trouble, or storms of life.

> *By day the Lord went ahead of them in a pillar of cloud to guide them on their way and by night in a pillar of fire to give them light, so that they could travel by day or night* (Exodus 13:21).

> *The Lord said to Moses: "Tell your brother Aaron not to come whenever he chooses into the Most Holy Place behind the curtain in front of the atonement cover on the ark, or else he will die, because I appear in the cloud over the atonement cover"* (Leviticus 16:2).

> *At that time the sign of the Son of Man will appear in the sky, and all the nations of the earth will mourn. They will see the Son of Man coming on the clouds of the sky, with power and great glory* (Matthew 24:30).

CLOWN: Not a serious person. Not taking God seriously. Childish.

COAT: Protective, covering, mantle.

> *The Lord God made garments [coat] of skin for Adam and his wife and clothed them* (Genesis 3:21).

> *He is to put on the sacred linen tunic, with linen undergarments next to his body; he is to tie the linen sash around him and put on the linen turban. These are sacred garments [coats]; so he must bathe himself with water before he puts them on* (Leviticus 16:4).

> *Take the garments [coats] and dress Aaron with the tunic, the robe of the ephod, the ephod itself and the breastpiece. Fasten the ephod on him by its skillfully woven waistband* (Exodus 29:5).

Clean: Righteousness.

Dirty: Not righteous, unclean.

COLLEGE: Promotion in the Spirit. Pertaining to the equipping season.

COLUMNS: Spirit of control and manipulation; obsessive or orderliness.

CONCEIVE: In process of preparation. To add. To multiply.

CONGREGATION: An appointed meeting. An assembly. Called together.

CORD: Something that holds things together. Enhances unity/love; or something that binds to cause restriction or bondage.

COUCH: Rest, relaxation, peace.

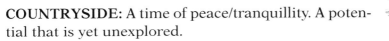

COUNTRYSIDE: A time of peace/tranquillity. A potential that is yet unexplored.

COURTHOUSE: Time of being judged or persecuted; trial.

COW: Food/source of enrichment; potential source of sin.

CRAWLING: Humility or to be humiliated; sign of judgment.

CROOKED: Distorted, not straight.

> *Every valley shall be raised up, every mountain and hill made low; the rough ground* [crooked] *shall become level* [straight], *the rugged places a plain* (Isaiah 40:4).

> *But those who turn to crooked ways the Lord will banish with the evildoers. Peace be upon Israel* (Psalm 125:5).

CROSSING STREET: Changing perspective.

CROSSROADS: Vital choice to make or change in position. Options.

CROWN: Symbol of authority. Seal of power. Jesus Christ. To reign. To be honored.

CRYING: Actual crying. A period of grief, outburst of sadness. Intense emotional expression.

CULTURAL CLOTHES: A call to the people of that culture; call to nation or that cultural affiliation.

CUP: Your portion in life; provision or responsibility.

CYMBALS: Instrument to praise God with. Could be used without genuine love.

DAM: The power of unity or gathering resources. Obstacle to flow. Reserve sustenance. Stillness..

DANCING, WORSHIP: Worshipping something—God or idol. A time of joy or rejoicing.

DARKNESS: Lack of light. Without spiritual direction.

DAUGHTER: Gift of God. Ministry that is your child in the Spirit. The child herself. Someone with similar qualities.

DAYTIME: The opportune time. A time of light. Season of good deeds. Season when things are revealed or understanding is gained.

DEAF: Not spiritually attentive. Not paying attention.

DEATH: What the Bible says more frequently about death is dying to self. Some measure of dying to self in an area. Separation from things of evil; actual physical death. The end of life on earth. Death is also overcoming the work of the flesh to resume communion with God.

DEER: Spiritual longing; symbol of hunger for the things of God; ability to take great strides; grace. Divine enabling. A deer is noted for swiftness, agility, and sure-footedness. Picture of graceful beauty.

> *As the deer pants for streams of water, so my soul pants for You, O God. My soul thirsts for God, for the living God. When can I go and meet with God?* (Psalm 42:1-2).

> *A loving doe, a graceful deer—may her breasts satisfy you always, may you ever be captivated by her love* (Proverbs 5:19).

> *The Sovereign Lord is my strength; He makes my feet like the feet of a deer, He enables me to go on the heights. For the director of music. On my stringed instruments* (Habakkuk 3:19).

DEN: Busy doing the wrong thing.

DESERT: Training; lack; testing. A place of reliance on God.

DEW: Blessings of God for all seasons. Condensed, moisturized air formed in drops during still, cloudless night indicates divine blessing on the earth. The Word of God.

May God give you of heaven's dew and of earth's richness—an abundance of grain and new wine (Genesis 27:28).

It is as if the dew of Hermon were falling on Mount Zion. For there the Lord bestows His blessing, even life forevermore (Psalm 133:3).

Let my teaching fall like rain and my words descend like dew, like showers on new grass, like abundant rain on tender plants (Deuteronomy 32:2).

Therefore, because of you the heavens have withheld their dew and the earth its crops (Haggai 1:10).

DIAMOND: Something to engrave with, something hard; stubbornness. Diamond as a pen nib. Valuable, precious, gift, majesty, beauty.

DIFFICULT WALKING: Difficult times of life. Facing opposition.

DINING ROOM: Feeding on the Word of God. A place of spiritual food. Table of the Lord.

DINOSAUR: Something in the distant past. Something big and terrible, but it has been dealt with by God. What used to be a major issue or hindrance in the past generation, but which no longer exists.

DIRTY CLOTH: False doctrine. Of a sinful nature.

Now Joshua was dressed in filthy clothes as he stood before the angel. The angel said to those who were standing before him, "Take off his filthy clothes." Then he said to Joshua, "See, I have taken away your sin, and I will put rich garments on you." Then I said, "Put a clean turban on his head." So they put a clean turban on his head and clothed him, while the angel of the Lord stood by (Zechariah 3:3-5).

DIRTY/DRY: Not pure spiritual things.

DIRTY/NEGLECTED: A place in need of attention.

DISEASE: Emotional upset, or it may be literal; bondage from the devil.

DITCH: Deception, a trap; fleshy desire.

DOCTOR: Jesus the healer. A person with healing anointing. Someone with caring service, minister. Symbol of healing anointing.

DOG: A gift that could be harnessed to do good, but may not be trusted. Could be versatile in function, but unpredictable. Man's best friend. A pet sin.

DONKEY: An enduring spirit, usable by the Lord. A gift that God could use if surrendered to Him.

DOOR: An opening. Jesus Christ. The way, a possibility, grace. Something to do with Jesus. Transition.

Set a guard over my mouth, O Lord; keep watch over the door of my lips (Psalm 141:3).

Therefore Jesus said again, "I tell you the truth, I am the gate [door] *for the sheep. All who ever came before Me were thieves and robbers, but the sheep did not listen to them. I am the gate* [door]*; whoever enters through Me will be saved. He will come in and go out, and find pasture"* (John 10:7-9).

After this I looked, and there before me was a door standing open in heaven. And the voice I had first heard speaking to me like a trumpet said, "Come up here, and I will show you what must take place after this" (Revelation 4:1).

DOWN: Spiritual descent/backslide. Falling away. Humiliation. Failure. Repositioning.

DRAGON: Satan. High demonic spirit. Great level of wickedness. Antichrist.

Then another sign appeared in heaven: an enormous red dragon with seven heads and ten horns and seven crowns on his heads (Revelation 12:3).

The great dragon was hurled down—that ancient serpent called the devil, or Satan, who leads the whole world astray. He was hurled to the earth, and his angels with him (Revelation 12:9).

DRAWING: Conceptualization.

Artist's paint: A means or method of illustration. To be fluent in expression.

Paint: Doctrine, truth, or deception.

DREAMING: To dream of dreaming means receiving a deeply spiritual message, or a much more futuristic message.

DRINKING: Receiving from the spiritual realm, whether good or bad. Receiving your portion in life; bearing your cross.

DRIVER: The one in command or control. The one who makes the decisions.

DRIVING IN REVERSE: Not going in correct direction with anointing.

DROUGHT: A period of lack without God.

DROWNING: Overcome by situation leading to depression. Overwhelmed to the point of self-pity.

DRUGS: Medication. Illicit drugs may mean counterfeit anointing.

DRUNKARD: Influenced by counterfeit source of anointing. Self-indulgence or error. Uncontrolled lust.

DUST: Temporary nature of humanity. Frailty of man. Curse. Symbolically may refer to humiliation. Dust may often mean a large number of something.

> *The Lord God formed the man from the dust of the ground and breathed into his nostrils the breath of life, and the man became a living being* (Genesis 2:7).

> *Your descendants will be like the dust of the earth, and you will spread out to the west and to the east, to the north and to the south. All peoples on earth will be blessed through you and your offspring* (Genesis 28:14).

> *Shake off your dust; rise up, sit enthroned, O Jerusalem. Free yourself from the chains on your neck, O captive Daughter of Zion* (Isaiah 52:2).

DYNAMITE: Holy Spirit "dynamus." Power/great spiritual power, whether good or bad.

EAR: Symbolic of the prophet. Hearing spiritual things that either build up or tear down. Need to be paying more attention.

EARTHQUAKE: Sudden release of great power. Judgment. Ground-shaking changes. Great shock. A time of trial. Release from prison.

> *As when fire sets twigs ablaze and causes water to boil, come down to make Your name known to Your enemies and cause the nations to quake before You! For when You did awesome things that we did not expect, You came down, and the mountains trembled before You. Since ancient times no one has heard, no ear has perceived, no eye has seen any God besides You, who acts on behalf of those who wait for Him* (Isaiah 64:2-4).

EAST: God's glory—the sun rising. East wind brings judgment/hardship.

EATING: Feeding on something, e.g. Word of God, or may be on something evil. Meditation and gaining greater understanding.

ECHO: Word coming back. Word sphere against living revealed. Repercussions.

EGG, SEED: Sustenance. The possibility for growth—potential and development in any manner, revelation. Delicate seed or promise.

EGYPT: Bondage/slavery. Refuge—Egypt was refuge for Jesus. Old sin. Pre-Christian life.

EIGHT: A new beginning. Circumcision of flesh.

EIGHTEEN: Bondage. God gave Israelites to Philistine for eighteen years.

> *He became angry with them. He sold them into the hands of the Philistines and the Ammonites, who that year shattered and crushed them. For eighteen years they oppressed all the Israelites on the east side of the Jordan in Gilead, the land of the Amorites* (Judges 10:7-8).

> *And a woman was there who had been crippled by a spirit for eighteen years. She was bent over and could not straighten up at all. When Jesus saw her, He called her forward and said to*

her, "Woman, you are set free from your infirmity." Then He put His hands on her, and immediately she straightened up and praised God. Indignant because Jesus had healed on the Sabbath, the synagogue ruler said to the people, "There are six days for work. So come and be healed on those days, not on the Sabbath." The Lord answered him, "You hypocrites! Doesn't each of you on the Sabbath untie his ox or donkey from the stall and lead it out to give it water? Then should not this woman, a daughter of Abraham, whom Satan has kept bound for eighteen long years, be set free on the Sabbath day from what bound her?" (Luke 13:11-16).

Getting the Ammonites and Amelikites to join him, Eglon came and attacked Israel and they took possession of the City of Palms. The Israelites were subject to Eglon King of Moab for eighteen years (Judges 3:13-14).

ELECTRICITY: Spiritual power; potential for God's flow.

Outlet for electricity: Possibility of being connected into the flow of the Holy Spirit.

Unplugged cord: Not connected to the power of the Spirit.

ELEMENTARY: The infant stage, not yet mature.

ELEVATOR: Moving up and down in levels of godly authority.

ELEVEN: Disorder confusion, lawlessness.

EMPLOYEE/SERVANTS: The one who is submitted to the authority. The actual person.

EMPLOYER/MASTER: Jesus. The authority, good or bad. Pastor. Evil leadership.

EXPLOSION: Quick outburst, generally positive. Sudden expansion or increase. Quick work or devastating change.

EYES: Seer's anointing.

Winking: Mockery or perversity; concealed intention or cunning person.

Closed: Ignorance; spiritually blind, mostly self-imposed.

FACE: Identity or characteristics. Image expression.

FACTORY: Structured service in God's vineyard.

FALLING: Loss of support. Falling out of favor. Entering a time of trial/darkness/sin.

FAMILY: The Christian or spiritual family. Group of people in covenant or spirit of oneness; unified fellowship.

FAN: Stirring up of gifting. Something that brings relief or comfort. Make fire hotter. Increasing circulation.

FARMER: One who plants, nurtures, cares for new Christians. Pastor capable of sowing and reaping harvest. Jesus Christ.

FATHER: Father God, supplier of needs. Natural father of the bloodline. One who provides. The head of home or place.

FATHER-IN-LAW: Father figure within the organization. An advisor, spirit of delegation, head of another organization.

FEATHERS: Protective spiritual covering. Weightless. Something with which to move in the spiritual realm. Presence of God.

> *He will cover you with His feathers, and under His wings you will find refuge; His faithfulness will be your shield and rampart* (Psalm 91:4).

> *Say to them, "This is what the Sovereign Lord says: A great eagle with powerful wings, long feathers and full plumage of varied colors came to Lebanon. Taking hold of the top of a cedar, he broke off its topmost shoot and carried it away to a land of merchants, where he planted it in a city of traders. He took some of the seed of your land and put it in fertile soil. He planted it like a willow by abundant water, and it sprouted and became a low, spreading vine. Its branches turned toward him, but its roots remained under it. So it became a vine and produced branches and put out leafy boughs. But there was another great eagle with powerful wings and full plumage. The vine now sent out its roots toward him from the plot where it was planted and stretched out its branches to him for water"* (Ezekiel 17:3-7).

FEEDING: To partake in a spiritual provision, good or evil.

FEET: A spiritual walk, heart attitude.

> ***Barefoot:*** Humble before the presence of God. One inner state—spiritual poverty. Reverence to God.

> ***Diseased:*** Spirit of offense.

> ***Kicking:*** Not under authority or working against authority.

> ***Lame:*** Crippled with unbelief, mindset, negative stronghold.

> ***Washing:*** Humble; duty of Christians.

FENCE: Protection. Security. Self-imposed. Limitation, stronghold.

> *How long will you assault a man? Would all of you throw him down—this leaning wall, this tottering fence?* (Psalm 62:3).

> *Then the king of the North will come and build up siege ramps and will capture a fortified* [fenced] *city. The forces of the South will be powerless to resist; even their best troops will not have the strength to stand* (Daniel 11:15).

FIELD: Life situation, things to do and accomplish. (Depends on the field and context.)

> *He gives rain on the earth, and sends waters on the fields* (Job 5:10 NKJV).

FIFTEEN: Mercy, grace, liberty, rest, freedom.

FIFTY: Period or time of outpouring, such as Pentecost. Number of Holy Spirit/jubilee/freedom/liberty.

FIGHT: To struggle with, to agonize, to war or resist something.

> *Contend, O Lord, with those who contend with me; fight against those who fight against me* (Psalm 35:1).

> *Fight the good fight of the faith. Take hold of the eternal life to which you were called when you made your good confession in the presence of many witnesses* (1 Timothy 6:12).

> *Remember those earlier days after you had received the light, when you stood your ground in a great contest* [fight] *in the face of suffering* (Hebrews 10:32).

FINGER: Means of discernment. Spiritual sensitivity, feelings.

Pointed finger: Accusations, persecution, instructions, direction.

Finger of God: Work of God, authority of God.

Clenched: Pride.

Thumb: Apostle.

Index: Prophet.

Middle: Evangelist.

Small: Pastor.

FIRE: God's presence. Trial, persecution, burning fervency, emotion, longing, aching and craving. Power. Holy Spirit. Anger or judgment/punishment. Lake of fire, very different from tongue of fire.

> *Then the Lord rained down burning sulphur on Sodom and Gomorrah—from the Lord out of the heavens* (Genesis 19:24).

FISH: New converts to the Lord. Newly recreated spirit of man. Miraculous provision of food.

> *"Come, follow me," Jesus said, "and I will make you fishers of men"* (Mark 1:17).

FIVE: Grace related to the fivefold ministry.

FLASH: Revelation or insight.

FLEA: Not plentiful. Inconvenience. Subtlety.

FLOOD: Judgment on those who use whatever power they have to inflict violence on others. Sin judged. Overcome. To be overcome and unable to recover. That which the Holy Spirit will use as a standard.

> *From the west, men will fear the name of the Lord, and from the rising of the sun, they will revere His glory. For He will come like a pent-up flood that the breath of the Lord drives along* (Isaiah 59:19).

> *I am going to bring floodwaters on the earth to destroy all life under the heavens, every creature that has the breath of life in it. Everything on earth will perish* (Genesis 6:17).

FLOWERS: Man's glory of the flesh that is passing away. An offering. Glory of God. Beautiful expression of love. Renewal. Spring.

> *That fading flower, his glorious beauty, set on the head of a fertile valley, will be like a fig ripe before harvest—as soon as someone sees it and takes it in his hand, he swallows it* (Isaiah 28:4).

> *But the one who is rich should take pride in his low position, because he will pass away like a wild flower* (James 1:10).

> *For, "All men are like grass, and all their glory is like the flowers of the field; the grass withers and the flowers fall"* (1 Peter 1:24).

Lily of the valley: Jesus.

Rose: Love, courtship, romance.

FLY (A FLY): Evil spirits. Corruption. To be possessed by evil spirit. Results of unclean actions.

> *As dead flies give perfume a bad smell, so a little folly outweighs wisdom and honor* (Ecclesiastes 10:1).

> *In that day the Lord will whistle for flies from the distant streams of Egypt and for bees from the land of Assyria* (Isaiah 7:18).

FLYING: Highly powered by the Holy Spirit.

> *Who are these that fly along like clouds, like doves to their nests?* (Isaiah 60:8).

> *Like birds hovering overhead, the Lord Almighty will shield Jerusalem; He will shield it and deliver it, He will "pass over" it and will rescue it* (Isaiah 31:5).

> *He mounted the cherubim and flew; He soared on the wings of the wind* (Psalm 18:10, 2 Samuel 22:11).

FOG: Not clear, uncertainty, concealed, vagueness. Wrath of God.

FOOD: Spiritual and physical nourishment, good or evil. To bring increase.

> *They should collect all the food of these good years that are coming and store up the grain under the authority of Pharaoh, to be kept in the cities for food* (Genesis 41:35).

FOREIGNER: A person outside the Christian faith (not a citizen of Heaven). Someone to be taught and cared for, and brought into the covenant.

FOREHEAD: Thought process and reasoning. Revelations. Retaining and recalling ability. Commitment to God.

FOREST: Growth in life (depending on the context). Place of danger and darkness where one can be easily lost and harmed. Confusion and lack of direction, uncultivated. A land covered with trees that are naturally planted is different from a park where man's hand is more evident.

> *The battle spread out over the whole countryside, and the forest claimed more lives that day than the sword* (2 Samuel 18:8).

FORTY: Testing period, season of trial.

> *Moses was there with the Lord forty days and forty nights without eating bread or drinking water. And he wrote on the tablets the words of the covenant—the Ten Commandments* (Exodus 34:28).

> *I brought you up out of Egypt, and I led you forty years in the desert to give you the land of the Amorites* (Amos 2:10).

> *Where for forty days he was tempted by the devil. He ate nothing during those days, and at the end of them He was hungry* (Luke 4:2).

FOUR: Worldly creation; four corners of the world; four seasons. Global implication or the four Gospels.

FOURTEEN: Double anointing. Recreation. Reproduction. Passover.

FOX: A cunning spirit. Craftiness, secretly, or counter-productive.

> *Tobiah the Ammonite, who was at his side, said, "What they are building—if even a fox climbed up on it, he would break down their wall of stones!"* (Nehemiah 4:3).

> *Catch for us the foxes, the little foxes that ruin the vineyards, our vineyards that are in bloom* (Song of Solomon 2:15).

Your prophets, O Israel, are like jackals [foxes] *among ruins* (Ezekiel 13:4).

He replied, "Go tell that fox, 'I will drive out demons and heal people today and tomorrow, and on the third day I will reach my goal'" (Luke 13:32).

FREEZER: Storing spiritual food for future time.

FRIEND: Brother or sister in Christ. Yourself. Showing to have similar qualities. Faithful person.

FROG: Evil spirit. Makes a lot of noise, boastful. Sorcery. Lying nature. Issuing curses.

If you refuse to let them go, I will plague your whole country with frogs (Exodus 8:2).

He sent swarms of flies that devoured them, and frogs that devastated them (Psalm 78:45).

Then I saw three evil spirits that looked like frogs; they came out of the mouth of the dragon, out of the mouth of the beast and out of the mouth of the false prophet (Revelation 16:13).

FRONT SIDE: Looking ahead, something in the future.

FRUITS: Source of nourishment. Means of increase. Reward of labor. To bear something or child. Harvest. Come to fullness. Gifts of the Spirit. Fruit of our labor. Fruit of the womb. Fruit of the Holy Spirit, consisting of all the Christian virtues.

FUEL: Source of energy. Source of food for the Spirit. Capable of reviving.

FURNACE: Source of heat, the heart, heated and painful experiences. Period of trial. Source of pruning. Center of holy activities.

Whoever does not fall down and worship will immediately be thrown into a blazing furnace (Daniel 3:6).

But as for you, the Lord took you and brought you out of the iron-smelting furnace, out of Egypt, to be the people of His inheritance, as you now are (Deuteronomy 4:20).

See, I have refined you, though not as silver; I have tested you in the furnace of affliction (Isaiah 48:10).

GALLOWS: A place of severe punishment. A place of nemesis or a place of death.

So they hanged Haman on the gallows he had pre-pared for Mordecai. Then the king's fury subsided (Esther 7:10).

GAP: Breach. A break in continuity; weak spot. A loophole. An opening.

You have not gone up to the breaks in the wall to repair it for the house of Israel so that it will stand firm in the battle on the day of the Lord (Ezekiel 13:5).

I looked for a man among them who would build up the wall and stand before Me in the gap on behalf of the land so I would not have to destroy it, but I found none (Ezekiel 22:30).

GARAGE: Symbolic of storage. Potential or protection.

GARBAGE: Abandoned things. Corruption. Reprobate or unclean. Unclean spirit; departure from all that is godly. Something that is thrown away. Opinion of life without Jesus.

GARDEN: A piece of land that is cultivated, signifying the life situation as planned by God. Field of labor in life. Place of increase, fruitfulness, and productivity. A place of rest or romance. Life of believer as a garden watered by the Holy Spirit.

Now the Lord God had planted a garden in the east, in Eden; and there He put the man He had formed (Genesis 2:8).

The Lord will guide you always; He will satisfy your needs in a sun-scorched land and will strengthen your frame. You will be like a well-watered garden, like a spring whose waters never fail (Isaiah 58:11).

The woman said to the serpent, "We may eat fruit from the trees in the garden" (Genesis 3:2).

Then the man and his wife heard the sound of the Lord God as He was walking in the garden in the cool of the day, and they hid from the Lord God among the trees of the garden (Genesis 3:8).

GARDENING: An area of labor. A place of reward, increase, or harvest. Putting things in order.

"Satan and his cohorts draw inspirations from and worship the elements of the earth, but as Christians we must only relate to these elements from the place of dominion given to Adam by God and redeemed to us by the precious blood of Jesus Christ. Many religions are already in this grave error—the error of worshiping the elements of nature. Imagery and scenes of the monumental celebration of worshiping rivers and other elements abound in our days. Joshua and Moses both spoke from the place of dominion; Moses commanded the ground and it obeyed him, and Joshua spoke to the sun and it stood still. Jesus Christ in His humanity rebuked the wind and punished the fig tree. These instances represent the correct and proper engagement of the elements of nature in spiritual warfare. We should always operate from the place of dominion rather than from the place servitude to nature."

More information about the relational consequences of the curse is found in my book, *The Final Frontiers.*[2]

GARMENT: Covering.

> ***Clean:*** Honor or mantle. The glory of God upon a person.

> ***Dirty:*** Mantle stained with sin.

GASOLINE: Source of energy. Faith-filled/prayer. Danger if not handled correctly, inflammable or potential for sudden explosion.

GATE: Doors, opening. Salvation. Entrance to something, such as building, grounds, or cities. In biblical days, business bargaining negotiations were conducted at the gates. Passage into or out of a place.

> *All these cities were fortified with high walls and with gates and bars, and there were also a great many unwalled villages* (Deuteronomy 3:5).

> *For he breaks down gates of bronze and cuts through bars of iron* (Psalm 107:16).

> *I will go before you and will level the mountains; I will break down gates of bronze and cut through bars of iron* (Isaiah 45:2).

> *The twelve gates were twelve pearls, each gate made of a single pearl. The great street of the city was of pure gold, like transparent glass* (Revelation 21:21).

The Lord loves the gates of Zion more than all the dwellings of Jacob (Psalm 87:2).

GIANT: A powerful spiritual being, e.g., an angel or demon. A challenging situation. Something that arouses fear.

We saw the Nephilim there (the descendants of Anak come from the Nephilim). We seemed like grasshoppers in our own eyes, and we looked the same to them (Numbers 13:33).

GIRDLE: To prepare for use; might or potency. To be made ready to show strength; gathering together of the strength within you.

GLOVES: Something that protects the means of service. Something that fits into another thing; protects the means of productivity.

GOAT: Pertaining to foolishness. Carnal, fleshly. Not submitting to authority. Walking into sin. Need for repentance. Miscarriage of judgment, e.g., scapegoat.

GOLD: Of God. Seal of divinity. Honorable. God's glory. Faithful; endurance; holiness that endures. Symbol of honor and high valor. Something valuable that endures.

I turned around to see the voice that was speaking to me. And when I turned I saw seven golden lampstands (Revelation 1:12).

Overlay it with pure gold, both inside and out, and make a gold molding around it (Exodus 25:11).

Make a table of acacia wood—two cubits long, a cubit wide and a cubit and a half high. Overlay it with pure gold and make a gold molding around it. Also make around it a rim a handbreadth wide and put a gold molding on the rim. Make four gold rings for the table and fasten them to the four corners, where the four legs are. The rings are to be close to the rim to hold the poles used in carrying the table. Make the poles of acacia wood, overlay them with gold and carry the table with them. And make its plates and dishes of pure gold, as well as its pitchers and bowls for the pouring out of offerings. Put the bread of the Presence on this table to be before Me at all times (Exodus 25:23-30).

In a large house there are articles not only of gold and silver, but also of wood and clay; some are for noble purposes and some for ignoble (2 Timothy 2:20).

GOVERNOR: The person who has the power in the place. Spiritual leader in the church, or of a geographical region or an evil principality. Authority; rulership; reigning.

GRANDCHILD: Blessing passed on from previous generation. Spirit passed on from the past generation. Generation inheritance, good or bad. Heir. Spiritual offspring of your ministry.

GRANDMOTHER: Generational authority over the person. Spiritual inheritance. Past wisdom or gifting. Parent church of a church plant.

GRAPES: Fruit of the Promised Land. Successful agriculture or success in life. Pleasant to the eyes. Evidence of fertility.

When I found Israel, it was like finding grapes in the desert; when I saw your fathers, it was like seeing the early fruit on the fig tree. But when they came to Baal Peor, they consecrated themselves to that shameful idol and became as vile as the thing they loved (Hosea 9:10).

"The days are coming," declares the Lord, "when the reaper will be overtaken by the plowman and the planter by the one treading grapes. New wine will drip from the mountains and flow from all the hills" (Amos 9:13).

Still another angel, who had charge of the fire, came from the altar and called in a loud voice to him who had the sharp sickle, "Take your sharp sickle and gather the clusters of grapes from the earth's vine, because its grapes are ripe" (Revelation 14:18).

When they reached the Valley of Eshcol, they cut off a branch bearing a single cluster of grapes. Two of them carried it on a pole between them, along with some pomegranates and figs (Numbers 13:23).

GRASS: Divinely provided; something meant to be maintained. Life. God's Word in seed form. Word of God; sustenance for animals.

Dried: Death to the flesh through repentance.

Mowed: Disciplined obedience.

GRASSHOPPER/LOCUST: A devastating situation. Instrument of God's judgment. Low self-esteem.

GRAVEYARD/GRAVE: Old tradition. Cultural reserve. Death. Demonic influence from the past. Buried potentials. Darkness, hell.

Let's swallow them alive, like the grave, and whole, like those who go down to the pit (Proverbs 1:12).

All your pomp has been brought down to the grave, along with the noise of your harps; maggots are spread out beneath you and worms cover you (Isaiah 14:11).

They came out of the tombs, and after Jesus' resurrection they went into the holy city and appeared to many people (Matthew 27:53).

GREY: Uncertainty, compromise, consisting of good and bad mixture.

GREEN: Life, good or evil. Provision. Rest and peace.

GROOM: Christ. Marriage. Headship.

GUARD: Ability to keep on the right path. Spirit of protection/to be vigilant.

GUEST: Spiritual messenger. An angel or evil presence.

GUN: Instrument of demonic affliction. Spoken words that wound. Power of words in prayer. Dominion through speaking the Word of God.

HAIL: Means of judgment against God's enemies. Something that can cause considerable damage to crops, property, and life. Means of punishment for the wicked.

Therefore, at this time tomorrow I will send the worst hailstorm that has ever fallen on Egypt, from the day it was founded till now (Exodus 9:18).

When Moses stretched out his staff toward the sky, the Lord sent thunder and hail, and lightning flashed down to the ground. So the Lord rained hail on the land of Egypt; hail fell and lightning flashed back and forth. It was the worst storm in all the land of Egypt since it had become a nation (Exodus 9:23-24).

I will execute judgment upon him with plague and bloodshed; I will pour down torrents of rain, hailstones and burning sulphur on him and on his troops and on the many nations with him (Ezekiel 38:22).

HAMMER: Living Word. Preaching the Word hard and fast. Capable of breaking something to pieces. Something that smoothes strong things such as metal or rocks. For building.

The craftsman encourages the goldsmith, and he who smoothes with the hammer spurs on him who strikes the anvil. He says of the welding, "It is good." He nails down the idol so it will not topple (Isaiah 41:7).

"Is not My word like fire," declares the Lord, "and like a hammer that breaks a rock in pieces?" (Jeremiah 23:29).

HANDS: Means of service. Means of expressing strength.

Clapping: Joy and worship.

Fist: Pride in one's strength; anger.

Covering face: Guilt or shame.

Holding hands: In agreement.

Left hand: Something spiritual.

Raised hands: Surrender or worshiping.

Right hand: Oath of allegiance. Means of power, of honor. Natural strengths.

Shaking hands: Coming to an agreement.

Stretched out hands: Surrender.

Trembling: To fear, spirit of fear; anxiety. Awe at God's presence.

Under thighs: In oaths.

Washing: Declaring innocence; to dissociate oneself.

HARLOT, PROSTITUTE: A tempting situation. Something that appeals to your flesh. Worldly desire. Pre-Christian habit that wants to resurrect. Enticement.

HARP: If used for God, praise and worship in Heaven and on the earth. Instrument for praise and worship. Could be used for idolatry.

HARVEST: Seasons of grace. Opportunities to share the gospel. Fruitfulness. Reward of labor and action.

HAT: Covering, protection, mantle, crown. Protection of the head.

HEAD: Lordship, authority. Jesus/God. Husband. Pastor. Boss. Mind, thoughts.

> ***Anointed:*** Set apart for God's service.

> ***Hands on heads:*** Signifying sorrow.

HEDGE: God's safeguard, security, safety. Literally means loose stonewall without mortar. Protection. Supernatural or prophetic protection. God as hedge around His people. Where the very poor find shelter.

> *Why have you broken down its walls* [hedge] *so that all who pass by pick its grapes?* (Psalm 80:12).

> *He then began to speak to them in parables: "A man planted a vineyard. He put a wall around it, dug a pit for the winepress and built a watchtower. Then he rented the vineyard to some farmers and went away on a journey"* (Mark 12:1).

HEEL: The crushing power.

HELICOPTER: Spirit-powered for spiritual warfare. One-man ministry.

HELMET: The awareness and inner assurance of salvation. God's promise.

HIGH SCHOOL: Moving into a higher level of walk with God; high level of training/equipping. Capable of giving the same to others.

HIGHWAY: Holy way; the path of life. Truth of God, Christ; Predetermined path of life, or path of life that enjoys high volume usage. May lead to good or evil destinations.

> ***Dead end:*** A course of action that will lead to nothing, that which will not persist.

Gravel (stony ground): Difficult path, a course that is not straight.

Muddy: Difficult path; not clear, uncertain path.

Construction: In preparation, change, not ready.

HILLS: A place of exaltation. Uplift high above the natural. Throne of God. Mount Zion.

HIPS: Reproduction. Relating to reproduction or supporting structure. May indicate seduction.

HONEY: Sweet; strength; wisdom. Spirit of God. The abiding anointing. The sweet Word of our Lord. Standard of measure for pleasant things. The best product of the land. Abundance. A land flowing with milk and honey. Food in times of scarcity.

Then their father Israel said to them, "If it must be, then do this: Put some of the best products of the land in your bags and take them down to the man as a gift—a little balm and a little honey, some spices and myrrh, some pistachio nuts and almonds" (Genesis 43:11).

He will not enjoy the streams, the rivers flowing with honey and cream (Job 20:17).

So I have come down to rescue them from the hand of the Egyptians and to bring them up out of that land into a good and spacious land, a land flowing with milk and honey—the home of the Canaanites, Hittites, Amorites, Perizzites, Hivites and Jebusites (Exodus 3:8).

Honey and curds, sheep, and cheese from cows' milk for David and his people to eat. For they said, the people have become hungry and tired and thirsty in the desert (2 Samuel 17:29).

HORNS: The source of anointed power. The power of a king, evil power.

HORSE: Of great strength, powerful in warfare. Spirit of tenaciousness, not double-minded. A ministry that is powerful and capable of competing. Strength under control, such as meekness. God's judgment.

Horse that kicks: Threatening, or opposition to the agreed terms.

Black: Lack.

Bay (flame-colored): Power, fire.

Pale: Spirit of death.

Red: Danger; passion; blood of Jesus.

White: Purity or righteousness.

Blue: Spiritual.

Brown: Repented, born-again.

Green: Life, mortal.

Grey: In between black and white. Vague, hazy.

Orange: Danger, evil.

Pink: Flesh. Relating to desire and decision based on the mind.

Purple: Something related to royalty. Noble in character. Riches.

Yellow: Gift from God; cowardliness, fear.

HOSPITAL: A gift of healing/anointing or caring or love. Edifying others. A place for treatment.

HOTEL: A place of gathering, a temporary place of meeting. A transit place of meeting, church; a transit situation.

HOUSE: One's spiritual and emotional house. Personality. Church.

HUSBAND: Jesus Christ. Actual spouse.

INCENSE: Prayer, worship, praises. Acceptable unto God.

IRON: Something of strength, powerful; strict rules; powerful strongholds.

IRONING: The process of correction by instructions, teaching. To talk things over. Working out problem relationships. Turning from sin.

ISLAND: Something related to the island. What the island is known for, or its name.

ISRAEL: The nation of Israel. The Christian community; the redeemed ones; authority that comes from God over men; people of God.

JERUSALEM: The establishment of peace. Chosen place by God. The city of God.

JEWELRY: Valuable possessions. God's people. Gifted person who has received abilities from the Lord. Something or person valued by the dreamer. Not to be given to those who will not value it.

JUDGE: Father God. Authority. Anointed to make decisions. Jesus Christ. Unjust ruler.

KANGAROO: Something that is not based on the truth. Prejudiced. Rushing to conclusion.

KEY: The authority to something, claim to ownership. Prophetic authority. Kingdom authority.

KISS: Coming to agreement, covenant. Seductive process. Enticement; deception or betrayal; betrayal from a trusted friend or brother/sister in Christ.

KITCHEN: A place of preparing spiritual food. Hunger for the work of God. A place of spiritual nourishment.

KNEELING: Surrender; praying; art of submission.

KNEES: Reverence; prayerfulness; submission.

KNIVES: Word of God. Speaking against someone.

LADDER: A means of change in spiritual position. Means of escape from captivity.

LAMB/SHEEP: Jesus. Believer. Gentleness. Blamelessness.

LAME: Shortcomings. A flaw in one's walk with God. Limitation.

LAMP: Source of light. Inward part of man or spirit. Holy Spirit.

LAND: Inheritance. Promise given by God.

Newly cleared land: Newly revealed area of God's promise.

Ripe on the land: Fruitful work of the ministry.

Bare earth or dust: Curse, bareness.

Neglected, unwanted land: Neglected promise or inheritance.

LAUGH: Rejoicing. Joy or sarcasm.

LAUGHING: Outburst of excitement or joy.

LAVA: Enemy.

LAWYER: Jesus Christ. The accuser of brethren. Pertaining to legalism. Mediator.

LEAD (METAL): Heavy burden; heavy thing.

LEAVEN: Sin that spreads to others. False belief system.

LEAVES: Trees with healthy leaves are planted by the rivers of life. Healing of the nation.

Dry leaves: Pressures of life.

LEFT: That which is of the Spirit. That which is not natural with man. God manifested through the flesh of man.

Who has gone into heaven and is at God's right hand—with angels, authorities and powers in submission to Him (1 Peter 3:22).

LEGS: Means of support. Spiritual strength to walk in life.

Female legs: Power of enticement.

LEOPARD: Powerful, either good or bad. Permanent. Unchanging character.

LEMON: Something gone sour; bitter doctrine. Hard to accept teaching.

LEVIATHAN: Ancestral spirit of demonic nature; difficult to eliminate—only God can deal with it.

LIBRARY: A place of knowledge. Schooling. Wisdom.

LICE: Concerted attempt to smear you. Accusation, shame.

LIFTING HANDS: Total surrender. Giving worship to God.

LIGHT: Illumination on the established truth. No longer hidden; to show forth.

> **Dim light:** Showing the need for the fullness of the knowledge of the Word.

> **Absence of light:** Lack of understanding, absence of God.

> **Small lamp or flashlight:** Walking in partial grounding of the Word, or pocket of wisdom.

LIGHTNING: God's voice; the Lord interrupting an activity to get man's attention. Something happening very quickly. God's power and mystery. Divine weapon. God's finger of judgment.

LIMOUSINE: Call of God. Pride or exhibitionism.

LION: Conquering nature of Jesus (majority of the time). A powerful spirit, good or bad.

LIPS: Word of God. Enticement. Means of testifying. Offering. Speak falsehood/accusation.

LIVING ROOM: Part of your personality that is opened to others to see.

LOST in what in the natural is a familial environment (DIRECTION): Indicating inner confusions or indecision in the dreamer.

MACHINES: Power and might of the Spirit. That which is powered by supernatural force.

MAGGOT: Filthiness or the lust of the flesh. Corruption.

MAN (UNKNOWN): A spiritual messenger, either God's messenger or evil. Jesus.

MANNA: God's miraculous provision. Coming directly from God. Glory of God. Bread of life.

MAP: Word of God. Instruction. Direction.

MARBLE: Beauty. Majesty of God.

MARK: Something that distinguishes. Symbol. To set apart. Mark of God or devil.

MARRIAGE: Going deeper into things of God (intimacy). A covenant process. Actual marriage. Jesus Christ's union with the Church.

MEAT: Something meant for the spiritually mature. Strong doctrine.

> *I gave you milk, not solid food, for you were not yet ready for it. Indeed, you are still not ready* (1 Corinthians 3:2).

> *But solid food is for the mature, who by constant use have trained themselves to distinguish good from evil* (Hebrews 5:14).

MERCY SEAT: Indicating the mercy of God. Kingship of the Lord. The throne of God. God's love.

MICE: Something that eats up valuables secretly. Devourer. Spirit of timidity or fear. Evil that can multiple rapidly.

MICROPHONE: Amplification of the Word of God. Preaching anointing. The prophetic ministry. Ability to influence many people.

MICROSCOPE: Need to look more carefully. Obtaining clearer vision. To magnify something,whether good or bad.

MICROWAVE OVEN: May indicate lack of patience. Looking for easy option. Quick acting process.

MIDDLE/JUNIOR HIGH: Medium level equipping by God.

MILK: Good nourishment. Elementary teaching.

MIRROR: Something that enables you to look more closely. Reflecting on something. Word of God revealing the need for change. Self-consciousness; vanity.

MISCARRIAGE: To lose something at the preparatory stage, whether good or bad. Plans aborted.

MONEY: God's favor. Spiritual and natural wealth. Spiritual authority, power. Man's strength. Greed.

MOON: Indicating the rulership. To reign in the night seasons. Light of God at dark season of life. Something bright in darkness.

> *God made two great lights—the greater light to govern the day and the lesser light to govern the night. He also made the stars* (Genesis 1:16).

MOON TO BLOOD: The Church being prosecuted. Something bright in darkness.

MORNING: The beginning of something. Light of God after dark season of life. Sins being revealed. Rejoicing, prayer time, time to lay a good foundation.

MOTH: Insect that dwells in dark places. Causes loss by deceitfulness. Corruption and deterioration.

MOTHER: The Church. Jerusalem. Actual person. Spiritual mother. Carer/teacher.

MOTHER-IN-LAW: A church that is not the dreamer's church. Actual person. False teacher.

MOTOR, ENGINE AND BATTERY: The source of power and of the anointing.

MOTORCYCLE: Spirit-powered personal ministry. Loner. Show-off pride or exhibitionism.

MOUNTAIN: Great power and strength, whether good or bad. A place of revelation or meeting with God or God's glory. Obstacle, difficulty.

MOUTH: Instrument of witnessing, good or bad. Speaking evil or good words. Something from which come the issues of life. Words coming against you.

MOVING: Change in spiritual and emotional well-being; Changing situation; a change is imminent.

MOVING VAN: A time or period of change, either in the natural or in the spirit.

MUSIC: Praise and worship, good or bad. Flowing in spiritual gift. Teaching. Admonishing. A message.

MUSTARD SEED: Faith. Value or power of faith. Sowing in faith. Word of God. God's promise.

He replied, "Because you have so little faith. I tell you the truth, if you have faith as small as a mustard seed, you can say to this mountain, 'Move from here to there' and it will move. Nothing will be impossible for you" (Matthew 17:20).

NAILS: Makes something more permanent. The way Jesus dealt with our sins.

NAME: The identity of something; designate; rank or status. Meaning of the name.

NATION: Could represent the characteristics of the nation. The calling related to the nation. The actual nation.

America: Cowboy.

France: Romance.

Germany: Hardworking. World War.

Jews: Business minded.

NECK: Stubborn, strong-willed.

Stiff-necked: Rebellious.

NEST: Security that is not real; God's place of rest.

NET: To trap, ensnare. The plans of the enemy. To win souls.

NEW: New condition.

NEWSPAPER: Proclamation. Bringing something to the public. Prophetic utterance.

NIGHT: Time of trial or difficulty. Lack of God's lights or understanding. Without involvement of the Spirit.

NINE: Fruit of the Spirit or gift of the Spirit; harvest.

NINETEEN: Faith, repentance.

NOISE: Irritation that is intrusive. Sound that draws attention.

NORTH: Refers to great powers that will come.

NOSE: Discerning spirit. Intruding into people's privacy. Discernment, gossiper.

NOSEBLEED: Strife. Need to strengthen your discerning.

OCEAN: Masses of people.

OIL: The anointing. Prosperity. Holy Spirit. Grace/mercy of God. Medicine. Joy.

OLD: Old ways. That which will give way to the new.

OLD MAN: Pre-Christian self. Spirit of wisdom.

ONE: New beginning. Unity (divinity). Deity.

ONE HUNDRED: Fullness. Hundredfold reward. The promise.

Isaac planted crops in that land and the same year reaped a hundredfold, because the Lord blessed him (Genesis 26:12).

ONE HUNDRED AND FIFTY: The promise and the Holy Spirit.

ONE HUNDRED AND TWENTY: The beginning of the work of Holy Spirit.

In those days Peter stood up among the believers (a group numbering about a hundred and twenty) (Acts 1:15).

ORANGE: Warning, danger ahead, caution needed.

OVEN: The heart of the matter. Of high intensity. Fervency.

OVERSLEPT: There is a chance of missing a divine appointment. To be behind in the divine schedule of things. To avoid over-indulgence or self-pity.

PAINTING: Creating a new image. Renew or revamp.

PARACHUTING: Bail out, escape and flee.

PARK: A place of rest, worship, tranquility. A temporary place. A place of peace. A place of romance. A place of meditation, exercise, and leisure.

PARROT: Something that mimics. Not the original.

PATH: The path of life. Personal walk with God. Directions in life.

PEACOCK: Something of pride. Generally, adornment of royal courts.

PEARL: Something of value. Established truth of God. Glory of Heaven.

PEN/PENCIL: Pertaining to writing. Words that are written. To make permanent.

PERFUME: Aroma of something. The glory of God. Fragrance of Holy Spirit or anointing.

PICTURE: Something relating to images. To keep in memory. To honor.

> *Frames:* Mindset; mentality.

> *Golden frames:* Divine seal.

> *Old frame:* Outdated.

PIG: Unclean spirit. Spirit of religion. Caged by mindset. Phony, not trustworthy. Selfish, hypocritical.

PILLAR: The main support of something. Spiritual and natural. Foundational truths.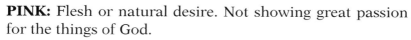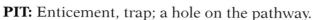

PINK: Flesh or natural desire. Not showing great passion for the things of God.

PIT: Enticement, trap; a hole on the pathway.

PLATTER: Something on which to present things.

PLAY: Life competition. Spiritual warfare/contention.

PLAYING: Reflective of true-life situation. The game of life.

PLOW: Preparing the heart to receive the Word of God. Cracking fallow grounds hardened by sin.

POISON: Evil and deadly teaching or doctrine.

POLICE: Spiritual authority. Having power to enforce purpose, whether good or bad. Pastor, elders. Angels or demons. Enforcer of a curse or of the law.

PORCH: Public part of the building, exhibition. Easily seen and openly displayed.

POSTAGE STAMP: The seal of authority. Authorization. Empowered.

POST-MORTEM: Examination of what has happened. Giving testimony.

POT: The vessel or container, e.g., tradition. A person.

PREGNANCY: In the process of reproducing; preparatory stage. The promise of God. The Word of God as seed. Prophetic word.

PREGNANCY, LABOR PAINS: Process of birthing something, whether good or bad. Final stages of trial or preparation; wilderness period.

PREACHER/PASTOR (PRIEST AND PROPHET): A person who represents God. Timely message from God. Spiritual authority.

PRISON: A place where a person is restricted and where human rights are limited. A place of bondage or confinement. Often indicates a place of depression, areas of stronghold bondage.

PRISONER: The lost soul.

PURPLE: Related to royalty. Kingly anointing or authority.

> *One of those listening was a woman named Lydia, a dealer in purple cloth from the city of Thyatira, who was a worshiper of God. The Lord opened her heart to respond to Paul's message* (Acts 16:14).

PURSE/WALLET: Treasure, heart, personal identity; precious and valuable.

> *Empty:* Bankrupt.

RABBIT: Evil spirit. Something capable of carnal multiplication.

RADIO: Continuous broadcasting of news, nuisance. Prophetic utterance. Teaching gospel.

RAFT: Without purpose or direction.

RAGS: Poverty, humility, or lack.

RAILROAD TRACK: Tradition, unchanging habit. Stubborn. Caution, danger.

RAIN: Blessings, God's Word. Outpouring of the Spirit. Hindrance, trial or disappointment.

> *Drought:* Lack of blessing. Absence of the presence of God.

RAINBOW: Sign of God's covenant. Sign of natural agreement.

RAINING: The blessing from God. Testing time or trial.

RAM: Satanic or of the occult.

RAT: Rubbish (sin), left out to eat. A passion that is unclean or something that feeds it.

REAP: Harvest. Reward of effort, good or bad.

REAPING: Reward of labor.

RED: Passion. Blood of Jesus. Strong feeling, danger, anger. Heated emotion. Zeal, enthusiasm.

REED: Weakness: spiritual or natural. Too weak to be relied on; not firm, coward.

REFRIGERATOR: Where "issues" are kept. Heart issues. Motivation. Thoughts. Storing up spiritual food for the right time.

> *Stored food:* Things stored in the heart.

> *Spoiled food:* To harbor a grudge, unclean thoughts or desires.

REFUGE: The place of protection, safety, or security.

REINS: A means of control or to restrain.

RENDING: Sorrow or disagreement. To tear apart as sign of anger. Grief, repentance, sorrow, disagreement.

REST: A state of stillness or inactivity, tranquility. A place where you can receive from God. Laziness.

RESTAURANT: A place of choice regarding the spiritual food you need. A place where the fivefold ministry is taught.

RESTING: Not in activity; lax.

RICE: Sustenance. Poor sustenance. Earthly. Lacking flavor.

RIGHT: Natural inclination, authority, or power. What you are naturally able to do.

RIGHT TURN: Natural change.

RING: Never-ending, unchanging, uninterrupted. Unity of purpose in a place. Covenant relationship. Relating to God's authority.

> *Wedding ring:* Symbol of our covenant with God. Marriage between man and woman.

> *Engagement ring:* Promise. Sign of commitment.

> *Rings worn as jewelry:* Vanity, worldliness.

RIVER: Movement of God. Flow of the Spirit. River as an obstacle. Trial.

> *Deep:* Deep things of God.

> *Muddy:* Operating in mixtures, flesh and spirit.

> *Dangerous currents:* Difficulty in moving in the flow of the Spirit. Danger ahead.

> *Dried up:* Lack of the presence of God, traditions or legalism. Empty of spiritual power.

ROACHES: Unclean. Something that can cause and thrive on sin.

ROBE: The true covering from God. Righteousness; right standing with God.

ROCK: Jesus Christ; solid foundation. Obstacle. A place of refuge. Stumbling block.

> *And drank the same spiritual drink; for they drank from the spiritual rock that accompanied them, and that rock was Christ* (1 Corinthians 10:4).

> *He is the Rock, His works are perfect, and all His ways are just. A faithful God who does no wrong, upright and just is He* (Deuteronomy 32:4).

ROCKET: A ministry or person with great power or potential for deep things of the Spirit. Capable of quick take-off and great speed.

ROCKING: Reflective.

ROCKING CHAIR: Long standing in nature, intercession, recollection, prayer, relaxation, old age.

ROD: Staff or scepter of authority. To guard. Discipline.

Even though I walk through the valley of the shadow of death, I will fear no evil, for You are with me; Your rod and Your staff, they comfort me (Psalm 23:4).

The rod of correction imparts wisdom, but a child left to himself disgraces his mother (Proverbs 29:15).

ROLLER COASTER: Something that moves up and down. Swings of season or moods. Faith needing more faith.

ROLLER SKATES: Skillful walk with God. Speedy progress. Fast but may be dangerous.

ROOF: Relating to the mind, thinking, meditation. Spiritual rather than the natural. Revelations from above; covering.

ROOT: The origin of something. The source of something. The heart of the matter, the means of sustenance or survival, the motives.

A shoot will come up from the stump of Jesse; from his roots a Branch will bear fruit (Isaiah 11:1).

In the morning, as they went along, they saw the fig tree withered from the roots (Mark 11:20).

ROPE/CORD: Something used in binding, either in covenant or in bondage.

ROUND (SHAPE): Never-ending. Favor, love, or mercy.

ROWBOAT: A ministry that intervenes for others. Offering earnest prayers.

ROWING: Working at something, to labor in spirit. Travailing in the spirit. Hard work.

RUG: To cover up something. Protection.

RUNNING: Trying to catch up with something. Hard work. Race.

SACRIFICE: To give up something. To lay down one's life for another. Something to cover up or wash away or to give up something.

But King David replied to Araunah, "No, I insist on paying the full price. I will not take for the Lord what is yours, or sacrifice a burnt offering that costs me nothing" (1 Chronicles 21:24).

SALT: Something that adds value. Something that preserves. Something that purifies. To make to last or to make more palatable.

You are the salt of the earth. But if the salt loses its saltiness, how can it be made salty again? It is no longer good for anything, except to be thrown out and trampled by men (Matthew 5:13).

Let your conversation be always full of grace, seasoned with salt, so that you may know how to answer everyone (Colossians 4:6).

SALT WATER: To add flavor. To cleanse.

SANCTUARY: A sacred place. A place set apart for spiritual offering, sacrifices. A place of immunity or rest. An asylum, a refuge. A sacred place reserved for communion with God, or gods or evil power.

Observe My Sabbaths and have reverence for My sanctuary. I am the Lord (Leviticus 26:2).

On the contrary, it is to be a witness between us and you and the generations that follow, that we will worship the Lord at His sanctuary with our burnt offerings, sacrifices and fellowship offerings. Then in the future your descendants will not be able to say to ours, "You have no share in the Lord" (Joshua 22:27).

SAND: Symbolic of work of flesh. Not suitable for foundation. Numerous. Seeds. Promises.

But you have said, "I will surely make you prosper and will make your descendants like the sand of the sea, which cannot be counted" (Genesis 32:12).

But everyone who hears these words of mine and does not put them into practice is like a foolish man who built his house on sand (Matthew 7:26).

SCEPTER: Staff of authority. Office. Staff of sovereignty.

The scepter will not depart from Judah, nor the ruler's staff from between his feet, until He comes to whom it belongs and the obedience of the nations is His (Genesis 49:10).

Your throne, O God, will last for ever and ever; a scepter of justice will be the scepter of Your kingdom (Psalm 45:6).

SCHOOL, CLASSROOM: Training period, a place of teaching. A ministry with teaching anointing.

SCORPION: Highly demonic spirit or any evil spirit. Something that could be poisonous.

SEA: Great multitude of people. Nations of the world. Unsettled, as the mark of sea. Something by which to reach the nations. Great obstacle.

Four great beasts, each different from the others, came up out of the sea (Daniel 7:3).

SEACOAST: Transition phase. Borderland.

SEAL: Confirmation or authenticity or guarantee. Mark of God's approval or belonging. Mark of evil.

SEA OF GLASS: Peaceful and clear. Symbol of revelation. Stillness/transparency.

SEAT: The power base. Rulership. Authority. Coming to rest. A place of mercy.

SEED: Word of God. Promise. Something capable of giving rise to many or greater things, whether good or bad.

SERPENT: Symbol of satan. Kingdom of the world. An accursed thing or cunning.

> ***Snake (if hung on a pole, stick, tree):*** Emblem of Christ on the cross.
>
> ***Viper:*** Gossip or persecution.
>
> ***Python:*** Spirit of divination.
>
> ***Rattles:*** Evil words against the dreamer.
>
> ***Fangs:*** Dangerous intentions coming against the dreamer.

Cobra: Vicious verbal attack, capable of spreading far, capable of forming hooded neck and can send off poison from a distance.

Anaconda: Attacks that will drain the dreamer of spirituality. Kills by squeezing out air (spiritual life) from the victim.

SEVEN: The number of perfection, earthly completion, or finished work. Rest. A time of blessing or holy time. Freedom.

Remember the Sabbath day by keeping it holy. Six days you shall labor and do all your work, but the seventh day is a Sabbath to the Lord your God. On it you shall not do any work, neither you, nor your son or daughter, nor your manservant or maidservant, nor your animals, nor the alien within your gates. For in six days the Lord made the heavens and the earth, the sea, and all that is in them, but He rested on the seventh day. Therefore the Lord blessed the Sabbath day and made it holy (Exodus 20:8-11).

These are the laws you are to set before them: If you buy a Hebrew servant, he is to serve you for six years. But in the seventh year, he shall go free, without paying anything (Exodus 21:1-2).

SEVENTEEN: Spiritual process of maturation. Not yet matured.

This is the account of Jacob. Joseph, a young man of seventeen, was tending the flocks with his brothers, the sons of Bilhah and the sons of Zilpah, his father's wives, and he brought their father a bad report about them (Genesis 37:2).

SEVENTY: Impartation of God's spirit/increase/restoration.

The Lord said to Moses: "Bring Me seventy of Israel's elders who are known to you as leaders and officials among the people. Have them come to the Tent of Meeting, that they may stand there with you. I will come down and speak with you there, and I will take of the Spirit that is on you and put the Spirit on them. They will help you carry the burden of the people so that you will not have to carry it alone (Numbers 11:16-17).

SEVENTY-FIVE: Period for purification and separation. Abraham was seventy-five when he set out from Haran.

So Abram left, as the Lord had told him; and Lot went with him. Abram was seventy-five years old when he set out from Haran (Genesis 12:4).

SEWAGE: Something that carries waste. Good appearance but carrying waste within. Waste could defile flesh.

SEWING: Putting together something. Amendment; union; counseling.

SEXUAL ENCOUNTER: Soulish desires.

Sexual encounter with old lover: You desire your old life.

SHADOW: Not the real thing, reflection of something. The spiritual cover. A place of safety, security. Only partially illuminated. Poor resemblance of. Delusion or imitation. Imperfect or lacking the real substance.

He who dwells in the shelter of the Most High will rest in the shadow of the Almighty (Psalm 91:1).

Dark shadows: Demons.

SHEPHERD: Jesus Christ,God.Leader, good or bad.Ability to separate goat from sheep. Selfless person.

Wherever I have moved with all the Israelites, did I ever say to any of their rulers whom I commanded to shepherd My people Israel, "Why have you not built Me a house of cedar?" (2 Samuel 7:7).

SHIELD: A protective thing. God's truth. Faith in God. Something trusted to protect based on past experience.

After this, the word of the Lord came to Abram in a vision: "Do not be afraid, Abram. I am your shield, your very great reward" (Genesis 15:1).

In addition to all this, take up the shield of faith, with which you can extinguish all the flaming arrows of the evil one (Ephesians 6:16).

The Lord is my strength and my shield; my heart trusts in Him, and I am helped. My heart leaps for joy and I will give thanks to Him in song (Psalm 28:7).

SHIP: A big ministry capable of influencing large numbers of people.

Battleship: Built for effective spiritual warfare.

Crashing: End of the ministry or end of one phase.

Fast: Operating its great power.

Large: Large area of influence.

Sinking: Out of line with the purpose of God, losing spiritual control.

Small: Small or personal.

On dry ground: Without the move of the Spirit. Moving more with the work of flesh. A miracle if moving on dry ground.

SHOES: Readiness to spread the gospel. Knowledge of the Word of God.

And with your feet fitted with the readiness that comes from the gospel of peace (Ephesians 6:15).

Boots: Equipped for spiritual warfare.

Does not fit: Walking in something you're not called to.

Giving away: Depending on the context, equipping others.

High heels: Seduction/discomfort.

Need of shoes: Not dwelling on the Word of God. In need of comfort or protection.

New shoes: Getting new understanding of the Gospel. Fresh mandate from God.

Putting on: Preparation for a spiritual journey.

Slippers: Too comfortable or too lax.

Snowshoes: Faith, walking in the Spirit, supported by faith in the Word of God.

Taking off: Honoring God, ministering to the Lord.

Taking someone else's shoes off: To show respect.

Tennis shoes: Spiritual giftedness. Running the race of life.

SHOPPING CENTER: Ministry that has multifaceted giftedness within its midst. Coming to a place of choices that may lead to not being single-minded. Could also indicate the various methods of the enemy strategies.

SHOULDER: The responsibility; the authority.

Broad shoulders: Capable of handling much responsibility.

Bare female shoulders: Enticement.

Drooped shoulders: Defeated attitude. Overworked; over-tired. Burned-out.

SHOVEL: Digging up something. To smear someone.

SICKLE: Reaping. Word of God. The harvest.

SIEVE: To separate the impure from the pure. Trial or testing.

For I will give the command, and I will shake the house of Israel among all the nations as grain is shaken in a sieve, and not a pebble will reach the ground (Amos 9:9).

SIFT: Separation by testing.

Simon, Simon, Satan has asked to sift you as wheat (Luke 22:31).

SIGN: A witness of something. A foreshadow. To draw attention to something.

Crossroad/intersection: A place for decision. Time for change.

Stop sign: Stop and pray for guidance.

Yield: A sign of submission.

SIGNATURE: Commitment and ownership or take responsibility for.

SILVER: Symbol of redemption. Understanding, knowledge. Something of valor, worldly knowledge, betrayal. Furnace of affliction.

SINGING: The words of the song = message from God. Rejoicing. Heart overflow.

SISTER: Sister in Jesus Christ. Actual person. Similar qualities in you.

SISTER-IN-LAW: Same as sister. A Christian in another fellowship. A relationship without much depth. Actual person. Person with similar qualities.

SITTING: A place of authority, position in power. Throne of God or seat of satan.

SIX: The number of man. Symbol of satan. Pride in the work of man.

SIX-SIX-SIX: Number of satan. Mark of the beast. Number of human hubris.

This calls for wisdom. If anyone has insight, let him calculate the number of the beast, for it is man's number. His number is 666 (Revelation 13:18).

SIXTEEN: Set free by love. The power of love or salvation. Sixteen characteristics of love mentioned in First Corinthians 13.

SKIING: Stepping out in faith. The power of faith. Smooth riding in God is provision. Making rapid process.

SKINS: The covering of; something closely linked and difficult to separate.

SKY: Above the natural. God's presence. Related to God or high things of the Spirit.

SKYSCRAPER: A ministry or person that has built-up structure to function on multi-level. A church or person with prophetic giftedness. High level of spiritual experience. Revelation.

SLEEPING: Being overtaken. Not being conscious of something. Hidden. Laziness. State of rest; danger. Out of control.

Overslept: In danger of missing a divine appointment. Prone to laziness.

SMILE: Sign of friendliness. Act of kindness. To agree with.

SMILING: Sign of friendship. Seductive process.

SMOKE: The manifested glory of God. Prayers of saints. Praise; worship. Sign of something. Hindrance.

SNAKE: Backbiting; divination; false accusations; false prophecies. Gossip; long tales; slander. See *Serpent.*

SNARE: A trap. The fear of man. Bring into bondage.

SNOW: Favor of God. Totally pure.

> *He spreads the snow like wool and scatters the frost like ashes* (Psalm 147:16).

> *As the rain and the snow come down from heaven, and do not return to it without watering the earth and making it bud and flourish, so that it yields seed for the sower and bread for the eater* (Isaiah 55:10).

> *As I looked, thrones were set in place, and the Ancient of Days took His seat. His clothing was as white as snow; the hair of His head was white like wool. His throne was flaming with fire, and its wheels were all ablaze* (Daniel 7:9).

> **Dirty snow:** No longer pure.

SOAP: Something that cleans. Forgiveness. Interceding for others.

SOCKS: Reflective of the state of the heart as the fertile ground for the Word of God. Peace. Protection of the feet.

> **White socks:** Heart and walk before God that is unblemished.

> **Dirty or torn socks:** Heart and walk before God that is blemished.

SOLDIER: Spiritual warfare. Call for more prayers fasting/worship. A period of trial or persecution.

SON: A ministry or gifting from God. Actual child has similar traits to you. Child of God.

SOUR: Corrupted. False.

SOUTH: A place of peace. The source of refreshment. The natural inclination.

SOWING: Planning for the future, good or bad. The art of spreading the Word of God.

SPEAKING: Revealing the contents of your heart. Proclamation.

SPEAR: Words, whether good or bad. Word of God. Evil words, curses.

SPIDER: An evil spirit that works by entrapping people. False doctrine.

SPOT: A fault. Contamination.

Without spot: Glorious church.

SPRINKLING: Spiritual change by washing away dirt. Cleansing, purifying, consecrating.

SQUARE: Tradition. Mindset. Worldly and blind to the truth.

STADIUM: Tremendous impact.

STAFF: Symbol of authority. Part of authority.

STAIRS: Means of bringing about changes.

Down: Demotion; backslide; failure.

Guardrail: Safety; precaution; warning to be careful.

STANDING: Firmness in faith. Committed to the belief. Not finished.

Straight: No crookedness but in the correct direction.

STARS: Important personality. Great number. Descendant. Supernatural. Jesus Christ.

Falling star: Apostate church.

STONE: Jesus Christ—chief cornerstone. Hard and sturdy foundation. Word of God. Defiance.

STONING SOMEONE: Involved in malicious accusation of others. Unforgiveness. Act of wickedness.

Dragged him out of the city and began to stone him. Meanwhile, the witnesses laid their clothes at the feet of a young man named Saul (Acts 7:58).

STORM: Trial. Testing period. Satanic attacks.

Before very long, a wind of hurricane force, called the "northeaster", swept down from the island. The ship was caught by the storm and could not head into the wind; so we gave way to it and were driven along (Acts 27:14-15).

White storm: God's power, revival.

STRAIGHT: To be fixed in attitude. Going in the right direction.

STUMBLING: To make mistakes, to fail, in error. Lack of the truth.

SUICIDE: Act of self-destruction, foolishness. Sinful behavior. Pride. Lack of hope.

SUITCASE: On the move. Transition. Private walk with God.

SUMMER: Time of harvest. The opportune time. Fruits of the Spirit.

SUN: The light of God. The truth. Glory of God.

SUPPER: The body and blood of Jesus. Marriage supper. God's provision. God's enabling power.

SWEATING: Signs of intense work of the flesh. Much work without Holy Spirit. Difficult and agonizing time.

SWEEPING: Getting rid of sinful things. Cleaning the place from evil. The process of making clean. Repentance. Correcting process.

SWEET: Something gratifying. Reflection in the Word of God. Communion with the Spirit.

SWIMMING: Moving in spiritual gifts. Prophetic utterance.

SWIMMING POOL: Church, place, or provision available for moving in the Spirit.

Dirty or dry: Corrupt or apostate.

SWING: Moving in ups and downs of life.

SWINGING: Full flow of peace.

 High: Overindulgence. Take unnecessary risks.

SWORD: Word of God. Evil words.

TABLE: A place of agreement or covenant. To iron out issues. Altar. Community, fellowship.

 You prepare a table before me in the presence of my enemies. You anoint my head with oil; my cup overflows (Psalm 23:5).

TAIL: The end of something. The least of something. The last time.

TAR: Covering; bitterness.

TARES: Children of darkness. Evil ones. Degenerates. Deceptive, e.g., grains.

TASTING: To experience something, good or bad. Judging something. Try something out.

TEA: A place or time of rest. Revelation or grace of God. Soothing.

TEACHER: Jesus Christ. Holy Spirit. Gift of God.

TEARS: Emotional sowing; mostly distress, but could represent brokenness. Joy.

TEETH: Wisdom, gaining understanding; to work something out.

 Baby teeth: Childish. Without wisdom or knowledge.

 Broken teeth: Inexperienced. Difficulty in coming to understanding.

 Brushing teeth: Gaining wisdom or understanding.

 False teeth: Full of reasoning of this world instead of pure spiritual understanding.

 Toothache: Tribulation coming; heartache.

TELEPHONE: Spiritual communication, good or evil. Godly counsel.

TELESCOPE: Looking or planning for the future. To make a problem appear bigger and closer.

TELEVISION: Visionary revelations or prophetic dreams. Prophetic utterance.

TEMPLE: A place of meeting with God. A place of refuge. God's habitation. Human body.

TEN: Law, government order and obligation. Responsibilities. Pastor. Testing trial.

TENT: Temporary covering. Flexible.

TEN THOUSAND: Army of the Lord. Battle readiness.

And he said: "The Lord came from Sinai, and dawned on them from Seir; He shone forth from Mount Paran, and He came with ten thousands of saints; From His right hand came a fiery law for them" (Deuteronomy 33:2 NKJV).

Now Enoch, the seventh from Adam, prophesied about these men also, saying, "Behold, the Lord comes with ten thousands of His saints" (Jude 1:14 NKJV).

TERMITES: Something that can cause hidden destruction.

THIEF: Satan. Deceiver. Secret intruder. Unexpected loss.

THIGH: Strength; flesh. To entice. Oath taken.

THIRTEEN: Rebellion; backsliding.

THIRTY: Beginning of ministry. Mature for God's work. Jesus was thirty when He began His ministry; Joseph was thirty when he became prime minister.

THORNS: Evil disturbance. Curse. Gossip.

THOUSANDS: Maturity approved.

THREE/THIRD: Witness; divine fullness; Godhead. Triumph over sin. Resurrection. Conform.

THREE HUNDRED: Chosen by God. Reserve of the Lord.

The Lord said to Gideon, "With the three hundred men that lapped I will save you and give the Midianites into your hands. Let all the other men go, each to his own place." So Gideon sent the rest of the Israelites to their tents but kept the three hundred, who took over the provisions and trumpets of the others. Now the camp of Midian lay below him in the valley (Judges 7:7-8).

THRONE: A seat of power. A place of authority. God's throne. Evil throne.

At once I was in the Spirit, and there before me was a throne in heaven with someone sitting on it. And the one who sat there had the appearance of jasper and carnelian. A rainbow, resembling an emerald, encircled the throne (Revelation 4:2-3).

THUMB: Apostolic; authority; soul power.

THUNDER: Loud signal from God. God speaking, touching. Warning or blessing.

TIN: Something of low valor. Not original, an imitation.

TITANIC: Big plan that is not going to work out.

TITLE/DEED: Ownership seal. Potential to possess something.

TONGUE: Powerful. National language. Something that cannot be tamed.

TORNADO: Distressing situation. Great trouble. Spiritual warfare.

TOWER: High spiritual thing. Supernatural experience. Great strength. Pride, e.g., the tower of Babel.

TRACTOR: Groundbreaking ministry. Prepare the mind to receive.

TRAIN: A large ministry that influences a lot of people. Move or send people out. Movement of God.

TREE: Leader, good or bad. Person or organization. Nations or kingdom.

Christmas: Celebrations.

Evergreen: Long-lasting, everlasting.

Oak: Great strength. Durable. Righteousness.

Olive: Anointed of God. Israel. Church. Anointing oil.

Palm: A leader who is fruit producing.

Tree stump: Tenacity or stubbornness. Retaining hope despite circumstances. Keeping the root in place.

Willow: Indicating sadness; defeat.

And provide for those who grieve in Zion—to bestow on them a crown of beauty instead of ashes, the oil of gladness instead of mourning, and a garment of praise instead of a spirit of despair. They will be called oaks of righteousness, a planting of the Lord for the display of His splendor (Isaiah 61:3).

These are the visions I saw while lying in my bed: I looked, and there before me stood a tree in the middle of the land. Its height was enormous (Daniel 4:10).

A shoot will come up from the stump of Jesse; from his roots a Branch will bear fruit (Isaiah 11:1).

But let the stump and its roots, bound with iron and bronze, remain in the ground, in the grass of the field. Let him be drenched with the dew of heaven, and let him live with the animals among the plants of the earth (Daniel 4:15).

TROPHY: Victory.

TRUCK: A personal ministry that brings provision.

TRUMPET: Voice of the prophet. The second coming of Christ. Proclaiming the good news. Blessing; promise.

To gather the assembly, blow the trumpets, but not with the same signal (Numbers 10:7).

For the Lord Himself will come down from heaven, with a loud command, with the voice of the archangel and with the trumpet call of God, and the dead in Christ will rise first (1 Thessalonians 4:16).

TUNNEL: A passage. A time or place of transition. Troubled or dark seasons of life.

He tunnels through the rock; his eyes see all its treasures (Job 28:10).

TWELVE: Government of God. Divine order. Discipleship. Government by election, theocracy.

TWENTY: Holiness and redemption.

TWENTY-FOUR: Complete order of God. Maturity or perfect government. Elders in the throne room.

> *Surrounding the throne were twenty-four other thrones, and seated on them were twenty-four elders. They were dressed in white and had crowns of gold on their heads* (Revelation 4:4).

TWO: Witnessing; confirmation. Division. Whole in marriage.

TWO HUNDRED: Fullness confirmed. Promise guaranteed.

TWO STORY: Multi-level giftedness. Symbolic of flesh and spirit. Multi-talented church.

UPSTAIRS: Pertaining to the Spirit. Pentecost. Zone of thought; great balance. Spiritual realm.

UPWARD MOTION: Moving onto higher spiritual things.

URINATING: Releasing pressure. Compelling urge or temptation. Repentance.

VAN (MOVING): A time or period of change, either in the natural or in the spirit. To walk.

VEIL: To conceal. To conceal glory or sin. To deceive. Blind to the truth. Lack of understanding.

> *Even to this day when Moses is read, a veil covers their hearts. But whenever anyone turns to the Lord, the veil is taken away* (2 Corinthians 3:15-16).

> *And even if our gospel is veiled, it is veiled to those who are perishing* (2 Corinthians 4:3).

VESSEL: People as instrument of use, for good or bad purposes. The Christian believers.

VINE: Jesus Christ. Christian believers.

> *I had planted you like a choice vine of sound and reliable stock. How then did you turn against Me into a corrupt, wild vine?* (Jeremiah 2:21).

> *I am the true vine, and My Father is the gardener* (John 15:1).

VINEYARD: A place planting; harvest. Heavenly Kingdom.

The vineyard of the Lord Almighty is the house of Israel, and the men of Judah are the garden of His delight. And He looked for justice, but saw bloodshed; for righteousness, but heard cries of distress (Isaiah 5:7).

VOICE: Message from God or devil. The Word of God. Godly instruction.

VOLCANO: Something sudden and explosive. Out of control and unstable; unpredictable. Judgment.

WALKING: Walking the path of life; life in the Spirit. Progress, living in the Spirit.

> *Difficulty:* Trials or opposition; evil opposition to destiny.

> *Unable to walk:* Hindrance to doing what you are called to do.

WALL: Obstacle, barrier, defense, limitation. Great hindrance. Blocking the view of presenting spiritual signs.

WAR: Spiritual warfare.

WASHING: To clean.

WASHBASIN: Means of cleansing. Prayers and intercession.

WASHCLOTH: Something that enhances the cleansing process.

WATCH: Need to be watchful. Time for something. Watch what is about to happen.

WATERMELON: Spirit-ruled soul. Fruitfulness.

WATERS: Move of the Spirit; Holy Spirit. Nations of the world.

> *Stagnant:* Instability or stale in the things of God.

> *Muddy or polluted:* Corrupted spiritual moves/sin/false doctrine.

> *Troubled water:* Troubled mind.

> *Water fountain:* God's Spirit welling up in man. Salvation.

> *Water well:* Revival coming.

> *Healing pool:* Time of refreshing.

WEEDS: Sinful nature or acts.

WEIGHT: Great responsibility, load, or burden.

WHEEL: Pertaining to life cycle. Long-lasting. Continuously.

WHIRLWIND: Powerful move in the Spirit, good or bad.

WHITE: Something that is pure, righteousness. God's glory, light of God. Innocence, blamelessness.

WIFE: Actual person. Someone joined to you in covenant. Spirit of submission. The Church. Israel; what or who you are called to.

WILDERNESS: Hard times. Place of trial/testing. Distant from God. Place of training. Place of provision.

WIND, BLOWING: Movement of the Spirit, usually good, but may be evil. Disappears quickly. Unstable. Difficult to understand.

WINDOW: Prophetic gifting. Revelation knowledge. Gaining insight.

WINE: Holy Spirit. Counterfeit spirit. Communion. Teaching; blessing.

> *Then I will send rain on your land in its season, both autumn and spring rains, so that you may gather in your grain, new wine and oil* (Deuteronomy 11:14).

> *No, new wine must be poured into new wineskins* (Luke 5:38).

> *Likewise, teach the older women to be reverent in the way they live, not to be slanderers or addicted to much wine, but to teach what is good* (Titus 2:3).

WINEPRESS: True doctrine; spiritual birthplace.

WINESKINS: The human body as a vessel. The Church. Saints.

WINGS: Prophetic. To be under the protection of God.

> *You yourselves have seen what I did to Egypt, and how I carried you on eagles' wings and brought you to Myself* (Exodus 19:4).

> *Have mercy on me, O God, have mercy on me, for in You my soul takes refuge. I will take refuge in the shadow of Your wings until the disaster has passed* (Psalm 57:1).

Each of the four living creatures had six wings and was covered with eyes all around, even under his wings. Day and night they never stop saying: "Holy, holy, holy is the Lord God Almighty, who was, and is, and is to come" (Revelation 4:8).

O Jerusalem, Jerusalem, you who kill the prophets and stone those sent to you, how often I have longed to gather your children together, as a hen gathers her chicks under her wings, but you were not willing! (Luke 13:34)

WINTER: Season of unfruitfulness. Latent period.

Pray that your flight will not take place in winter or on the Sabbath (Matthew 24:20).

Do your best to get here before winter. Eubulus greets you, and so do Pudens, Linus, Claudia and all the brothers (2 Timothy 4:21).

WITCH: Spirit of rebellion. Non-submission. Manipulative person. Spirit of control.

For rebellion is as the sin of witchcraft... (1 Samuel 15:23 NKJV).

WOLF: A tendency to destroy God's work. False minister. Opportunistic person.

WOMAN (UNKNOWN): A messenger from God or satan. An angel or demonic spirit. Seducing spirit.

WOOD: Life. Dependence on flesh. Humanity. Carnal reasoning. Lust.

WORK AREA: The place or time of your service.

WORM: Something that eats from the inside, often secretly. Not obvious on the surface. Disease; filthiness.

WRESTLING: Struggling with something in the Spirit or real life. To battle. Perseverance. To contend with, struggle.

YARD: The opened part of your personality. Behind or past.

YEAR: Time of blessing or judgment.

YELLOW: Hope; fear; mind.

YOKE: Bondage. Tied to something; usually evil, but sometimes good. Enslaved.

ZION: A place of strength. A place of protection. God's Kingdom.

Here am I, and the children the Lord has given me. We are signs and symbols in Israel from the Lord Almighty, who dwells on Mount Zion (Isaiah 8:18).

Their bloodguilt, which I have not pardoned, I will pardon. The Lord dwells in Zion! (Joel 3:21)

But on Mount Zion will be deliverance; it will be holy, and the house of Jacob will possess its inheritance (Obadiah 1:17).

PART 3

Other Symbolic Overtones

In What The Watchman Receives

Actions and Feelings

FEELINGS OR EMOTIONS: Feelings in dreams are expressions of what the truest situation is in the life of the dreamer. They come without the moderating effect of social norms, mind-sets, prejudices, or pretences. Sometimes, the feeling expressed by the dreamer may be incongruous to what the dreamer thinks he or she is. If this happens, it is often because there are suppressed desires or hidden hurts, wounds, or scars in the life of the dreamer that could resurrect. By and large, most feelings in dreams are usually the reflection of the degree or intensity with which an actual event will eventually happen. However, in my experience, in over 80 percent of cases, the following feelings are symbolized as indicated below.

Anger: Anger.

Bitterness: Bitterness.

Hatred: Hatred.

Joy: Happiness.

Love: Love.

Sadness: Lack of joy.

Tears: Deep emotional move, could either be for a pleasant or unpleasant reason.

FLYING: The dreamer has the potential to soar high in the things of the Spirit. Divine miraculous intervention, especially the provision of escape from danger or acceleration towards destiny.

HUNGRY: Inspiration to desire spiritual food. Lack of adequate spiritual nourishment.

INABILITY TO MOVE: This may indicate hindrances to the divine purposes in the life of the dreamer. Call for intensification of spiritual warfare.

INDIFFERENT: Not considerate. Resistant. Perseverance. Carefree.

RUNNING: (Consider the context of the dream.) Accelerated pace of events is approaching—either towards or away from something.

SLEEP: To be overtaken by something beyond your control.

THINKING: A time of study, reflection, meditation, and intellectual exercise.

WALKING: The normal routine or run of life events; the expected pace of progression.

On gravel, on stones: Hard times.

On sand: May indicate not having sound foundation on the aspect of life the dream addresses.

On swampy, moldy path: May indicate sticky situation, hard times, or hindrances.

On clear waters: Moving in the Spirit and grace of God.

On dirty waters: Dabbling in wrong doctrines.

On a straight path with near infinite view: Many places to go in life.

WORRYING: Uncertain times, insecurity. Consider the context of its occurrence.

Schools/Schooling

*Note the level of school education in the dream.

SCHOOL BUILDING: May indicate a place of learning, church, or professional institute.

PRIMARY SCHOOL: Indicates the fundamental things of life.

SECONDARY SCHOOL: Indicates the equipping period of life.

TERTIARY SCHOOL: Indicates the definite place of specialized call on the dreamer's life.

HIGH SCHOOL: Moving into a higher level of walk with God. Capable of giving same to others.

DELAY/HINDRANCES OR DISTURBANCES DURING EXAMINATIONS: May be indications of negative influences that are at play in deciding the desired placement. It could represent personal weaknesses that are standing in the way of the dreamer.

END OF SCHOOL SEASON: Indicates the completion of the equipping season.

EXAMINATION: At the verge of a promotion.

FAILING EXAMINATIONS: May mean one is not meeting the requirement for the desired placement.

INABILITY TO GET TO THE SCHOOL PREMISES: Indicates you are not in the right place for the required equipping. Extraneous hindrances to the dreamer's drive to achieve required equipping.

INABILITY TO LOCATE A CLASSROOM: May indicate inner uncertainty about definite vocation or call of God in the dreamer.

LATENESS: May indicate inadequate preparation for a time of equipping.

OLD SCHOOL TIME OR PLACE: May indicate similar time or season of experience and importance is at hand or imminent.

NOT FINISHING A TEST: Could mean inadequate preparation.

PASSING EXAMINATIONS: Confirms divine approval for the promotion.

PREPARING FOR EXAMINATION: A season preceding a promotion.

RECEIVING OR GIVING A LECTURE: The theme of the lecture is the message for the dreamer, or for the people or occasion.

RUNNING OUT OF PAPER, INK, OR PEN: Could indicate inadequate knowledge for the desired placement.

Parts of the Human Body

BEARD: To have respect for authority.

So Hanun seized David's men, shaved off half of each man's beard, cut off their garments in the middle at the buttocks, and sent them away. When David was told about this, he sent messengers to meet the men, for they were greatly humiliated. The king said, "Stay at Jericho till your beards have grown, and then come back" (2 Samuel 10:4-5).

Messy: Insanity.

Trimmed: Respectable or sane.

BELLY: Feelings, desires. Spiritual well-being. Sentiment. Humiliation.

They conceive trouble and give birth to evil; their womb [belly] *fashions deceit* (Job 15:35).

Whoever believes in Me, as the Scripture has said, streams of living water will flow from within [from his belly] *him* (John 7:38).

For such people are not serving our Lord Christ, but their own [belly] *appetites. By smooth talk and flattery they deceive the minds of naive people* (Romans 16:18).

BONES: The substance of something. The main issue. Long lasting.

Moses took the bones of Joseph with him because Joseph had made the sons of Israel swear an oath. He had said, "God will surely come to your aid, and then you must carry my bones up with you from this place" (Exodus 13:19).

Once while some Israelites were burying a man, suddenly they saw a band of raiders; so they threw the man's body into

Elisha's tomb. When the body touched Elisha's bones,the man came to life and stood up on his feet (2 Kings 13:21).

BONES, SKELETON: Something without substance or flesh. Something without details.

EYES: The means of seeing.To want something.The seer's anointing.
Closed eyes: Spiritual blindness. Ignorance, mostly self-imposed.
Winking: Concealed intention or cunning person.

FACE: Who the person is.The identity of the person.The reflection of the heart of the person. Identity or characteristics. Image expression.

FEET: Symbol of the heart or thought pattern. The part of the body that comes in contact with the earth. The lower members of the Church. Not to be ignored. Have tendency to be ignored.

And with your feet fitted with the readiness that comes from the gospel of peace (Ephesians 6:15).

"Do not come any closer," God said."Take off your sandals, for the place where you are standing is holy ground" (Exodus 3:5).

If the foot should say,"Because I am not a hand, I do not belong to the body," it would not for that reason cease to be part of the body (1 Corinthians 12:15).

Bare foot: Humble before the presence of God. Lack of studying the Word of God. Lack of preparation.
Diseased: Spirit of offense.
Lame feet: Crippled with unbelief, mind-set.Negative stronghold.
Kicking: Not under authority or working against authority.
Overgrown nails: Lack of care or not in proper order.
Washing: Humility or Christian duty.

FINGERS: Image of activity,whether human or divine. Image of sensitivity. Denoting power or authority. Assigning blame. Unit of measure. For battle.

Then Pharaoh took his signet ring from his finger and put it on Joseph's finger.He dressed him in robes of fine linen and put a gold chain around his neck (Genesis 41:42).

The magicians said to Pharaoh,"This is the finger of God." But Pharaoh's heart was hard and he would not listen,just as the Lord had said (Exodus 8:19).

Then you will call,and the Lord will answer;you will cry for help,and He will say: Here am I. If you do away with the yoke of oppression, with the pointing finger and malicious talk (Isaiah 58:9).

For your hands are stained with blood, your fingers with guilt. Your lips have spoken lies, and your tongue mutters wicked things (Isaiah 59:3).

Each of the pillars was eighteen cubits high and twelve cubits in circumference; each was four fingers thick,and hollow (Jeremiah 52:21).

The young men who had grown up with him replied,"Tell these people who have said to you,'Your father put a heavy yoke on us, but make our yoke lighter'—tell them, 'My little finger is thicker than my father's waist'" (1 Kings 12:10).

Praise be to the Lord my Rock,who trains my hands for war,my fingers for battle (Psalm 144:1).

Clenched: Pride or boastfulness.

Finger of God: Work of God or authority of God.

Fourth: Teacher.

Index: Prophet.

Little: Pastor.

Middle: Evangelist.

Pointed finger: Accusations or persecutions. Instruction or direction.

Thumb: Apostle.

FOREHEAD: That which is prominent and determines the identity of something or someone.

Therefore the showers have been withheld, and there has been no latter rain. You have had a harlot's forehead; you refuse to be ashamed (Jeremiah 3:3 NKJ).

They will see His face, and His name will be on their foreheads (Revelation 22:4).

HAIR: Cover, or something numerous, or man's glory. Protection, beauty, and identification. Mark of beauty or pride. Uncut hair is symbol of covenant. Long hair is a shame for men but glory for women. Sign of good age or dignity.

Whenever he cut the hair of his head—he used to cut his hair from time to time when it became too heavy for him—he would weigh it, and its weight was two hundred shekels by the royal standard (2 Samuel 14:26).

Because you will conceive and give birth to a son. No razor may be used on his head, because the boy is to be a Nazirite, set apart to God from birth, and he will begin the deliverance of Israel from the hands of the Philistines (Judges 13:5).

Does not the very nature of things teach you that if a man has long hair, it is a disgrace to him, but that if a woman has long hair, it is her glory? For long hair is given to her as a covering. If anyone wants to be contentious about this, we have no other practice—nor do the churches of God (1 Corinthians 11:14-16).

As I looked, thrones were set in place, and the Ancient of Days took His seat. His clothing was as white as snow; the Hair of his head was white like wool. His throne was flaming with fire, and its wheels were all ablaze (Daniel 7:9).

Grey hair is a crown of splendor; it is attained by a righteous life (Proverbs 16:31).

Baldness: Grief and shame.

Haircut: Getting something in correct shape or cutting off evil or bad habit or tradition.

Long and well maintained: Covenant and strength.

Long on a man: Probably rebellious behavior or covenant relationship.

Long on a woman: Glory of womanhood. Wife or submissive church.

Long and unkempt: Out of control.

Losing hair: Loss of wisdom or glory.

Out of shape: Not in order.

Shaving: Getting rid of things that hinder or things that are dirty.

Short on a woman: Probably lack of submission or manliness.

HANDS: Power.Personal service, taking action on behalf of someone. A person in action. Means of service. Means of expressing strength.

The fear and dread of you will fall upon all the beasts of the earth and all the birds of the air, upon every creature that moves along the ground,and upon all the fish of the sea; they are given into your hands (Genesis 9:2).

So they called together all the rulers of the Philistines and said,"Send the ark of the god of Israel away; let it go back to its own place, or it will kill us and our people."'For death had filled the city with panic; God's hand was very heavy upon it (1 Samuel 5:11).

My Father,who has given them to Me, is greater than all; no one can snatch them out of My Father's hand (John 10:29).

Stretch out your hand to heal and perform miraculous signs and wonders through the name of your holy servant Jesus (Acts 4:30).

The Lord rewards every man for his righteousness and faithfulness. The Lord delivered you into my hands today, but I would not lay a hand on the Lord's anointed (1 Samuel 26:23).

The Lord says to my Lord:"Sit at my right hand until I make your enemies a footstool for your feet" (Psalm 110:1).

But Israel reached out his right hand and put it on Ephraim's head, though he was the younger, and crossing his arms, he put his left hand on Manasseh's head, even though Manasseh was the firstborn (Genesis 48:14).

Do not neglect your gift,which was given you through a pro-phetic message when the body of elders laid their hands on you (1 Timothy 4:14).

For this reason I remind you to fan into flame the gift of God,which is in you through the laying on of my hands (2 Timothy 1:6).

Clapping: Joy and worship.

Fist: Pride in one's strength.

Covering face: Anger. Guilt or shame.

Holding: In agreement.

Left hand: Something spiritual.

Place on the right hand: Position of honor.

Put hand on the head: Blessings. Ordination.

Raised: Surrender or worshipping.

Right hand: Oath of allegiance; means of power of honor, natural strengths.

Shaking hands: Coming to an agreement. Surrender.

Stretched out hands: In security or anger.

Striking: Demonstrating strength or anger.

Trembling: To fear; spirit of fear; anxiety/awe at God's presence.

Under thighs: In oaths.

Washing: Declaring innocence or to dissociate oneself.

HEAD: Leader. To take responsibility. Be proud of something. Godordained authority—husband. Christ. Christ as head of all people.God as the Father and head of Christ.

And Moses chose able men out of all Israel,and made them heads over the people: rulers of thousands,rulers of hundreds,rulers of fifties,and rulers of tens (Exodus 18:25 NKJ).

If anyone goes outside your house into the street, his blood will be on his own head;we will not be responsible.As for anyone who is in the house with you,his blood will be on our head if a hand is laid on him (Joshua 2:19).

Now I want you to realize that the head of every man is Christ, and the head of the woman is man, and the head of Christ is God (1 Corinthians 11:3).

For the husband is the head of the wife as Christ is the head of the church, His body, of which He is the Savior (Ephesians 5:23).

Instead, speaking the truth in love, we will in all things grow up into Him who is the Head, that is, Christ (Ephesians 4:15).

And He is the head of the body, the church; He is the beginning and the firstborn from among the dead, so that in everything He might have the supremacy (Colossians 1:18).

He has lost connection with the Head, from whom the whole body, supported and held together by its ligaments and sinews, grows as God causes it to grow (Colossians 2:19).

And you have been given fullness in Christ, who is the head over every power and authority (Colossians 2:10).

Anointed: Set apart for God's service.

Covered with the hand: Signifying sorrow.

HEART: Most mentioning of the heart in Scripture is almost never in literal terms. The seat of affection. The seat of intellect. Innermost being.

Do not trust in extortion or take pride in stolen goods; though your riches increase, do not set your heart on them (Psalm 62:10).

The Lord saw how great man's wickedness on the earth had become, and that every inclination of the thoughts of his heart was only evil all the time (Genesis: 6:5).

Blessed are they who keep His statutes and seek Him with all their heart (Psalm 119:2).

The Lord was grieved that He had made man on the earth, and His heart was filled with pain (Genesis 6:6).

HEEL: The crushing power.

HIPS: Reproduction. Relating to reproduction or supporting structure.

KNEES: Sign of expression of relationship. Submission, blessing, or fear. Submission to Christ. Blessing. A measure of faith.

> *Then,at the evening sacrifice,I rose from my self-abasement,with my tunic and cloak torn,and fell on my knees with my hands spread out to the Lord my God* (Ezra 9:5).

> *That at the name of Jesus every knee should bow, in heaven and on earth and under the earth, and every tongue confess that Jesus Christ is Lord,to the glory of God the Father* (Philippians 2:10-11).

> *Why were there knees to receive me and breasts that I might be nursed?* (Job 3:12)

> *Your words have supported those who stumbled;you have strengthened faltering knees* (Job 4:4).

> *They are brought to their knees and fall,but we rise up and stand firm* (Psalm 20:8).

> *Strengthen the feeble hands,steady the knees that give way* (Isaiah 35:3).

> ***Trembling knees:*** Weakness or fear.

LEGS: Means of support. Spiritual strength to walk in life. Symbol of strength. Object of beauty. Something you stand on—your foundational principles.

> *His pleasure is not in the strength of the horse, nor His delight in the legs of a man* (Psalm 147:10).

> *Then I saw another mighty angel coming down from heaven. He was robed in a cloud, with a rainbow above his head; his face was like the sun,and his legs were like fiery pillars* (Revelation 10:1).

> *His legs are pillars of marble set on bases of pure gold.His appearance is like Lebanon,choice as its cedars* (Song 5:15).

> *How beautiful your sandaled feet, O prince's daughter! Your graceful legs are like jewels,the work of a craftsman's hands* (Song 7:1).

> *His face turned pale and he was so frightened that his knees knocked together and his legs gave way* (Daniel 5:6).

I heard and my heart pounded,my lips quivered at the sound;-decay crept into my bones,and my legs trembled.Yet I will wait patiently for the day of calamity to come on the nation invading us (Habakkuk 3:16).

Legs giving way: Giving up on the issue.

Female legs: Power to entice.

LIPS: Reflects the quality of the heart. Lying lips. Can determine outcome in life. Issuing deception. Object of seduction.

Let their lying lips be silenced,for with pride and contempt they speak arrogantly against the righteous (Psalm 31:18).

He who guards his lips guards his life, but he who speaks rashly will come to ruin (Proverbs 13:3).

Words from a wise man's mouth are gracious, but a fool is consumed by his own lips (Ecclesiastes 10:12).

The Lord says:"These people come near to Me with their mouth and honor Me with their lips, but their hearts are far from Me.Their worship of Me is made up only of rules taught by men (Isaiah 29:13).

His cheeks are like beds of spice yielding perfume.His lips are like lilies dripping with myrrh (Song 5:13).

MOUTH: Instrument of witnessing. Speaking evil or good words. Something from which comes the issues of life.Words coming against you.

NECK: Associated with beauty. A place to secure something valuable. Capture and subjection. Cut off or break.

Outstretched: Arrogance.

Long neck: Noisy.

Risk the neck: To take risk.

Stiff-necked: Stubbornness.

Are they not finding and dividing the spoils: a girl or two for each man, colorful garments as plunder for Sisera, colorful garments embroidered, highly embroidered garments for my neck—all this as plunder? (Judges 5:30)

They will be a garland to grace your head and a chain to adorn your neck (Proverbs 1:9).

Let love and faithfulness never leave you; bind them around your neck, write them on the tablet of your heart (Proverbs 3:3).

In His great power God becomes like clothing to me; He binds me like the neck of my garment (Job 30:18).

The Lord has appointed you priest in place of Jehoiada to be in charge of the house of the Lord ; you should put any madman who acts like a prophet into the stocks and neck-irons (Jeremiah 29:26).

Therefore in hunger and thirst, in nakedness and dire poverty, you will serve the enemies the Lord sends against you. He will put an iron yoke on your neck until He has destroyed you (Deuteronomy 28:48).

Who risked their own necks for my life, to whom not only I give thanks, but also all the churches of the Gentiles (Romans 16:4 NKJ).

NOSE: Discerning spirit. Discernment, good or bad. Intruding into people's privacy. Gossiper.

SHOULDERS: The responsibility, the authority. Something, person or animal on which burden or load is laid or can be placed. Something that can be of good for work. Governmental responsibility. Sign of unity – shoulder to shoulder. Captivity.

For as in the day of Midian's defeat, you have shattered the yoke that burdens them, the bar across their shoulders, the rod of their oppressor (Isaiah 9:4).

For to us a child is born, to us a son is given, and the government will be on His shoulders. And He will be called Wonderful Counselor, Mighty God, Everlasting Father, Prince of Peace (Isaiah 9:6).

Then will I purify the lips of the peoples, that all of them may call on the name of the Lord and serve Him shoulder to shoulder (Zephaniah 3:9).

He says, "I removed the burden from their shoulders; their hands were set free from the basket" (Psalm 81:6).

They tie up heavy loads and put them on men's shoulders, but they themselves are not willing to lift a finger to move them (Matthew 23:4).

Bare female shoulders: Enticement.

Broad: Capable of handling much responsibility.

Drooped: Defeated attitude, overworked, overtired, burnt-out.

TEETH: Primary symbol of strength. Image of good consumption by breaking down into tiny bits. To simplify into its smallest bits for easy processing for wisdom. Power.

And there before me was a second beast, which looked like a bear. It was raised up on one of its sides, and it had three ribs in its mouth between its teeth. It was told, "Get up and eat your fill of flesh!" (Daniel 7:5)

Like the ungodly they maliciously mocked; they gnashed their teeth at me (Psalm 35:16).

But the subjects of the kingdom will be thrown outside, into the darkness, where there will be weeping and gnashing of teeth (Matthew 8:12).

Baby teeth: Immaturity.

Breaking of teeth: Defeat and/or losing wisdom.

Brushing teeth: Gaining understanding.

False teeth: Wisdom of this world.

Gnashing of teeth: Sign of taunt, division or regret and sorrow.

Toothache: Trial, problems.

BUILDINGS

PERSONALITIES OR STRUCTURE OF AN ORGANIZATION

I will show you what he is like who comes to Me and hears My words and puts them into practice. He is like a man building a house, who dug down deep and laid the foundation on rock. When the flood came, the torrent struck that house but could not shake it, because it was well built (Luke 6:47-48).

CHURCH BUILDING: Pertaining to church, ministry, or the call of God.

COURTROOM: Being judged. Under scrutiny. Persecution, trial.

CURRENT HOUSE: The dreamer's make-up.

FACTORY: A place of putting things together. A place of protection. A church.

>*Foundation:* Something on which the person or object stands on.
>
>*Idle:* Not put into proper use.
>
>*Factory in good state:* Good standing.
>
>*Factory ruins:* Needing attention.

FAMILY HOME: Related to the past. Something from the past influencing the present. Something from the bloodline.

>**House:**
>
>*High-rise:* Multitalented ministry; multiple ministries in one place.
>
>*Mobile home:* A transitory situation. Character in transition. Temporary place.
>
>*Moving home:* Changes in personality.

New: New personality, either natural or spiritual.

Old: Past or something inherited. If in good state, then it is righteous or good from the past. If in bad state, then it is sin or weakness that runs in a family.

Shop: A place of choices. Business related venue.

Under construction: In process of formation.

LIBRARY: Time or place of knowledge; education.

OFFICE BUILDING: Relates to secular jobs, the dreamer's office life.

Parts of a Building

BACK: Something in the past or unexpected.

BATHROOM: A period of cleansing; entering a time of repentance. A place of voluntary nakedness. Facing reality in individual life.

BEDROOM: A place of intimacy. A place of rest or where you sleep and dream. A place of covenant or a place of revelation.

FRONT: Something in the future.

KITCHEN: A plea of nourishment; heart.The mind or intellect, where ideas are muted in the natural realm.The heart (Spirit).Where revelations are received and nurtured for the equipping of others.

ROOF: The covering.

SITTING ROOM: That which is easily noticed by the public. The revealed part.

States of a Building

CRACKED WALL: Faulty protective measures. Not adequately protected.

LEAKING ROOF: Inadequate spiritual cover.

MODERN: Current doctrine up-to-date.

NEGLECTED: Lack of maintenance.

OLD-FASHIONED: Tradition or old belief.

Spiritual Significace of Numbers

God speaks through numbers a great deal, and the Bible is full of evidence of God's arithmetic. Numbers are high-level forms of symbolism. I have put together some numbers and their generally accepted scriptural relevance or meaning. The spiritual significance of numbers given here is based on the Word of God, and I have found it very useful in my personal experience.

ONE: Unity. The number of God. The beginning, the first. Precious.

There is one body and one Spirit—just as you were called to one hope when you were called—one Lord, one faith, one baptism; one God and Father of all, who is over all and through all and in all (Ephesians 4:4-6).

I and the Father are one (John 10:30).

That all of them may be one, Father, just as You are in Me and I am in You. May they also be in Us so that the world may believe that You have sent Me. I have given them the glory that You gave Me, that they may be one as We are one (John 17:21-22).

Make every effort to keep the unity of the Spirit through the bond of peace (Ephesians 4:3).

And I will pour out on the house of David and the inhabitants of Jerusalem a spirit of grace and supplication. They will look on Me, the one they have pierced, and they will mourn for Him as one mourns for an only child, and grieve bitterly for Him as one grieves for a firstborn son (Zechariah 12:10).

A mediator, however, does not represent just one party; but God is one (Galatians 3:20).

TWO: Union, witnessing or confirmation. It could also mean division depending on the general context of the events or revelation.

> *The man said, "This is now bone of my bones and flesh of my flesh; she shall be called 'woman,' for she was taken out of man." For this reason a man will leave his father and mother and be united to his wife, and they will become one flesh* (Genesis 2:23-24).

> *But if he will not listen, take one or two others along, so that every matter may be established by the testimony of two or three witnesses* (Matthew 18:16).

> *He is a double-minded man, unstable in all he does* (James 1:8).

> *So God made the expanse and separated the water under the expanse from the water above it. And it was so. God called the expanse "sky." And there was evening, and there was morning—the second day* (Genesis 1:7-8).

> *Then the king said, "Bring me a sword." So they brought a sword for the king. He then gave an order: "Cut the living child in two and give half to one and half to the other"* (1 Kings 3:24-25).

THREE: Resurrection, divine completeness and perfection. Confirmation. The trinity of Godhead. Restoration.

> *Therefore go and make disciples of all nations, baptizing them in the name of the Father and of the Son and of the Holy Spirit* (Matthew 28:19).

> *For as Jonah was three days and three nights in the belly of a huge fish, so the Son of Man will be three days and three nights in the heart of the earth* (Matthew 12:40).

> *Jesus answered them, "Destroy this temple, and I will raise it again in three days"* (John 2:19).

FOUR: Creation or to rule or to reign. On the fourth day of creation, God made two great lights—the sun and the moon—to rule the day and the night.

> *And God said, "Let there be lights in the expanse of the sky to separate the day from the night, and let them serve as signs*

to mark seasons and days and years, and let them be lights in the expanse of the sky to give light on the earth." And it was so. God made two great lights—the greater light to govern the day and the lesser light to govern the night. He also made the stars. God set them in the expanse of the sky to give light on the earth, to govern the day and the night, and to separate light from darkness. And God saw that it was good. And there was evening, and there was morning—the fourth day (Genesis 1:14-19).

Also before the throne there was what looked like a sea of glass, clear as crystal. In the center, around the throne, were four living creatures, and they were covered with eyes, in front and in back. The first living creature was like a lion, the second was like an ox, the third had a face like a man, the fourth was like a flying eagle. Each of the four living creatures had six wings and was covered with eyes all around, even under his wings. Day and night they never stop saying: 'Holy, holy, holy is the Lord God Almighty, who was, and is, and is to come" (Revelation 4:6-8).

FIVE: Grace or the goodness of God. Fivefold ministry.

It was He who gave some to be apostles, some to be prophets, some to be evangelists, and some to be pastors and teachers (Ephesians 4:11).

SIX: The number of man. Weakness of humanity or the flesh. Can mean evil or satan. God created man on the sixth day.

Then God said, "Let us make man in Our image, in Our likeness, and let them rule over the fish of the sea and the birds of the air, over the livestock, over all the earth, and over all the creatures that move along the ground." So God created man in His own image, in the image of God He created him; male and female He created them (Genesis 1:26-27).

Nebuchadnezzar the king made an image of gold, whose height was sixty cubits and its width six cubits. He set it up in the plain of Dura, in the province of Babylon (Daniel 3:1 NKJ).

SEVEN: Completeness or spiritual perfection. Rest. Blessing. Redemption.

Thus the heavens and the earth were completed in all their vast array. By the seventh day God had finished the work He had been doing; so on the seventh day He rested from all His work.And God blessed the seventh day and made it holy,because on it He rested from all the work of creating that He had done (Genesis 2:1-3).

But in the days when the seventh angel is about to sound his trumpet, the mystery of God will be accomplished,just as He announced to His servants the prophets (Revelation 10:7).

The seventh angel poured out his bowl into the air, and out of the temple came a loud voice from the throne, saying, "It is done!" (Revelation 16:17)

At the end of every seven years you must cancel debts.This is how it is to be done:Every creditor shall cancel the loan he has made to his fellow Israelite. He shall not require payment from his fellow Israelite or brother, because the Lord's time for cancelling debts has been proclaimed (Deuteronomy 15:1-2).

EIGHT: New birth or new beginning. The circumcision of male children of Israel on the eighth day is a type of new birth.

On the eighth day,when it was time to circumcise Him,He was named Jesus,the name the angel had given Him before He had been conceived. When the time of their purification according to the Law of Moses had been completed,Joseph and Mary took Him to Jerusalem to present Him to the Lord (as it is written in the Law of the Lord,"Every firstborn male is to be consecrated to the Lord") (Luke 2:21-23).

For the generations to come every male among you who is eight days old must be circumcised, including those born in your household or bought with money from a foreigner— those who are not your offspring (Genesis 17:12).

NINE: Fruit of the Spirit. Harvest or the fruit of your labor. Nine gifts of the Spirit.

But the fruit of the Spirit is love, joy, peace, patience, kindness, goodness, faithfulness, gentleness and self-control. Against such things there is no law (Galatians 5:22-23).

*To one there is given through the Spirit the message of wis-
dom, to another the message of knowledge by means of the
same Spirit, to another faith by the same Spirit, to another
gifts of healing by that one Spirit, to another miraculous powers, to another prophecy, to another distinguishing between
spirits, to another speaking in different kinds of tongues, and
to still another the interpretation of tongues* (1 Corinthians
12:8-10).

TEN: Law and responsibility. Tithe is a tenth of our earning, which
belongs to God. It is also the number for the pastoral. Judgment.
Ten plagues upon Egypt.

ELEVEN: Confusion, judgment, or disorder.

TWELVE: Government.The number of apostleship.

*One of those days Jesus went out to a mountainside to pray,and
spent the night praying to God.When morning came,He called
His disciples to Him and chose twelve of them,whom He also
designated apostles* (Luke 6:12-13).

*Jesus said to them,"I tell you the truth,at the renewal of all
things, when the Son of Man sits on His glorious throne, you
who have followed Me will also sit on twelve thrones,judging
the twelve tribes of Israel"* (Matthew 19:28).

THIRTEEN: Thirteen evil thoughts from the heart listed. Rebellion or spiritual depravity.

*For from within, out of men's hearts, come evil thoughts, sex-
ual immorality, theft, murder, adultery, greed, malice, deceit,
lewdness, envy, slander,arrogance and folly* (Mark 7:21-22).

FOURTEEN: Deliverance or salvation.The number of double
anointing.

*Thus there were fourteen generations in all from Abraham to
David, fourteen from David to the exile to Babylon, and fourteen from the exile to the Christ* (Matthew 1:17).

FIFTEEN: Rest, mercy.

*Mordecai recorded these events, and he sent letters to all the
Jews throughout the provinces of King Xerxes, near and far,*

to have them celebrate annually the fourteenth and fifteenth days of the month of Adar as the time when the Jews got relief from their enemies, and as the month when their sorrow was turned into joy and their mourning into a day of celebration. He wrote them to observe the days as days of feasting and joy and giving presents of food to one another and gifts to the poor (Esther 9:20-22).

Say to the Israelites:"On the fifteenth day of the seventh month the Lord's Feast of Tabernacles begins,and it lasts for seven days.The first day is a sacred assembly; do no regular work" (Leviticus 23:34-35).

SIXTEEN: Love—sixteen things are said of love.

Love is patient,love is kind.It does not envy,it does not boast,it is not proud. It is not rude, it is not self-seeking, it is not easily angered, it keeps no record of wrongs. Love does not delight in evil but rejoices with the truth.It always protects,always trusts,always hopes,always perseveres. Love never fails. But where there are prophecies, they will cease; where there are tongues, they will be stilled; where there is knowledge, it will pass away (1 Corinthians 13:4-8).

SEVENTEEN: Immaturity.Transition.Victory.

Joseph, a young man of seventeen, was tending the flocks with his brothers, the sons of Bilhah and the sons of Zilpah, his father's wives, and he brought their father a bad report about them (Genesis 37:2).

Jacob lived in Egypt seventeen years, and the years of his life were a hundred and forty-seven (Genesis 47:28).

And on the seventeenth day of the seventh month the ark came to rest on the mountains of Ararat (Genesis 8:4).

EIGHTEEN: Bondage.

Then should not this woman,a daughter of Abraham,whom satan has kept bound for eighteen long years,be set free on the Sabbath day from what bound her? (Luke 13:16)

The Israelites were subject to Eglon king of Moab for eighteen years (Judges 3:14).

He became angry with them. He sold them into the hands of the Philistines and the Ammonites,who that year shattered and crushed them. For eighteen years they oppressed all the Israelites on the east side of the Jordan in Gilead,the land of the Amorites (Judges 10:7-8).

NINETEEN: Faith. Nineteen persons mentioned in Hebrews chapter 11.

Now faith is being sure of what we hope for and certain of what we do not see. This is what the ancients were commended for… (Hebrews 11:1-32).

TWENTY: Redemption (silver money in the Bible).

THIRTY: Blood of Jesus. Dedication.The beginning of service. Salvation.

Then one of the Twelve—the one called Judas Iscariot—went to the chief priests and asked,"What are you willing to give me if I hand Him over to you?" So they counted out for him thirty silver coins (Matthew 26:14-15).

Count all the men from thirty to fifty years of age who come to serve in the work in the Tent of Meeting.This is the work of the Kohathites in the Tent of Meeting: the care of the most holy things (Numbers 4:3-4).

Joseph was thirty years old when he entered the service of Pharaoh king of Egypt.And Joseph went out from Pharaoh's presence and traveled throughout Egypt (Genesis 41:46).

David was thirty years old when he became king,and he reigned forty years (2 Samuel 5:4).

FORTY: Trial. Probation.Testing or temptation.

Remember how the Lord your God led you all the way in the desert these forty years, to humble you and to test you in order to know what was in your heart, whether or not you would keep His commands.He humbled you,causing you to hunger and then feeding you with manna,which neither you nor your fathers had known,to teach you that man does not live on bread alone but on every word that comes from the mouth of the Lord.Your clothes did not wear out and your feet did not swell during these forty years.Know then in your heart that as a man disciplines his son,so the Lord your God disciplines you (Deuteronomy 8:2-5).

Jesus, full of the Holy Spirit, returned from the Jordan and was led by the Spirit in the desert,where for forty days He was tempted by the devil.He ate nothing during those days,and at the end of them He was hungry (Luke 4:1-2).

So he got up and ate and drank.Strengthened by that food,he traveled forty days and forty nights until he reached Horeb, the mountain of God (1 Kings 19:8).

On the first day, Jonah started into the city. He proclaimed:"-Forty more days and Nineveh will be overturned" (Jonah 3:4).

FIFTY: Number of the Holy Spirit. Jubilee, liberty.The number for the Holy Spirit: He was poured out on the day of Pentecost which was fifty days after the resurrection of Christ.

Consecrate the fiftieth year and proclaim liberty throughout the land to all its inhabitants. It shall be a jubilee for you; each one of you is to return to his family property and each to his own clan (Leviticus 25:10).

SIXTY: Pride or arrogance.The image that Nebuchadnezzar set up was sixty cubits high.

Nebuchadnezzar the king made an image of gold, whose height was sixty cubits and its width six cubits. He set it up in the plain of Dura, in the province of Babylon (Daniel 3:1 NKJ).

SEVENTY: Universality or restoration. Israel lived in exile for seventy years after which they were restored.

In the first year of his reign,I,Daniel,understood from the Scriptures, according to the word of the Lord given to Jeremiah the prophet, that the desolation of Jerusalem would last seventy years (Daniel 9:2).

EIGHTY: Beginning of a high calling or becoming spiritually acceptable.

Moses was eighty years old when he started his ministry to deliver the Israelites.

NINETY OR NINETY-NINE: Fruits are ripe and ready. Abraham was ninety-nine years old when God appeared to him.

When Abram was ninety-nine years old, the Lord appeared to him and said, "I am God Almighty; walk before Me and be blameless" (Genesis 17:1 KJV).

ONE HUNDRED: God's election of grace. Children of promise. Full reward. Abraham was one hundred years old when his son Isaac (child of promise) was born.

Abraham was a hundred years old when his son Isaac was born to him (Genesis 21:5).

ONE THOUSAND: The beginning of maturity; mature service or full status.

Multiples or Complex Numbers

For these numbers, the meaning lies in the way it is pronounced rather than as it is written.

Example:

2872 is pronounced "Two thousand, eight hundred, seventy-two."

Two thousand = confirmed spiritual maturity or mature judgment.

Eight hundred = new beginning into the promises.

Seventy-two = confirmed, completed, and restored.

CONTACT INFORMATION

For additional copies of this book and other products from Cross House Books,
contact: info@crosshousebooks.co.uk.

Please visit our Website for product updates and news at
www.crosshousebooks.co.uk.

OTHER INQUIRIES

CROSS HOUSE BOOKS
Christian Book Publishers
245 Midstocket Road, Aberdeen, AB15 5PH, UK

info@crosshousebooks.co.uk
publisher@crosshousebooks.co.uk

"The entrance of Your Word brings light."

Do you want to become a published author
and get your book distributed worldwide
by major book stores?

Contact:
info@crosshousebooks.co.uk
www.crosshousebooks.co.uk.
or write to
CROSS HOUSE BOOKS
245 Midstocket Road, Aberdeen, AB15 5PH, UK

MINISTRY AND CONTACT INFORMATION

The Father's House is a family church and a vibrant community of Christians located in Aberdeen, Scotland, United Kingdom. The Father's House seeks to build a bridge of hope across generations, racial divides, and gender biases through the ministry of the Word.

You are invited to come and worship if you are in the area.

For location, please visit the church's Website:
www.the-fathers-house.org.uk

For inquiries:
info@the-fathers-house.org.uk
Call: 44 1224 701343

By Dr. Joe Ibojie

Times of Refreshing Volume 1

Times of Refreshing allows you to tap in to daily supernatural experiences! Overflowing with inspiring messages, comforting prayers, and Scriptures that bring His presence to you, these daily boosts of God's love are just what the Doctor ordered for a healthy mind, body, and spirit. Best-selling author and Pastor Bishop Joe Ibojie and Pastor Cynthia Ibojie bring 365 days of hope and refreshment into your personal space.

Times of Refreshing Volume 2

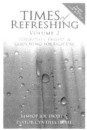

Times of Refreshing Volume 2 gives readers the ability to tap in to daily supernatural experiences! As with *Times of Refreshing Volume 1,* Volume 2 overflows with inspiring messages, comforting prayers, and Scriptures that bring His presence home. These daily boosts of God's love are just what the Divine Doctor ordered for a healthy mind, body, and spirit. Each page includes a Scripture and God-given message, as well as space for interactive exchanges of the reader's written word with His. An added bonus is a listing of Scriptures to read the Bible in a year. Prophetic Prayer Points conclude this volume of encouraging and motivating messages of daily living the supernatural, victorious life in God's Kingdom.

Times of Refreshing Volume 3

Each volume of *Times of Refreshing* is filled with daily inspiration, love, and hope. Beginning with a Scripture passage and followed with insights straight from the throne of God, readers worldwide have been strengthened and motivated to pursue their daily destiny. A few inspirational questions conclude the day's devotion, prompting a search into the inner being to discover truths from the Lord— nuggets of His devotion and wisdom. And for those who have never read the entire Bible, on every page are Scripture references from the Old and New Testaments so the Bible can be read in a year's time. Pastors Joe and Cynthia Ibojie authored *Times of Refreshing* out of united prayer and compassionate hearts.

Times of Refreshing Volume 4—NEW

Best-selling author Bishop Joe Ibojie and his wife, Pastor Cynthia Ibojie, have again combined their unique prophetic gifting with rare vision into the mysteries of God as they offer *Times of Refreshing Volume 4* for everyone yearning to find daily peace and solace by stepping into God's presence. As with the first three very popular volumes of *Times of Refreshing, Volume 4* includes a Scripture, Holy Spirit-inspired message, and questions designed to provoke thought and soothing meditation. There is also a convenient list of Scriptures so you can read the Bible in a year—everything you need to make each and every day a supernatural, victorious experience!

Revelations Training Manual

Revelations Training Manual takes you into the depths of God's holiness and desire to communicate with His children. It is possible to understand your dreams and revelations from God—and with the wisdom shared in this manual, your spiritual questions will be answered.

How You Can Live an Everyday Supernatural Life

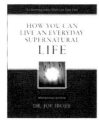

This comprehensive manual is the perfect training ground for every believer! Filled with practical and easy-to-implement ways to achieve a supernatural lifestyle, readers can immediately put into practice the God-given advice, insights, and revelations. Essential keys are presented that open the doors into a realm of divine and intimate relationship with God. He welcomes all to enjoy daily spiritual and physical miracles, signs, and wonders—naturally in the supernatural. Senior Pastor Joe Ibojie is a worldwide Bible and prophetic teacher.

Destined for the Top

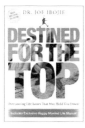

Destined for the Top presents simple and proven successful answers to life's most complex questions. Divided into two parts—Life Issues and Family Issues—you can be at the top of your game in every aspect of your life by knowing what and who to avoid during your journey to the top. Through an added feature of thought-provoking questions at the end of each chapter, you will learn how to strengthen your spirit, invest in your potential, and realize how fickle your feelings really are. You will discover how God's wisdom and love through you propels you toward fulfilling your destiny!

The Final Frontiers—Countdown to the Final Showdown

The Final Frontiers—Countdown to the Final Showdown peers pro-foundly into the future. It expertly explores the emerging cosmic involvement of the seemingly docile elements of nature and their potential to completely alter the ways of warfare. Christians must not allow the things that are supposed to bless them to become instruments of judgment or punishment. *The Final Frontiers* pro-vides you with a practical approach to the changing struggles that confront humanity now and in your future.

The Watchman: The Ministry of the Seer in the Local Church

The ministry of the watchman in a local church is possibly one of the most common and yet one of the most misunderstood minis-tries in the Body of Christ. Over time, the majority of these gifted people have been driven into reclusive lives because of relational issues and confusion surrounding their very vital ministry in the local church.

The Justice of God: Victory in Everyday Living

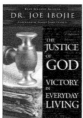

Only once in awhile does a book bring rare insight and godly illumi-nation to a globally crucial subject. This book is one of them! A sem-inal work from a true practitioner, best-selling author, and leader of a vibrant church, Dr. Joe Ibojie brings clarity and a hands-on perspective to the Justice of God. *The Justice of God* reveals: How to pull down your blessings; How to work with angels; The power and dangers of prophetic acts and drama.

Illustrated Bible-Based Dictionary of Dream Symbols— BEST SELLER

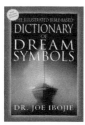

Illustrated Bible-Based Dictionary of Dream Symbols is much more than a book of dream symbols. This book is a treasure chest, loaded down with revelation and the hidden mysteries of God that have been waiting since before the foundation of the earth to be uncovered. Whether you use this book to assist in interpreting your dreams or as an additional resource for your study of the Word of God, you will find it a welcome companion.

EXPANDED AND ENRICHED WITH EXCITING NEW CONTENT

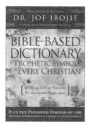

Bible-Based Dictionary of Prophetic Symbols for Every Christian

The most comprehensive, illustrated Bible-based dictionary of prophetic and dream symbols ever compiled is contained in this one authoritative book! *The Bible-Based Dictionary of Prophetic Symbols for Every Christian* is a masterpiece that intelligently and understandably bridges the gap between prophetic revelation and application— PLUS it includes the expanded version of the best selling *Illustrated Bible-Based Dictionary of Dream Symbols.*

How to Live the Supernatural Life in the Here and Now— BEST SELLER

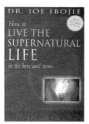

Are you ready to stop living an ordinary life? You were meant to live a supernatural life! God intends us to experience His power every day! In *How to Live the Supernatural Life in the Here and Now* you will learn how to bring the supernatural power of God into everyday living. Finding the proper balance for your life allows you to step into the supernatural and to move in power and authority over everything around you. Dr. Joe Ibojie, an experienced pastor and prolific writer, provides practical steps and instruction that will help you live a life of spiritual harmony.

Dreams and Visions Volume 1—BEST SELLER

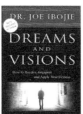

Dreams and Visions presents sound scriptural principles and practical instructions to help you understand dreams and visions. The book provides readers with the necessary understanding to approach dreams and visions by the Holy Spirit through biblical illustrations, understanding of the meaning of dreams and prophetic symbolism, and by exploring the art of dream interpretation according to ancient methods of the Bible.

Available in Italian and Koream translations.

Dreams and Visions Volume 2

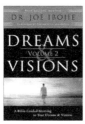

God speaks to you through dreams and visions. Do you want to know the meaning of your dreams? Do you want to know what He is telling and showing you? Now you can know! *Dreams and Visions Volume 2* is packed full of exciting and Bible-guided ways to discover the meaning of your God-inspired, dreamy nighttime adventures and your wide-awake supernatural experiences!

By Dr. Fred Addo

The Enemy Called Worry

Worry gives birth to many sins and affects a person's spiritual development and physical health. There is a way to eliminate worry from your life and move forward into your God-given destiny. This book gives you every weapon needed to proclaim victory over *The Enemy Called Worry!*

40 Names of the Holy Spirit

The names of God represent a deliberate *invitation to you* to take advantage of what God can and wants to be in your life. Whatever you call Him is what He will become to you. Do you know all of His names? How much deeper would you like to know the Comforter? You will learn: Seven Symbols of the Holy Spirit; Names of the Holy Spirit; Seven Things *Not* to Do to the Holy Spirit; Twentyfold Relationship with the Holy Spirit; Fourfold Presence of the Holy Spirit; Seven Keys to Receiving the Holy Spirit Baptism—and much more!

By Pastor Emmanuel O. Emmanuel

Growing God's Kingdom

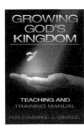

Written by an experienced Bible scholar and beloved pastor, the insights and depth of God's word is thoughtfully shared so that newborn Christians and mature believers alike can understand and appreciate. Prefaced with an intriguing prophecy, *Growing God's Kingdom* contains practical principles that reveal the importance of God's mandate to share the gospel. You will learn about being mentored and mentoring those next in line to inherit God's riches.

From Rogue to Revivalist: Impacting the Nations with Revival

From Rogue to Revivalist is the fascinating, true story of a young man whose early life resembles nothing of his later life—although each stage was preparing him for the miracles God performs through him today. Set in exotic and not-so-exotic countries world-wide, the journey leads readers into mesmerizing and shocking scenes that prove God's ultimate protection for all who call upon His name. Laced with dozens of personal testimonies from people healed by God's touch, this book is sure to impact every reader. Pastor Kul Bal travels worldwide as a healing revivalist.

The Odyssey of a Judicial Career

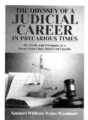

In this comprehensive treatise, three-time Chief Justice Samuel William Wako Wambuzi sets the record straight regarding the events of a country shaken to its cultural, military, political, and legal core. As a distinguished scholar and judicial genius, he presents the facts in a way that people of all walks of life will appreciate the historical significance of Uganda's struggles while enjoying the everyday life of a man with strong family ties.

21st Century Psalms

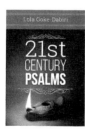

A beautiful collection of writings including heartfelt prayers, conversations with God, and lessons learned firsthand from the Holy Spirit. When you embrace open two-way communication and sweet fellowship with your awesome God, He reveals Himself in incomprehensible ways. Each psalm exposes the brilliance of His majesty and you'll realize that He will be to you what you need Him to be—Warrior, Comforter, Defender, Prince of Peace, Avenger, Redeemer...